A WELL-EXECUTED FAILURE

THE SULLIVAN CAMPAIGN AGAINST THE IROQUOIS, JULY–SEPTEMBER 1779

Major General John Sullivan.
Portrait by Tenney, from a pencil sketch by Trumbull,
courtesy of the New Hampshire Historical Society.

A WELL-EXECUTED FAILURE

THE SULLIVAN CAMPAIGN AGAINST THE IROQUOIS, JULY–SEPTEMBER 1779

Joseph R. Fischer

THE UNIVERSITY OF SOUTH CAROLINA PRESS

© 1997 University of South Carolina

Cloth edition published by the University of South Carolina Press, 1997
Paperback edition published in Columbia, South Carolina,
by the University of South Carolina Press, 2008

www.sc.edu/uscpress

Manufactured in the United States of America

17 16 15 14 13 12 11 10 09 08   10 9 8 7 6 5 4 3 2 1

The Library of Congress has cataloged the cloth edition as follows:
Fischer, Joseph R., 1953–
 A well-executed failure : the Sullivan campaign against the Iroquois,
July–September 1779 / Joseph R. Fischer.
  p. cm.
 Includes bibliographical references and index.
 ISBN 1-57003-137-1
 1. Sullivan's Indian Campaign, 1779. 2. Sullivan, John, 1740–1795.
3. New York (State)—History—Revolution, 1775–1783.
 I. Title.
 E235.F57 1997
 973.3'35—dc20   96—25192

ISBN 978-1-57003-837-2 (pbk)

Contents

List of Figures   vi

Preface   vii

Acknowledgments   ix

Chapter 1. Introduction   1

Chapter 2. The Frontier in Flames: 1778   9

Chapter 3. Strategy and Operations   34

Chapter 4. Tactics   61

Chapter 5. Logistics   102

Chapter 6. Leadership   129

Chapter 7. Civil-Military Relations   157

Chapter 8. Conclusions   191

Notes   198

Selected Bibliography   244

Index   256

FIGURES

Fig. 1. Sullivan Expedition, July–October 1779   3

Fig. 2. Treaty of Fort Stanwix, 1768   12

Fig. 3. Continental Army's 1779 Campaign against the Iroquois   51

Fig. 4. Sullivan's Movement Formation   74

Fig. 5. Sullivan's Formation for Combat   76

Fig. 6. Army's Encampment at Tioga   78

Fig. 7. Battle of Newtown   88

Fig. 8. Boyd Ambush   98

Preface

In the summer of 1779 the Continental army attempted its first Indian campaign. Major General John Sullivan, commanding four brigades of Continental regulars, marched westward from New Jersey and New York with the mission of punishing the Iroquois Confederation for the series of raids that had devastated western settlements in New York and Pennsylvania in 1778.

Sullivan's army entered the Iroquois homelands in August 1779. Brushing aside Tory-Iroquois attempts to stop them, Sullivan's soldiers torched forty towns and villages and destroyed 160,000 acres of corn. The immediate effect of the offensive was to compel the remnants of the Iroquois to take refuge with their British supporters at Fort Niagara. The long-term goal of removing the Iroquois from the war, however, eluded Washington's grasp. More dependent than ever on the British, they resumed their raids the following year.

The failure of the Sullivan expedition to achieve its strategic objectives has largely overshadowed the contribution a study of the campaign can make to understanding the Continental army at midwar. The four brigades Washington assigned to Sullivan were a representative slice of the army, and their performance provides an opportunity to answer many important questions concerning the army's condition and development. To what extent had Washington developed a strategic plan for the war? How was intelligence collected, evaluated, and processed? What kinds of tactics and doctrine guided the army's actions, and to what extent were homegrown solutions applied to fighting in the North American wilderness? How well did the supply system work? How did officers and noncommissioned officers motivate and lead their men? How well did soldiers respond to the army's leadership style, particularly given the army's social composition? From a broader perspective the campaign also sheds light on the nature of the relationship existing among the Continental army, the civil governments, and the people of those regions in the interior most victimized by Tory and Indian raiding parties.

A study of the campaign reveals that Washington was making progress in the development of the Continental army, but the results were uneven. Despite the best efforts of Nathanael Greene, Washington's quartermaster general, the supply system threatened failure in all the army's endeavors. The army's leadership varied in quality and competency. Furthermore, the lack of an adequate working relationship among leaders at the national, state, and army levels created considerable friction, tried Washington's patience, and endangered the cause in the name of provincialism.

To Washington's credit, the accomplishments of Sullivan's army indicate that the Continental army had developed a marked degree of sophistication in the areas of operational planning, preparation of intelligence, and tactics. The army was not the equal of its British counterparts, but it had significantly narrowed the performance gap. Given the strategic situation facing Great Britain in 1779, victory required smashing Washington's army in a battle of annihilation. The showing turned in by Sullivan's men indicated that this had become no small task.

Acknowledgments

It has been nearly thirty-five years since I read my first roadside historical marker on the Sullivan campaign. From a little boy's perspective it seemed the stuff of high adventure. My father no doubt tired of hearing me plead for him to stop every time another marker appeared. The journey from the curiousity of a seven-year-old to this interpretation of what the event demonstrates about the Continental army and its foes has been a long one, but one that I did not make alone.

I am indebted to many people for their advice and assistance in the writing of this book. Gary Gallagher was the first to encourage me to see where a study of Sullivan's army might lead. He has been both a friend and critic. Whatever talents I bring to this profession I owe in large measure to him. Carol Reardon patiently read my work and offered her insights on eighteenth-century military history. John Shy taught me how to weave campaign history into the broader social context in which all armies operate. John Frantz, my first mentor in this profession, provided his usual patient confidence in my skills even when I was not so sure of them myself. Christine White provided fresh insights into the material and was a constant source of encouragement.

I am very thankful for the contributions of Charlotte Walter and Jack Hetrick. Regardless of the archive's posted hours, Charlotte and Jack always insured that the holdings of the Northumberland County Historical Society were available when needed. Dr. Frank Lorenz at Hamilton College offered similar support and expertise with Samuel Kirkland's papers.

Several other good friends have also had a part in the writing of this book. Charles Schoffstall, one of the finest teachers I have ever had the good fortune to know, graciously agreed to accompany me on a canoe trip to retrace the steps of Sullivan's army along the Susquehanna River. The Susquehanna on an August day can be hot and slow. Chuck always found a way to make the journey into an educational experience. His knowledge of physical geography and geology proved particularly insightful in understanding the effect of the valley's terrain on Sullivan's logistics. Scott Dratch contributed to the maps and graphics that accompany this study. Over more cups of coffee than I can count, Dr. Susan Shirk challenged my ideas and showed me new ways to look at the people and events that we historians see only dimly through the darkened glass of time. My running buddy, Dr. William Blair, was a constant source of support and friendly criticism, especially when the road seemed too long and the finish line beyond reach. Nancy Adams, a special friend, took up where Bill finished, encouraging me through to the final completion of this labor.

Finally, I am indebted to my parents. Estalene Fischer, my mother, has patiently seen me through the years that have gone into this. As for my father, Russell J. Fischer, who passed away long before this book's first words were written, it is to his memory that I dedicate this study of the Continental army.

A Well-Executed Failure

The Sullivan Campaign against the Iroquois, July–September 1779

1

INTRODUCTION

In the spring of 1779 the United States entered its fifth year of war in its bid for independence from England. It had been a long and trying experience thus far for the new nation. What many Americans had hoped would be a short contest now seemed to have no end in sight. General Henry Clinton's army in New York City and Newport, Rhode Island, remained a constant threat to the rebellion's future. Over the winter, however, that army had remained relatively quiet, as British leaders in Whitehall rethought their strategy to account for changes in the military situation. France's entry into the conflict in 1778 had widened the war and forced the British to turn their attention southward to the Caribbean, Georgia, and the Carolinas. General George Washington intended to make use of the respite his opponents offered.

On 17 March 1779 Major General John Sullivan received an express packet from Washington. The correspondence arrived by way of Major General Horatio Gates in Boston.[1] In the letter Washington revealed that he intended to send part of his army against the Iroquois Confederacy in New York during the spring. With an anticipated strength of at least four thousand soldiers, the campaign would be the largest independent command created in the North since the Saratoga campaign. Given the magnitude of the undertaking, Washington offered it first to Gates, with instructions that he pass the appointment to Sullivan if he believed himself not up to the mission.[2] Gates declined the offer, excusing himself under the pretext that the rigors of such an expedition on the frontier called for the services of a younger man than he.[3] Sullivan responded with only slightly more enthusiasm, claiming that his own failing health and the demands of family business kept him from rendering an answer.[4] After pondering the offer for nearly a week, Sullivan decided to accept. Turning his command over to Brigadier General John Glover, Sullivan departed Providence, Rhode Island, and began the journey to Middlebrook, New Jersey, to confer with Washington.[5]

Sullivan thus far had not enjoyed a particularly successful military career. He had commanded the withdrawal of the American expeditionary force from Canada in 1776. At Brooklyn Heights the British outflanked his forces, and Sullivan himself was captured in the ensuing confusion. After his exchange he performed admirably at Trenton, only to find himself again the subject of criticism when his division crumbled and fled at Brandywine Creek. Sullivan had his share of critics both in and out of the army. The onetime New Hampshire lawyer could be pompous and seldom missed an opportunity to spar with his critics. Aware of Sullivan's faults, Washington nonetheless found many of his subordinate's traits to his liking, particularly his knack for detailed planning. The nature of the campaign Washington envisioned required such skills.

In the six months that separated his appointment from the completion of the offensive, Sullivan found his talents as well as his patience sorely tested. Because of circumstances largely beyond his control, he failed to have his army ready to move before the end of July 1779. Once the march began, however, he executed Washington's instructions to the letter, returning triumphant two months later to the grassy river plain near Fort Sullivan at Tioga, Pennsylvania (fig. 1). A thirteen-gun salute and cheering garrison greeted Sullivan and his men, behind whom lay the ruins of the once powerful Iroquois nation.[6] The army had brought a whirlwind of destruction to their Tory and Indian adversaries during the campaign in the Iroquois country. Their torches had reduced forty Iroquois towns and villages to ashes and destroyed 160,000 bushels of corn, which would have fed many in the coming winter. The soldiers had girdled the bark on thousands of fruit trees, leaving them to wither and die in the frost-touched autumn mornings.[7]

INTRODUCTION

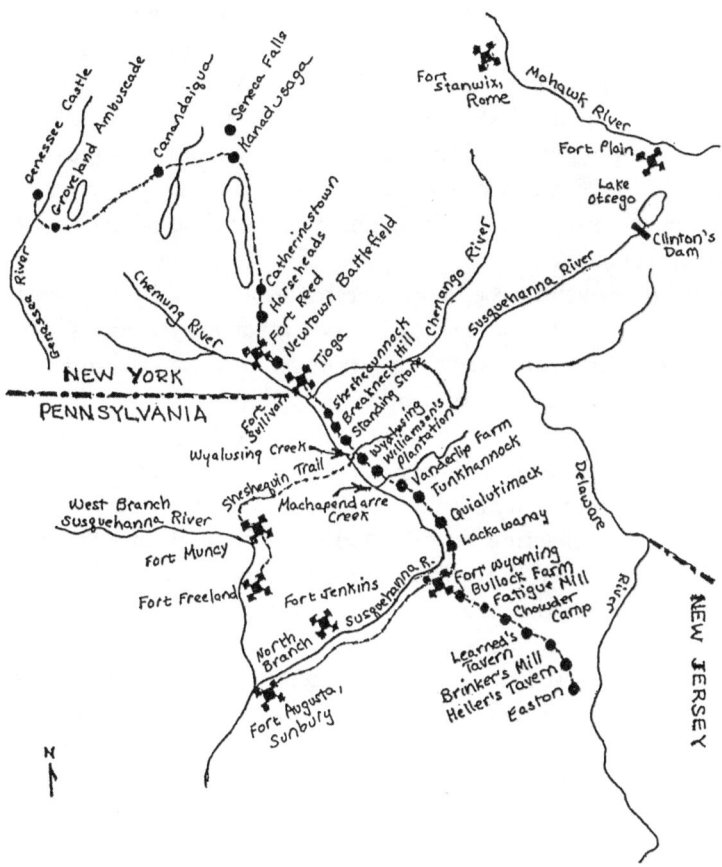

Fig. 1. Sullivan expedition, July–October 1779 (courtesy of the Northumberland County Historical Society, Sunbury, Pennsylvania).

Neither the Iroquois nor their allies had offered much resistance. Falling back in anger and frustration before Sullivan's advancing army, nearly three thousand inhabitants of the stricken villages finally found refuge with the British at Fort Niagara. Even there the nightmare did not end. The following winter proved to be one of the hardest on record. Snow piled several feet deep in the forests of northwestern New York made hunting difficult. With supplies short and several thousand refugees still camped outside the fort, British officers found themselves unable to cope with the problem. Hunger, scurvy, and other diseases took their toll. Attempts to convince the refugees to take up temporary residence with allied tribes in Canada met with only partial success. The Iroquois would emerge from the winter of 1779–80 much weakened but still unbroken. Motivated by revenge, they resumed their attacks against the frontier settlements with the coming of spring.

Sullivan's strike into the Iroquois heartland stands out as the Continental army's single major undertaking in 1779. Involving the efforts of fifteen regiments of infantry and one of artillery, it demonstrated the complexities of eighteenth-century military campaigning. Unlike other campaigns conducted against Indians during the war, it involved almost exclusively experienced regulars.[8] The operation required months of preparation by quartermaster and commissary agents to organize a supply base capable of sustaining an army operating in the wilderness. The work that Washington and his staff dedicated to the intelligence preparations proved no less impressive. Despite all this, the Sullivan expedition has received scant attention from modern scholars of American military history.

The campaign lacked the dramatic luster of other events of the Revolutionary War. Only a handful of combatants lost their lives in battle and few civilians died as a direct result of the operation.[9] Only one small-scale battle outside the Delaware village of Newtown (near present-day Elmira, N.Y.) on the Chemung River and two smaller skirmishes occurred during the entire campaign. Several additional factors may help explain the lack of emphasis historians have given the event. First, Sullivan's opposition consisted almost entirely of Tory irregulars and Iroquois warriors, because the theater contained no large British army to challenge Sullivan. Second, the border war occurred in one of the most sparsely populated areas of the colonies, well away from the public eye and largely out of the news. Finally, the resumption of raids against the settlements the following spring clearly challenged Sullivan's contention that the raid had been a tremendous success. As the war dragged on, it appeared increasingly insignificant to the larger outcome.

Early histories of the American Revolution by nationalist school historians gave the Sullivan expedition little attention. In George Bancroft's

History of the United States the author accorded it only a passing glance, blaming Sullivan's "insatiable demands on the government of Pennsylvania" for delaying the expedition's start and largely ignoring its place in the overall war effort.[10] Benson Lossing provided a much better account in *Pictorial Field Book of the Revolution*. He judged the expedition a failure but defended the army's leadership for the damage inflicted on Iroquois culture. "To us, looking upon the scene from a point so remote, it is difficult to perceive the necessity that calls for a chastisement so cruel and terrible," he wrote. "But that such necessity seemed to exist we should not doubt for it was the judicious and benevolent mind of Washington that conceived and planned the campaign, and ordered its rigid execution in the manner in which it was accomplished."[11] Lossing left the military aspects of the operation largely unexplored.

Local historians from Pennsylvania's Susquehanna Valley and New York's Finger Lakes region attempted to raise the stature of the campaign to commemorate its centennial in 1879. A. Tiffany Norton grounded his *History of Sullivan's Campaign against the Iroquois* in primary materials, relying upon the journals and letters of some of the expedition's participants but largely ignoring British, Tory, and Indian sources. The book is a simple campaign narrative, long on patriotism and short on analysis. Overstating his case, Norton declared the campaign "one of the most important military movements of the Revolutionary War." Yet he neglected to explain how its results worked to bring the British to the peace table or modified the results of peace negotiations.[12]

David Craft, a minister and local historian from Athens (Tioga), Pennsylvania, published a briefer account the same year Norton's study appeared. It contained much of the same patriotic rhetoric and ethnocentrism. Craft stressed that Sullivan's efforts determined "whether the American Indian, with his deeply rooted prejudices, with his unconquerable aversion to civilization, with his undisguised hatred for religion and the cultures of the European, was longer to stand in the way of human progress."[13] Failing to use the numerous primary sources available for study, Craft also badly misunderstood the participants of the event and misinterpreted its significance. The Iroquois possessed one of the most advanced political and social structures to be found anywhere in North America. Craft's insistence on passing judgments on who was "civilized," particularly when starvation of the

Iroquois constituted the campaign's primary purpose, demonstrated the social Darwinism of the author.

Twentieth-century historians have produced journal articles on the expedition or discussed it as part of broader works. Most have been summaries of Norton's and Craft's narratives, but a few stand out for their examination of issues left untouched by these earlier authors. Alexander C. Flick first searched archival materials in Ottawa and London to add a better understanding of Sullivan's opponents. He also advanced the idea that the campaign accomplished more than punitive goals: (1) curbing the power of New York's Tory elements, (2) cutting off a key source of British grain supplies, and (3) helping the United States stake a claim to the western lands south of the Great Lakes during negotiations leading up to the Treaty of Paris.[14] Howard Swiggett's *War out of Niagara,* a history of the British side of the frontier war in New York and Pennsylvania, agreed with Flick's findings and subscribed to Craft's and Norton's idea that the campaign was far more significant than most historians believed.[15] Christopher Ward took up the issue of Sullivan's expedition in *The War of the Revolution.* His campaign narrative examines Washington's aims, summarizes the campaign's execution, and concludes with a discussion of its impact. Taking issue with Flick, Ward judged the effort a failure that tied the Iroquois even more closely to the British while conceding that their anemic inability to mount any serious opposition to the Americans probably dealt a serious blow to the League's military prestige.[16]

More recent articles by Morris Bishop and Donald R. McAdams have taken opposite views concerning the success of the operation. Bishop argues that Sullivans's expedition may not have finished the Iroquois but did push back the frontier and cut the heart out of the League.[17] Although agreeing about the level of destruction Sullivan and his men inflicted, McAdams insisted that the expedition failed completely to bring peace to the frontier by crushing the Indians; both the size and frequency of Indian-Tory raids increased over the war's remaining years.[18] Barbara Graymont provided the best account of the Iroquois side of the campaign in *The Iroquois in the American Revolution.* She emphasized that Sullivan had indeed cut a swath through the Iroquois homelands that irreparably damaged the Iroquois, but he failed to break their spirit. More dependent than ever on the British, the Iroquois approached the remaining years of the war motivated by an intense desire for revenge.[19] The campaign also complicated postwar dealings between the Confederation and the United States. In 1790 the Seneca chief Cornplanter reminded Washington of the legacy of the general's decision: "When your army entered the country of the Six Nations, we called you Town Destroyer and to this day when that name is heard our women look behind them and turn pale, and our children cling close to the necks of their mothers."[20] In *The War of American Independence* Don Higginbotham briefly touched on the campaign, lauding Washington and Sullivan for their efforts in planning and executing the undertaking. Like McAdams and Graymont, Higginbotham questioned its success, pointing out that, although "the Sullivan expedition provided Americans with an example of how to conduct Indian warfare, it was no more decisive in its outcome than Clark's dazzling stroke along the Wabash."[21] Robert Middlekauff's *The Glorious Cause* ignores the campaign entirely.[22]

The point of contention for all the major works on Sullivan's expedition has been the focus on its strategic impact. Flick's view that the campaign helped the United States lay claim to the western lands south of the Great Lakes stands out as the strongest statement in this regard. But Flick overstates his case and offers no evidence in support. American claims to the Ohio Valley, championed by influential land speculators both in and out of the Continental Congress, rested on colonial charters rather than military conquest. That Britain agreed to accept American claims on the region came about for two reasons. First, British ministers, particularly Lord Shelburne, simply did not value the territory enough to make retaining it a point of contention. They believed that the Appalachians would prove a barrier to trade with the Atlantic seaboard, making the region's future settlers economically dependent on British Canada.[23] Second, John Jay's astute diplomatic maneuvering effectively froze the French out of the treaty negotiations and prevented the imposition of a more restrictive boundary on the United States.[24] George Rogers Clark's exploits had little to do with the final settlement, and Sullivan's figured not at all, as neither campaign produced a permanent American military presence in the region.

Previous research largely ignores the contribution a study of the Sullivan campaign can make to understanding the Continental army at midwar. The militia units and volunteers assembled to contain the British army in Boston in 1775 represent American society's first attempt to field an army.

With its ranks dominated by untrained farmers and its leadership only slightly more experienced, the force possessed few attributes of a European army. Through a combination of factors, not the least of which was luck, it managed to survive the opening years of the conflict. Sullivan's expedition provides an opportunity to answer many important questions concerning the army's condition and development in the middle years of the war. To what extent had Washington developed a strategic plan for the war? How was intelligence collected, evaluated, and processed? What kind of tactics and doctrine guided the army's actions, and to what extent were homegrown solutions applied to fighting in the North American wilderness? How well did the supply system work? How did the Continental officers and noncommissioned officers motivate and lead their men? How well did soldiers respond to the army's leadership style, particularly given the army's social composition?

From a broader perspective the campaign also sheds light on the nature of the relationship existing among the Continental army, the civil governments, and the people of those regions in the interior most victimized by Tory and Indian raiding parties. Washington undertook this campaign largely to quiet the pleadings of the Continental Congress and state governments to do something to bring the raids to an end.[25] He ordered the expedition with great reluctance and only after it became clear that more decisive options simply were not viable. Given the circumstances, he undoubtedly expected cooperation in support of the project. Was this an unreasonable expectation, given the problems facing public officials at both the state and national levels? To what extent were they able to support the expedition? Because Sullivan's force represents one of the largest independent commands ever detached from the main Continental army, answers to these questions provide an insightful picture of the Continental army at the war's midpoint.

A study of the campaign reveals problems in the army. The tenuous nature of the supply system threatened failure in all of its endeavors. Furthermore, the lack of an adequate working relationship among leaders at the national, state, and army levels created considerable friction, tried Washington's patience, and endangered the cause in the name of provincialism. The campaign's accomplishments, however, suggest that the army had made considerable strides during the first years of the fighting.

2

THE FRONTIER IN FLAMES: 1778

The roots of the Sullivan expedition lay in the American leadership's inability to confine the conflict to the seaboard. The settled interior of the Middle Colonies served as the strategic rear for the Continental army, providing supplies and a safe haven for the army should the British push it from the coast.[1] Commissary officers found these farming regions of Pennsylvania and New York particularly well suited for providing food and fodder. Farther to the west, new lands were being brought into production and in the short span of thirteen years that separated the French and Indian War from the Revolution, settlers had made considerable strides toward developing them into some of the most productive grain-producing regions in the colonies. For British commanders controlling these areas seemed one of the surest ways to cripple Washington and his army. Failing this, disrupting the harvest could yield the same result.

Settlers had only recently opened much of Pennsylvania's and New York's western lands to cultivation. The French and Indian War and Pontiac's Rebellion temporarily had stopped the westward march of settlers, but, with the coming of peace, Iroquois resentment as well as that of Mingo, Shawnee, and Delaware peoples living along a rapidly shifting frontier had risen as white encroachments resumed. The focus of much of the friction existing between whites and Indians centered in the Ohio Valley, although the disposition of lands in Pennsylvania's and New York's Susquehanna Valley were also contested. To defuse the situation and to permit the repositioning of British soldiers eastward to deal with mounting civil tensions, the Board of Trade had ordered William Johnson, its superintendent of Indian affairs in the northern district, to negotiate a new treaty line that would provide a clearer boundary between the English settlements and Indian lands.[2] The board's instructions for the new treaty not only assumed a westward shift of the Proclamation of 1763 boundary to accommodate existing settlements but also anticipated demands for new lands.

The Iroquois acted as principal spokesmen for the Indian tribes during negotiations, claiming that the tribes of the Ohio Valley had been dependents of the Six Nations. Iroquois claims to these lands were dubious at best. Nonetheless, it had long been the contention of the English Crown that the Iroquois had conquered the Indian peoples of the Ohio Valley. On the eve of the French and Indian War, British cartographer Lewis Evans published his *General Map of the Middle British Colonies in America with an Analysis giving much attention to the boundaries of the Six Nations "Confederates."* According to Evans's map, the Mississippi River formed the western terminus of the Iroquois Confederacy. The myth of an expansive Iroquois empire served as a convenient justification for British claims to the trans-Appalachian West in their contest with the French.[3] Although the Iroquois insisted on seeing themselves as independent of the British Crown, England's rulers saw things differently. The Iroquois and all the lands they had conquered, or claimed they had conquered, became part of the English view of their own empire.[4] Perpetuating the myth also simplified the process of opening these lands to settlement. Instead of having to deal with the various tribes settled along the Ohio, the Crown's Indian agents only had to come to the Iroquois.

What the Iroquois hoped to achieve was a treaty that provided a clear boundary between white and Indian settlements while at the same time insuring that no restrictions existed to the continuation of commerce between the two peoples. Iroquois sachems wanted assurances that roads and waterways would remain open and that they would retain hunting rights to any lands ceded to the whites.[5] Most important, the Iroquois hoped to eliminate the sources of conflict between the English and themselves by using the Ohio lands as a means of diverting white settlement toward Kentucky and western Virginia. This could only be done at the expense of the Ohio tribes.

Several thousand Indians, to include tribal leaders of the Iroquois, Shawnee, and Delaware tribes along with representatives from the colonies of New Jersey, New York, Pennsylvania, and Virginia, gathered at Fort Stanwix to discuss the terms of the treaty. Like many past treaties involving Indian lands, this one had its public version in which key leaders postured for interested listeners and a private side in which the real business was conducted. Signed in 1768, the Treaty of Fort Stanwix opened more lands to white settlement than even the board had directed or the tribes of the Ohio had wanted.[6] The new boundary in Pennsylvania ran from the Ohio River to the west branch of the Susquehanna, then cross-country to the Susquehanna's north branch. In New York the line followed the Susquehanna to the headwaters of the Unandilla River, ending on Wood Creek west of Fort Stanwix (fig. 2).[7] The Iroquois achieved their aim of keeping the waterways open for commerce by insisting that the rivers themselves serving as treaty boundaries remain on the Indian side of the dividing line. On the west branch of the Susquehanna, for example, where the treaty opened the valley to white settlement as far as Tiadaghton Creek, this was done by drawing the boundary line along the river's western and southern shores.[8]

Within the Iroquois Confederation the treaty found mixed support. In exchange for the concessions the Iroquois received what they at first thought would be a clear set of boundaries separating their lands from that of white settlers. The problem was that cartographers who produced maps showing the lands to be open to white settlement misrepresented the geography of the Susquehanna Valley during treaty discussions then produced corrected maps once the treaty was signed. The result was to create confusion and suspicion among the Iroquois. Land speculators and common farmers proved eager to take advantage of the situation, and a growing reluctance on the part of England to use force against errant whites guilty of treaty violations complicated the problem. On the Susquehanna's west branch the propensity of whites to disregard treaty agreements became a continuing problem.

Fig. 2. Treaty of Fort Stanwix, 1768 (broken line represents new settlement line).

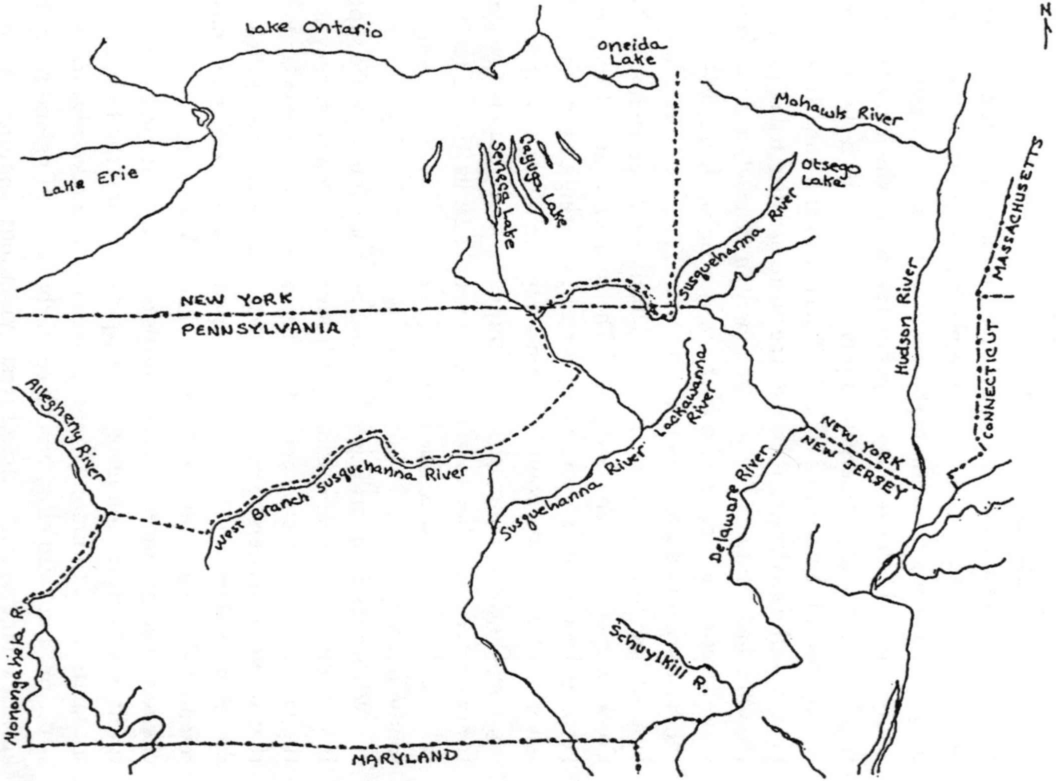

Outside the Iroquois Confederation the treaty proved a diplomatic blunder. The Shawnee in particular realized that the Iroquois had not looked after their interests and had instead sold their tribal hunting lands without providing compensation. As a result, the Shawnee took an active step in helping to form a competing union of western tribes bent on opposing further white encroachments. Because of their readiness to sell lands that belonged to other native peoples, Iroquois influence over the tribes of the Ohio decreased at the same time British authorities began to place additional pressure on the Confederation to insure the compliance of their wards. The outbreak of Lord Dunmore's War in 1774 gave stark testimony to the inability of the Iroquois either to control the tribes of the Ohio, particularly the Shawnee, or to force the British to deal with the white encroachments that precipitated the war.[9]

The rivers of New York and Pennsylvania provided access into the newly opened lands. By the time of the Revolution the settlement line in New York had pushed up the Mohawk River to German Flats and included a series of smaller settlements just east of Otsego Lake in Cherry Valley. In Pennsylvania settlers from Connecticut had occupied the Wyoming Valley, precipitating a land dispute with Pennsylvania's government, which refused to recognize Connecticut's claim to the area. North of Wyoming settlement thinned significantly, although a few small farms dotted the bottom land along the Susquehanna's east bank nearly as far north as Tioga. Several abandoned Indian villages still marked the trail northward from Wyoming. The largest of these was the old Moravian mission of Friedenshütten (tents of peace) located along the river not far from Wyalusing. Following the Treaty of Fort Stanwix the Moravians elected to relocate the settlement to the Ohio Valley.[10] On the west branch settlers from New Jersey had opened farms upriver as far as Pine Creek. This influx of white settlers coexisted for a time with small Indian villages from a variety of tribes who had settled in the area following the Lancaster Treaty of 1744.

The new lands proved exceptionally rich. Land companies in the Susquehanna described the area in almost utopian terms. One advertisement claimed "that fresh Settlers frequently do not till the Land for the First Crop but only rake the ground clean, then sow the Wheat."[11] Travelers to the area did not find the boast to be too far afield. Philip Vickers Fithian, a missionary to the Susquehanna River settlements, enthusiastically described the area's pastoralism:

By ten I left Town [Sunbury], West Branch of the Susquehannah [*sic*]; The Road lies along the River and after leaving Town a Mile, such a fertile, level, goodly Country I have perhaps never seen. Wheat & Rye, thick and very high; Oats I saw in many Places, yet green, and full as high, in general through the field, as a six railed Fence! Pokes, and Elders higher than my head, as I sat on my Horse! And the Country is thick inhabited, and grows to be a little open. . . . The Woods are musical, they are harmonious. Bells tinkling from every Quarter, make a continued, and a charming Echo. Cows returning home; Sheep, and Horses grazing through the Woods, and these all round, in every Part, make, surely, a transporting Vesper![12]

Along the Mohawk, Scottish and German farmers made up the majority of the new settlers; in Pennsylvania, Scotch-Irish, English, and to a lesser extent Germans drove the settlement line westward. At the time of the Revolution most of these new homesteads were subsistence endeavors. Times were changing, however. Many farmers, especially in the middle Susquehanna Valley, began to find increasing opportunities for trade beyond the limits of their valleys. The commencement of military operations in 1775 accelerated this trend.[13] The small village of Sunbury, built south of Fort Augusta at the confluence of the North and West Branches of the Susquehanna River, served as the area's hub for the shipment of agricultural products to eastern markets. By 1775 Sunbury contained one hundred houses and was connected by road to Reading and by water to Harris Ferry. Northumberland, a smaller sister village, had grown across the river to help ship the ever growing agricultural surplus of the area. Fithian described Northumberland's wharves as being "as *busy* & *noisy* as a Philadelphia Ferry House."[14] Commissary officers searching the backcountry for farmers willing to sell their grain became a frequent sight. In addition, state governments saw grain surpluses as a commodity exchangeable for badly needed hard currency.[15] Both the Continental Congress and the state governments correctly believed it in their best interests to keep these border regions out of the war.

The numerous Native American nations that lay just beyond the western fringes of the white settlements threatened the security of the backcountry. In the South the Cherokee opted for war in May 1776 against

The Frontier in Flames: 1778

the rebellious colonists of the Carolinas and Georgia, who had been openly encroaching on tribal lands. The decision proved a disaster for the Cherokee, and by the summer of 1777 the tribe's chiefs found themselves forced to sign two peace treaties, surrendering their claims to lands in South Carolina as well as parts of North Carolina and Virginia. The defeat of the Cherokee benefited the Americans in their war against Great Britain, for harsh terms of the peace treaty effectively intimidated other southern tribes into remaining out of the conflict. Farther north in the Ohio Valley the effect of the Cherokee defeat was not so pronounced. The Shawnee and a few members of the Delaware cast their lot with the British, believing their future threatened if England's rebelling colonies gained their independence. Most of the Delaware elected to remain neutral, although Moravian ministers such as David Zeisberger applied subtle pressure on tribal leaders to back the American cause.[16]

In western New York the Iroquois Confederation offered a particular challenge. Formed for defensive purposes, the Confederation emerged over time into the most powerful Native American tribal organization of the colonial period, although by the time of the American Revolution its power was clearly on the decline.[17] Consisting originally of the Onondaga, Oneida, Seneca, Cayuga, and Mohawk tribes, the League expanded to include the Tuscarora, following the loss of their lands in the Carolinas at the conclusion of the Tuscarora War of 1711–13.[18] Beginning in about 1675 the Confederation also undertook a policy to enhance the security of Iroquoia by accepting Indian refugees from both former enemies and allies. Shawnee, Delaware, Nanticoke, Conoy, and others found themselves welcomed into the Confederacy. Rather than allow them access to land inside the Iroquois homelands, however, the League settled these displaced peoples along the Susquehanna and Allegheny watersheds, where they could help guard the natural avenues of approach into Iroquoia. To provide further support to Iroquois claims to the Susquehanna Valley, the League maintained a token presence in settlements along the river and retained loose oversight powers in the person of Shikellamy, an Oneida headman who resided at Shamokin (present-day Sunbury) until his death in 1747.[19] Frederick Post, a Moravian missionary living along the Susquehanna in 1759, recorded his understanding of Iroquois settlement policy:

They settle these New Allies on the Frontiers of the White People and give them this as their Instruction. "Be Watchful that no body of the White People may come to settle near you. You must appear to them as frightful Men, & if notwithstanding they come too near give them a Push. We will secure and defend you against them. . . . The Chain of Union between the several Indian Nation is of that nature, that if we have War with one of them, we have also war with them all.[20]

As a political-military entity, Iroquois power extended across the New York and Pennsylvania frontiers into the Ohio River Valley. Throughout the colonial period every major dynastic war on the North American continent involving England and France caught the Iroquois in the middle. Courted by both sides and in the end unable to remain neutral during King William's War (1689–97), the Confederation suffered the brunt of the fighting. Rather than risk further loss, Iroquois diplomatic policy adhered to a measured neutrality in the next two dynastic contests. When the Seven Years' War came, the Iroquois attempted to continue this policy but finally found themselves drawn into the conflict. However valuable were their contributions to the final British victory, the Confederation emerged from the war politically and diplomatically weakened.

During the first half of the eighteenth century Iroquois independence was based on a delicate combination of military power and diplomatic finesse. The Confederacy adhered to a course that effectively played off England against France while maneuvering among the interests of Virginia, Pennsylvania, and New York concerning trade and the opening of new lands. It used its position of influence among the Europeans as well as the power of the League's tribal alliance to manipulate other tribes.[21] The French and Indian War badly eroded the Confederacy's position, and, as war clouds gathered in 1775, tribal leaders feared the worst. A war between England and its colonies threatened to sweep the League forward to its doom. Regardless of which side won the contest, the League would be faced with a new reality, one in which it no longer enjoyed room for diplomatic maneuver. Once in this position, the continued existence of the League rested on the victor's whim.

The Frontier in Flames: 1778

Volckert P. Douw and Turbutt Francis, the First Continental Congress's commissioners to the Iroquois, made it clear as early as August 1775 that the Continental Congress strongly favored Iroquois neutrality.[22] "This is a family quarrel between us and Old England," they told Iroquois sachems. "You Indians are not concerned in it. We don't want you to take up the hatchet against the king."[23] In no hurry to rush into a conflict they did not understand, Abraham, a Mohawk sachem, responded on behalf of the Confederation:

> We have fully considered this Matter. The Resolutions of the Six Nations are not to be broken or altered. When they resolve the Matter is fixed. This then is the Determination of the Six Nations. Not to take any part, but as it is a family Affair to sit still and see you fight it out. We beg you will receive this as infallible it being in full Resolution. For we bear as much Affection for the King of England's Subjects upon the other Side of the Water as we do for you born upon this island.[24]

Iroquois sachems made it clear to the two agents that their neutrality was not unconditional. If the Americans persisted in waging war against their former king, then the Iroquois demanded that the fighting be kept to the east, far from tribal homelands. Fearing the impact of war on trade relations, sachems insisted that their hunting rights as well as access to the various trading posts along the frontier not be impeded. Furthermore, Loyalist friends of the Iroquois, such as Sir John Johnson and the Reverend Mr. John Stuart, missionary to the Mohawk, were not to be disturbed. Later the Iroquois added another condition by warning the Americans against any military expedition to seize the British outpost at Detroit.[25]

At the start of the Revolutionary War, Whitehall also wanted to keep the Iroquois as well as other Indian nations out of the conflict. The British did not expect a protracted war and desired to avoid adding the uncertainties of an Indian conflict to the contest. Given the political-military problem that the rebelling colonies caused for Britain, the decision to keep the Indians out of it demonstrated considerable logic. Success required combining two difficult and related tasks—that of defeating the rebel army while at the same time finding a way to pacify the population. British leaders such as Lord George Germain mistakenly believed that the people responsible for fomenting the rebellion enjoyed the support of only a small part of the colonial population. Once British forces crushed rebel military power in an area, so Germain's thinking went, the majority of the population would willingly resume its support for the Crown; the pacification problem, therefore, did not loom as large as the military one.[26] An Indian war would threaten this assumption. During the French and Indian War the raids and ambushes that characterized Indian tactics had claimed the lives of combatants and noncombatants alike. Should Britain deliberately start an Indian war, the scars it left behind might threaten pacification.[27]

Within the British military considerable disagreement existed on the utility of Indians. Some British commanders believed that Indians could contribute to the British cause without endangering pacification if kept under tight control. The Americans themselves had provided an opening to justify their use. The Mohicans of Stockbridge elected as early as the siege of Boston to provide warriors to serve in Massachusetts' militia companies. Painted for war, they, along with some of the frontier riflemen from Pennsylvania and Virginia, made a practice of sniping at British sentries. When the British became more respectful of their adversaries' marksmanship, the Mohicans adopted an approach more closely akin to psychological warfare. They would approach as close as possible to British lines, yelling insults and making a great show of displaying their scalping knives. When opportunity presented itself, a few added a note of levity to the situation by turning to display their buttocks to British ships positioned offshore.[28]

Lieutenant General Thomas Gage held mixed opinions regarding the use of Indians. He perceived the Mohicans as domesticated and therefore possessing the fighting qualities of neither Indian nor European. During the French and Indian War he wrote: "These Indians were last campaign so great a nuisance to the army and did no manner of service. Some people say they were not properly managed. I own myself ignorant of the management that is proper for those gentry; can only say that neither orders nor entreatys [sic] could prevail on them to do service, always lying drunk in their hutts [sic], or firing round the camp."[29] The Mohicans he found outside his lines at Boston in 1775 did not shake his earlier opinions; however, Gage was not one to generalize the military prowess of one tribe as being indicative of all Indian nations. It had been Gage, after all, who had penned the official report on Braddock's ill-fated expedition to the forks of the Ohio. In his findings Gage noted that one of the major factor's in the defeat was "the want of Indians or of other irregulars to give timely notice of the enemy's approach."[30] The Americans' decision to employ the Stockbridge Mohicans provided a pretext for British authorities in Canada to recruit from tribes along the St. Lawrence. Writing to the earl of Dartmouth, Gage argued that "we need not be tender of calling upon the Savages, as the Rebels have shewn [sic] us the example, and brought all they could down upon us here."[31] Gage urged Major General Guy Carleton, commander of the Canadian theater early in the war, to push the Indians into a declaration of war against the Americans.[32] Carleton did not share Gage's enthusiasm and doubted whether the contributions of Native American warriors would be worth the cost involved in bringing them into the fray. He feared that Indians would be largely worthless in battle while at the same time requiring considerable logistical support to keep them in the field.[33]

The British view on the use of Indians began to change as Whitehall developed a strategy for the war. The first evolution of the British strategic plan, the Hudson Valley plan put forth in the fall of 1775, saw New England as the center of rebellion. Seizing control of the Hudson River to cut off New England from the rest of the colonies represented the first step. Once New England was isolated, British armies could then invade east from the Hudson Valley, while a British army based in Rhode Island raided north and south along the coast.[34] These British forces operating along the Hudson might require the service of guides and scouts, roles well matched to the skills of Indians. The initial plan contained a number of flaws; most important, it failed to address genuine colonial vulnerabilities. The causes of the war went far beyond New England's dissatisfaction with British policy. In 1777 an inept attempt to execute this plan led to the British disaster at Saratoga.[35]

Saratoga changed Britain's strategic problem. A war intended to bring thirteen wayward colonies back under the Crown's control had grown to threaten the empire's existence. The addition of France to the war caused a contraction of British military operations in the thirteen colonies to meet the wider threat now looming over the empire. British leaders shifted their attention to the West Indies, where they expected a French challenge for control over the sugar islands.[36] The military actions of 1777—Saratoga,

Germantown, and Brandywine—had sobered British commanders about their opponent's capabilities.[37] Increasingly, Germain believed it unlikely that his commanders could draw Washington into a decisive battle. General Henry Clinton's task, if he could not shatter the Continental army on the battlefield, would be to fix it in place, while detached elements of the British army worked to conquer the southern states. Once under the protection of the British army, Loyalist militias would take on the task of securing and pacifying a population that American Loyalists had assured them was largely pro-British.[38] This plan had the added advantage of concentrating the British military effort closer to the West Indies, where the French navy threatened British possessions.

Under this plan Indian involvement in the North, particularly that of the Iroquois, played a significant role. Ideally, raids against New York's and Pennsylvania's western settlements, areas that Washington depended on for food and fodder, would force the diversion of Continental soldiers to defend these regions. The American failure to seize and hold Canada early in the war meant that the British retained control of the St. Lawrence River and their forts along the Great Lakes. These posts provided British generals with the means to keep a military force working against these rear areas supplied from Montreal and Quebec. Washington's army occupied increasingly well-fortified positions in the Hudson Highlands around West Point. Diverting large numbers of Washington's soldiers to frontier defense could weaken the army in the Highlands and make it vulnerable to attack by British forces from New York City. Should Washington elect to defend the frontier with militia, a politically unpopular course of action in both Pennsylvania and New York, the impact on civilian morale could only play into British hands. At the very least a successful campaign capable of driving in the frontiers and disrupting the food-producing regions of the settled interior threatened the Continental army's source of supplies.[39] Washington might find himself unable to provide either manpower or supplies to oppose British operations in the South.

To make the strategy viable, however, required the active assistance of the Confederation and its allies to provide badly needed manpower as well as expertise. British garrisons stationed along the frontier were too few to present a significant threat. Should American Indian agents gain the neutrality of the tribes or, worse, their support, the strategy fell apart. Instead of providing a means to weaken the Americans, the need to divert resources to secure the Great Lakes posts would have the opposite effect.

Iroquois hunting parties had been a common sight in the frontier regions of Pennsylvania and New York. With the coming of war, they vanished as the Iroquois considered how to react. The problem of what to do became the dominant issue at Onondaga in 1776. Increasingly, tribal sachems found themselves pressured to side with the British. Tory leaders such as John and Guy Johnson enjoyed considerable status among the tribes, thanks largely to their relationship to the now deceased William Johnson. John Butler proved no less influential and even more energetic in manipulating Iroquois sympathies. From inside the Confederation, Molly Brant, Sir William Johnson's widow and the head of a society of Six Nation matrons, stood as an unwavering proponent of Iroquois involvement on the side of the British. As Daniel Claus, a longtime subordinate of William Johnson, remarked concerning Molly, "one word from her goes farther with them than a thousand from any white Man without Exception who in general must purchase their Interest at a high rate."[40] Molly's younger brother, Joseph Brant, an Anglicized Mohawk, also demonstrated an untiring desire to bring his people over to the English cause. Schooled at Eleazar Wheelock's Indian Charity School in Connecticut, Joseph was fluent in the English language and held a sound understanding of his adversaries. Both British and Loyalist officers took a liking to Joseph, and Carleton promoted him to the rank of captain. Over the course of the border war Joseph would become one of the most feared of Iroquois war leaders.[41]

The British diplomatic offensive to bring the Iroquois into the conflict dates to the spring of 1776. In a council held in late May and early June a condescending John Butler appealed directly to Iroquois fears, warning them of their fate should the Americans win:

> Your Father the Great King has taken pity on you and is determined not to let the Americans deceive you any longer—tho' you have been so foolish as to listen to them last year and to believe all their wicked stories—they mean to cheat you and should you be so silly as to take their advice and they should conquer the King's Army, their intention is to take all your Lands from you and destroy your people, for they are all mad, foolish, crazy and full of deceit—

> They told you last Fall at Pittsburgh that they took the Tom Hawk out of your Hands and buried it deep and transplanted the Tree of Peace over it. I therefore now pluck up that Tree, dig up the Tom Hawk, and replace it in your hands with the Edge toward them that you may treat them as Enemies.[42]

The council pondered the speech for several days before answering Butler. Speaking on behalf of the full council, Kayashuta, a Seneca, replied:

> It is three nights since you told me the Americans, with whom you are at War, are all mad, foolish, crazy and full of deceit, and that their intentions toward us are bad. . . . I now tell you that you are the mad, foolish, crazy and deceitful person—for you think we are fools and advise us to do what is not in our interest. The Americans on the contrary are the wise people so far as they have yet spoke to us—for what they advise us is in our Interest to follow—they tell us your quarrel is between yourselves and desire us to sit still and they tell us right. But you want us to assist you which we cannot do—for suppose the Americans conquer you what would they then say to us. I tell you Brother you are foolish and we will not allow you to pluck up the Tree of Peace nor raise the Hatchet. We are strong and able to do it ourselves when we are hurt.

Neither Butler nor some of the pro-British Iroquois assembled were willing to accept the council's decision. The following day a Mohawk speaker attempted to rebut Kayashuta's answer. The maneuver failed. Flying Crow, another Seneca, provided the council's final response to Butler's appeal for war:

> You have called us here to open Our Eyes, to break the Peace we live in with our American Brethren and to ask our help to fight them. . . . We have now lived in Peace with them a long time and we resolve to continue to do so as long as we can—when they hurt us it is time enough to strike them. If you are so strong Brother, and they but as a weak Boy, why ask our assistance? It is true I am tall and strong but I will reserve my strength to strike those who injure me. If you have so great plenty of Warriors, Powder, Lead and Goods, and they are so few and little of either, be strong and make

good use of them. You say their Powder is rotten—We have found it good. You say they are mad, foolish, wicked, and deceitful—I say you are so and they are wise for you want us to destroy ourselves in your War and they advise us to live in Peace. Their advice we intend to follow.[43]

Butler's diplomatic offensive had failed for the moment, although he had gained the sympathy of a number of key Iroquois leaders. He was soon to receive support. Brant arrived in the Iroquois country in the autumn, after participating in the New York campaign against Washington's army. Believing the Americans were bent on eventually pushing the Iroquois from their lands, he set out to visit the Confederacy's villages to argue the Crown's case. In the months that followed Butler's and Brant's efforts started to bear fruit, as Major General Philip Schuyler and the rest of the American delegation began to lose ground in council contests for the heart of the Iroquois. As early as 20 May 1776, Brant succeeded in involving some of the Mohawk in combat alongside British forces at the Battle of the Cedars, as American forces withdrew in defeat from Canada. At Fort Niagara in September 1776 a secret meeting of League warriors from the Seneca, Cayuga, Onondaga, and Mohawk tribes as well as a large number of warriors from the Wyandot, Mississauga, Delaware, Nanticoke, and Conoy declared their loyalty to England and sent a warning to the Oneida and Tuscarora to end their ties with the Reverend Samuel Kirkland and others favoring the American cause. Clearly, the unity of the Confederation was coming unglued. Only the outbreak of an epidemic at Onondaga in January 1777, which killed ninety people, including three sachems, temporarily crippling the League's decision-making process, prevented the rift from coming out into the open.

Many white settlers, particularly in lands recently opened by the Treaty of Fort Stanwix, sensed the gathering storm among the Iroquois tribes and feared the worst. In Sunbury, Robert Fruit, the chairman of Northumberland County's Committee of Correspondence, noted that the "Indians who have been among us have now withdrawn to their towns. We'll see them soon as enemies."[44] Fruit's dim view of the future proved well founded thanks to the Continental Congress's shortcomings.

The Continental Congress fought an uphill battle from the beginning in their efforts to maintain Iroquois neutrality. The Congress wished to replace the Crown as the chief arbitrator of Indian affairs but soon discovered itself unable to match the British record in Indian relations. By the time of the Revolution the Iroquois had grown to rely on whites for key supplies and services that they could not provide for themselves. British military officers and Indian agents had provided over the preceding decades both muskets and powder, replacing bows and arrows for hunting and war. The British also placed gunsmiths at trading posts to repair broken weapons. The Continental Congress could not consistently provide these supplies and services to the Iroquois. Keeping an army in the field already had taxed the Congress to the limits. Money for Indian affairs claimed low priority. Iroquois and Delaware Indians who attempted to maintain their neutrality in the first years of the war constantly complained that they lacked the supplies the British generously provided their supporters. The Congress's problems were not limited to a paucity of supplies. At times the Iroquois particularly lamented the lack of clarity in American Indian policy. At Albany in 1775, for example, agents of the Continental Congress informed the representatives of the Six Nations and other tribes that the United States desired them to remain neutral. A year later the Congress authorized the commander-in-chief to recruit two thousand paid Indian auxiliaries, declaring that "it was highly expedient to engage the Indians in the service of the United State."[45] Finally, the Congress found itself at a disadvantage due to the diplomatic experience of their Indian agents, who lacked the expertise and stature of their Loyalist opponents.

The generally accepted interpretation of the diplomatic battles for the Iroquois' loyalty holds that the British eventually won the support of three of the Confederacy's six Indian nations. Thanks largely to the labors of their Indian agent and resident minister, Reverend Kirkland, and the persistence of Schuyler, the Americans managed to force the Onondaga into neutrality and eventually won the active support of the Oneida and Tuscarora nations.[46] Kirkland's affiliation with the Boston Board of Commissioners and Harvard College did focus Oneida and Tuscarora attention on rebellious Boston, making them more susceptible to American arguments; nonetheless, this explanation of the Confederacy's disintegration is too simplistic.

Most Iroquois, regardless of tribal affiliation, found the war to be confusing and more than a little frightening. During the first two years of the

The Frontier in Flames: 1778

conflict the Confederation remained officially neutral, although this neutrality hid deepening splits within the tribes, as the Seneca and Cayuga slipped gradually under Butler's and Brant's spell. Relying on the British at Fort Niagara rather than the Americans at Albany for manufactured goods, these two western tribes experienced constant British pressure to abandon neutrality. For the Mohawk at the eastern door to the Longhouse, their proximity to white settlements made them particularly vulnerable to contentious land disputes they had little hope of winning. The Treaty of Fort Stanwix had left nearly all Mohawk lands to the east of the treaty line and, therefore, within the bounds and jurisdiction of the colony of New York. Only the British Crown, through its Indian agents, stood between the Mohawk and the eventual dispossession of their lands at the hands of land-hungry farmers.

The Confederacy split apart in July 1777, following a council meeting at Irondequoit, near Fort Oswego. Butler finally carried the day here. After lavishing numerous gifts on the assembled Indians, Butler reminded them of King George's love for his Iroquois people and of their duty to support him in his time of need. Brant, in a fiery address, warned his listeners that neutrality would eventually bring disaster to the League. Overwhelmed by an abundant supply of British goods as well as a long litany of pro-British speakers, the pro-neutrality faction of the assembled tribes began to give ground until, finally, the majority of warriors present opted for war.[47] Most of the assembled Indians came from the Seneca. This did not bode well for the Americans, as the Seneca alone accounted for half of the manpower the Confederation could field in the event of war. Over time other tribes reluctantly followed, but, with the exception of the Seneca, few offered a united front in support of the British. As the unity of the Confederation slowly came undone, the frontier regions of Pennsylvania and New York prepared for the worst.

The Battle of Oriskany in August 1777 marked the first significant Iroquois involvement in the fighting. Butler, along with twenty Tory rangers and four hundred Indians, mostly from the Seneca, ambushed General Nicholas Herkimer's one thousand–strong relief column within five miles of Fort Stanwix. When the killing stopped, nearly half of Herkimer's militia lay dead or wounded. Butler suffered only thirty-three killed and twenty-nine wounded. The Seneca suffered the brunt of the losses—sixteen dead, including five chiefs. Mary Jemison recalled the distress Oriskany caused the Seneca:

> Previous to the battle of Fort Stanwix, the British sent for the Indians to come and see them whip the rebels; and at the same time stated that they did not wish to have them fight, but wanted to have them just sit down, smoke their pipes, and look on. Our Indians went, to a man; but, contrary to their expectation, instead of smoking and looking on, they were obliged to fight for their lives; and in the end of the battle were completely beaten, with great loss in killed and wounded. . . . Our town exhibited a scene of real sorrow and distress, when our warriors returned, recounted their misfortunes, and stated the real loss they had sustained in the engagement. The mourning was excessive, and was expressed by the most doleful yells, shrieks, and howlings, and by inimitable gesticulations.[48]

The results pulled the Seneca deeper into the war. Revenge provided a motive for continued involvement, although their losses made them reluctant to take part in other pitched battles.[49] It also signaled a deepening split within the Confederation. Sixty Oneida from the Indian settlement of Oriska had chosen to serve as scouts for Herkimer, in effect involving themselves in combat against the Seneca. In September Schuyler finished what Butler had started; the last semblance of Iroquois unity disappeared when most of the Oneida and Tuscarora nations agreed to take up the hatchet on behalf of the American cause.[50] The conflict became for the Iroquois what it had already become for the whites, a civil war pitting brother against brother.

As British strategy began to shift to the southern theater following the Saratoga disaster, this contest for allegiance of the uncommitted tribes in the Confederation assumed increasing importance to Whitehall's plans. British and Tory officers working out of Fort Niagara doubled their efforts. Now focused on disrupting Washington's sources of supply and forcing the diversion of Continental regulars to the frontier defense, they envisioned a guerrilla war aimed at decimating the settlements along the Susquehanna and Mohawk Rivers.

Along the seaboard the 1778 campaign season in the Middle Colonies opened quietly. Facing the threat of a much wider war with the entry of

France, Whitehall dispatched the earl of Carlisle to America in a last attempt to find peace. The Carlisle Commission possessed the authority to grant the colonies autonomy within the empire as an incentive to bring the fighting to an end.[51] The attempt failed when both the Congress and Washington refused to meet with the Crown's representatives. Events had proceeded too far now for Carlisle's offer to find much support. Militarily, American fortunes appeared to be looking up. In June the Continental army fought Clinton's regulars to a draw at Monmouth, New Jersey, the battle proving to be the year's only major engagement between the two main armies. Washington also attempted a combined operation with the French navy against the British garrison stationed in Newport, Rhode Island, but this effort failed, when Comte Charles Hector d'Estaing, commanding the French fleet, withdrew his vessels for repairs after a storm separated his fleet from his British opponent.

On the frontier, however, the war did not ebb. With the coming of spring, Tory and Indian parties increased the frequency of their raids. In Pennsylvania attacks against settlements on the Susquehanna's west branch increased in intensity, while John Butler's devastating raid on the Wyoming Valley on 3 July 1778 touched off a general panic. After securing the peaceful surrender of two small blockhouse forts, Fort Wintermoot and Fort Jenkins, Butler's combined force of eight hundred Iroquois warriors, Tory rangers, and British regulars pressed on to the largest fortification in the area, Forty-fort. The post's commander refused Butler's terms. Lacking the ability to carry out a siege, the Tory leader opted instead to burn the two captured forts and feign a withdraw, hoping to lure patriot forces into battle. The ploy worked, as four hundred soldiers largely consisting of local militia struck out in pursuit and soon stumbled into an ambush. Butler's men flanked and quickly shattered the patriot line.[52] When the militia broke and ran, the Indians gave chase, killing nearly every soldier who fell into their hands.

This no-quarter brand of war was not unusual and was practiced by both sides. Nonetheless, as news of the battle spread, the story took on a decidedly sensationalist tone, with accusations that Butler and his Iroquois allies had tortured and killed prisoners with abandon. One account held that Henry Pensil, a militiaman from the valley, had been discovered hiding in some bushes by his brother, a soldier in Butler's Rangers. Pensil fell to his knees and begged his brother to spare his life. He was still begging when his brother shot him through the head.[53] Another story held that Esther (Catherine) Montour, a half-blood Indian who had lived for years near Tioga, had accompanied the raid and reigned over the systematic execution and scalping of sixteen prisoners.[54] Little evidence exists to support the stories. Butler made a point of boasting to Lieutenant Colonel Mason Bolton, Fort Niagara's commanding officer, that, during "the destruction of this settlement, not a single person has been hurt of the Inhabitants, but such as were in arms."[55] Regardless of the probable truth of Butler's contention, in the hysteria that followed the event most settlers chose to believe the worst. Patriot settlers departed their farms in droves for safe haven in more secure settlements to the east. Robert Covenhoven, one of the valley's settlers, described the exodus:

> I took my family safely to Sunbury, and came back in a keel-boat to secure my furniture. Just as I rounded a point above Derrstown [now Lewisburg, Pa.] I met the whole convoy from all the forts above. Such a sight I never saw in my life. Boats, canoes, hog-troughs, rafts hastily made of dry sticks, every sort of floating article, had been put in requisition, and were crowded with women and children and plunder. Whenever an obstruction accurred [*sic*] at any shoal or ripple, the women would leap out into the water and put their shoulders to the boat or raft, and launch it again into deep water. The men of the settlement came down in single file, on each side of the river, to guard women and children.[56]

Lieutenant Colonel Thomas Hartley, commanding the Eleventh Pennsylvania downstream at Fort Augusta, realized that he did not have the capability of defending the vast stretch of frontier now being rapidly depopulated. He elected instead to raid Tioga, the staging area for Butler's attack on Wyoming. He wrote to the Continental Congress that the operation "would probably induce the Savages to remove to a greater distance from the Settlements."[57] Hartley attempted to supplement his regiment with militia from the Susquehanna Valley but found his pleas largely unheeded. With a force of two hundred men he departed on 21 September 1778 from Muncy following the Sheshequin Path to the Susquehanna River just below Tioga.[58] Finding it abandoned, he destroyed the village. He had planned to push on to the nearby village of Chemung. This changed when his scouts brought word that Walter Butler had gathered a force twice his size at Chemung and would soon move to contest the raid. Fearing the worst, Hartley chose instead to withdraw back to Wyoming by way of the river. The withdrawal did not go unopposed. Hartley's men fought their way past several parties of Indians attempting to block their way.[59]

In New York the situation proved much the same. At the end of May, Brant and his men fell on Cobleskill, burning most of the settlement to the ground and killing whatever livestock his Tories and Indians could not take with them. Brant then moved west to Springfield and Andrustown. These villages suffered a similar fate. In early July another raid struck Minisink along the Delaware River. The coming of fall brought no respite for the frontier settlements. In September Brant torched German Flats. The effect of these attacks proved to be as the British commanders in Canada and New York City had hoped. Frontier settlements had trouble bringing in the harvest, despite a good growing season. In addition, the almost unbroken series of successful raids had undermined the confidence of settlers in both their state militia and in the Continental army, for neither had been able to protect them. A settler's committee writing to Governor George Clinton from Canajoharie made this frustration clear:

> Woeful Experience teaches us militia are by no means a Defence for any Part of the Country. Strange as it may appear to your Excellency, it is no less true, that our Militia by Desertion to the Enemy and by Enlistments into our Service, are reduced to less than seven hundred Men. Indeed if these 700 would do their Duty and act like Men, we might perhaps give the Enemy a Check, so as to give Time to the Militia from below to come up, but, Sir, they are actuated by such an ungovernable Spirit that it is out of the Power of any Officer in this County to command them with any Credit to himself—for notwithstanding the utmost Exertion the Officers have nothing but Blame in return.[60]

Desperate for some sort of solution for his stricken frontiers, New York's governor, George Clinton, pressed for a punitive expedition against Unandilla on the upper Susquehanna. The village had served as a Tory-Indian rendezvous point for raids against settlements along Lake Otsego and Cherry Valley. This mission fell to Lieutenant Colonel William Butler commanding the Fourth Pennsylvania. Consisting largely of Scotch-Irish farmers from the western counties, with four companies of Morgan's Rifles attached, the regiment represented one of the more seasoned of Continental regiments.[61] Washington had attached the rifle companies to the regiment to make it better suited to the kind of frontier warfare the commander-in-chief believed likely while the unit was stationed at Schoharie. Butler's men carried the war back to the Iroquois and their Tory allies on 10 October, burning Unandilla and other nearby villages.[62]

The Unandilla raid failed in its object. Instead of humbling the Iroquois, it accomplished the opposite. Walter Butler, with a group of Tory rangers and Seneca warriors, fell on Cherry Valley in November. Before this raid the border war had displayed a degree of civility seldom seen in previous frontier conflicts. The British did recognize the negative aspects of being the perpetrators of a blood bath and continuously strove to rein in their Indian allies. Houses, barns, and livestock had been fair game in the war of torches, but the parties of Tories and Indians had left civilians largely unharmed. This changed with Cherry Valley. Butler lost control over his Indians, and thirty-three civilians died in what can only be called a massacre. Following the tragedy the Indians defended their actions, arguing that they had been the victims of past rebel injustices. They complained first that they had been falsely accused of committing a massacre at Wyoming, when in fact great care had been taken to guard against harming civilians. Second, they believed themselves betrayed by several detachments of Wyoming soldiers manning the valley forts who had capitulated under a flag of truce. Many of these soldiers, after agreeing to lay down their arms for the duration of the war, had marched with Hartley against the Delaware and Iroquois settlements near Tioga.[63] Finally, one of the Mohawk chiefs offered William Butler's raid against Unandilla as an additional justification for the excesses of Cherry Valley.[64]

The excuses offered had a hollow ring to them, and British leaders, particularly Germain, found themselves forced to redouble their efforts to prevent any recurrence of the unfortunate incident. Chastising the offending warriors for their sins was one way to do this, but it had been done before and was beginning to lose its effect on the audience. Another way was to find a role model for Britain's Indian allies, and Brant fit the part nicely. Germain had Brant promoted to the rank of "colonel of Indians" and directed that prints of George Romney's portrait of the chief be circulated among Iroquois villages as a demonstration of British esteem for his accomplishments.[65]

Winter brought a temporary peace to the frontier. Many of the most significant communities in these regions lay in ashes, and most of their residents had fled eastward. Hartley's and Butler's efforts to stem the tide of Tory-Indian raids had angered the Iroquois but did little more than cause them some temporary inconvenience. Washington asked Brigadier General Edward Hand, the ranking Continental army officer in the region, to consider the possibility of a winter campaign against the Indian villages along the Susquehanna and Chemung Rivers. Little came of the idea. The terrain as well as the condition of Continental army logistics made such an undertaking difficult, if not impossible.

Few families still braving conditions on the frontiers were sad to see the year end. The Continental Congress's diplomatic efforts to keep the frontiers quiet had now clearly failed. War had come to the prosperous valleys of Pennsylvania and New York, leaving them smoking ruins. If 1779 was not to be a repeat of 1778, Washington realized that something would have to be done to beat back this threat. He understood that the western theater was not the place in which the war could be won, because the British had little of strategic significance there. Victory could come only through operations carried out along the seaboard. Nonetheless, the problems of the nation's western regions threatened the war effort. If left to continue, the raids would certainly undermine civilian morale in the two key states of Pennsylvania and New York. Furthermore, the constant pressure against the frontiers and settled regions farther east threatened one of the army's key sources of food and fodder. Yet any diversion of a large army to this theater had to come at the expense of the more strategically important eastern theater. For Washington the problem for the new campaign season became that of deciding where to use his already overcommitted army to achieve the greatest good.

As 1778 ended, the British fleet controlled the waters along the eastern seaboard, but British ground forces remained confined to the ports of New York and Newport, Rhode Island, while Whitehall shifted the strategic focus southward. Early in the new year Germain laid out his plans for the

British army in the colonies. His plan reflected the evolving nature of British strategy and marked a clear departure from the previous emphasis on New England. He instructed Henry Clinton to lure Washington's army into a decisive battle. If this proved impossible, "keep him in the Highlands so that the inhabitants of the land can be free to renounce the authority of the Congress, and return to their allegiance to his Majesty." Germain granted Clinton freedom to use his naval assets, along with two corps of ground forces numbering four thousand soldiers each, to attack seaports in New England and Chesapeake Bay. He encouraged Clinton to take advantage of the discontent among settlers in Vermont who were claiming their independence from New York by giving "them reason to expect that King George will erect their Country into a 'separate Province' and confirm every Occupant that shall give proofs of his return to his Duty, in the possession of that ungranted Lands he occupies."[66] To support Clinton, Germain noted, "A considerable diversion will be also directed to be made on the side of Canada by a succession of Parties of Indians, supported by a Detachment of Troops there, alarming and harassing the Frontiers, and making incursions into the Settlements."[67]

Germain felt certain that the combined pressure of Clinton's operations and backcountry raids would make it impossible for Washington to mount any operation against either Canada or the Five Nations while undercutting popular support for the war.[68] Clinton believed himself temporarily unable to carry out his instructions, as he had sent five thousand soldiers to St. Lucia in the West Indies and another three thousand to Florida at the end of 1778. Rather than risk defeat, he intended to wait for reinforcements or the return of some of his detachments before executing the plan. The delay provided his adversary an opportunity to strike first.

Washington saw 1779 as a year of opportunity for the rebel cause. He noted the British reluctance to resume the offensive and intended to take advantage of the opening this afforded. By this time Washington had clearly adopted a strategy of exhaustion, focused on finding ways to make the British position expensive and eventually untenable. Washington found himself facing several strategic options as the new year approached. He could attempt to expel British forces from New York. He estimated this would require more than twenty thousand soldiers, and the presence of the British fleet could severely complicate the operation. A second possibility envisioned another attack on Newport. As before, this required the availability of the French fleet. The prospects for this remained unclear. Another invasion of Canada using either the Hudson River–Lake Champlain route to the St. Lawrence River or up the Connecticut River toward Montreal represented the third possibility. Some members of the Continental Congress strongly favored this idea, and Washington had instructed Lafayette to lay the groundwork for it during the preceding year. Nonetheless, concerns over logistics and the difficulty of the terrain made Washington uncertain of its practicality. The final possibility required that British forces along the coast be kept in their seaport towns while a detachment of the Continental army marched westward to deal with the threat to the frontiers.[69] The preceding year's toll on frontier settlements had produced considerable political pressure from other members of the Congress as well as state governments of the affected areas for a military solution to their problems. The art of operational strategy involves evaluating whether desired military objectives can be obtained given the capabilities at hand.[70] Washington examined carefully the relationship between these two facets of operational strategy before deciding on a western campaign.

3

STRATEGY AND OPERATIONS

George Washington seldom found time to conduct long-range planning or the opportunity to execute such plans. For much of the war British commanders forced Washington to adopt a reactive rather than proactive strategy, and his operational approach to battle reflected this.

This has led to some confusion. Historians such as James Thomas Flexner and Russell Weigley have accused him of waging a Fabian strategy designed to bring decision through attrition.[1] There is truth in this, as his strategy following the disastrous New York campaign illustrates, but it does not describe adequately Washington's abilities as a strategist. Dave R. Palmer in *The Way of the Fox,* argued that Washington possessed a unique sense of timing and was seldom content to react. Depending on circumstances, Washington frequently sought opportunities that would allow him to pit his fledgling army against his foe when the odds were in his favor. This particularly characterized American strategy from January 1778 to 1781.[2] As in most protracted wars involving democratic societies, success rests to a great extent on public support. A Fabian strategy assumes a public will to support the war beyond the patience and fortitude of one's adversary. Washington never accepted such an assumption. In a nation that produced a considerable economic surplus during the war years, the army's chronic problems with personnel and supply shortages pointed to a fragile

American base of support. With time an uncertain ally, victory rested on a measured but opportunistic offensive approach to the war.

Washington envisioned an offensive-defensive strategy. With Major General William Howe's decision to pull his army from Boston in March 1776, Great Britain temporarily lost the power to oppose the colonial drift toward independence. Once the Second Continental Congress declared independence in July 1776, colonial strategy became defensive in nature, seeking to preserve the status quo and oppose any British attempt to reestablish control. It was not long before Howe's men landed on Long Island. Realizing the tenuous nature of public support for independence, the Continental Congress prodded Washington to respond. The ill-fated campaign that followed was primarily defensive, but, following his army's flight into New Jersey, Washington demonstrated a desire to seek every reasonable opportunity to attack his foes, to limit their operational reach and inhibit their ability to pacify the population. Preserving the army's existence became the most important limiting factor to this strategy.[3] Lose the army and one loses the war—the equation was that simple. Before the war shifted to the South, Washington depended on areas of Pennsylvania, New Jersey, New York, and Connecticut for badly needed supplies.[4] With much of the area beyond the reach of British naval power, Washington expected to use the region's farms to provide his army with food and fodder.[5] Success rested on denying control of these areas to the British and their Tory allies, to limit the majority of Britain's ground forces to the port cities, where only the Royal Navy could supply them. With little or no room to maneuver, British forces confined there might prove lucrative targets. The British navy's control of the coastal waterways, however, made siege operations against occupied port cities difficult. To trap and destroy a British army along the coast required a naval force to counter that of the British. The entry of France into the war following Saratoga appeared to give Washington access to the naval power he wanted. From the first months of the French alliance, Washington sought opportunities to use the French fleet in combined operations against the British. Until Yorktown his efforts met with little success. French naval commanders served as dutiful guardians of the fleet, seldom involving their ships in high-risk engagements. Often finding himself without naval support, the commander-in-chief focused on operations designed to keep the British army out of the interior.

The Sullivan expedition falls into this category. Washington as well as the Continental Congress believed that punishing the Iroquois in their homelands around the Finger Lakes of New York would bring some semblance of peace and order to agricultural areas critical to the support of Continental army. They intended the campaign to provide a psychological lift to a region that believed itself slighted by the Congress and the army. Finally, if the operation succeeded, they hoped to deny the British a source of grain for their western garrisons and perhaps even force the Crown to support their Indian allies, adding yet another drain on Britain's war chest.[6]

Sullivan's Indian campaign offered the commander-in-chief little opportunity to influence the outcome of the war immediately or significantly, and for this reason he was somewhat reluctant to undertake the campaign. However, Washington's work in planning the campaign, particularly his operational and intelligence efforts, highlight his abilities as a military commander. His performance stands as all the more remarkable considering his lack of military training. Washington, as his biographer James Thomas Flexner argued, was not really a soldier but, rather, a "citizen in arms."[7] He had read widely in military subjects, but much of his skill came from experience and an ability to learn from mistakes. Don Higginbotham offered high praise for Washington as well as his subordinates during the Sullivan expedition, describing the campaign as "unpretentious in its aims and accomplishments" but also "one of the best planned and best executed operations of the Revolution."[8]

The geographic scope of the campaign says much about Washington's willingness to take significant risks for an operation with a limited objective. Sending nearly one-third of his army into the wilderness of Pennsylvania and New York with Henry Clinton's redcoats only two days' march from West Point stands out as risky in the extreme. Most eighteenth-century commanders only reluctantly made large detachments from their army and usually only for a short time.[9] Seldom did these detached units operate far from the main theater of conflict. The reason was simple. Even in the better traveled terrain of Europe, command and control represented the most difficult challenge for generals.[10] During the French and Indian war opposing armies quickly learned that waging an offensive campaign into the American wilderness was even more difficult. Rivers dictated the routes generals could take. Roads had to be built to waterways, while quartermaster officers secured wagons from a usually less than cooperative populace. In 1756 the French enjoyed all the advantages of having a continuous water line of communications stretching from Louisbourg to Fort Niagara, and British armies more than once suffered defeat trying to overcome the problems inherent in attacking it. In 1779 this advantage of military geography fell to the British, yet Washington willingly risked sixteen regiments of his best soldiers on a journey that took them nearly three hundred miles from the Hudson Valley.

Meticulous planning based on sound intelligence represented Washington's most notable contribution to Sullivan's expedition. Based on his information, the commanding general provided a clear statement of objectives, a flexible operational concept permitting multiple routes of access to the objective, and a reasonably accurate understanding of both the terrain and the enemy's capabilities. Washington also designed and implemented a deception plan to keep British commanders guessing about Sullivan's objective until it was too late to react. These efforts in counterintelligence paid dividends. A review of Tory and British correspondence reveals that Sullivan's foes possessed all the information they needed to take action against the expedition if they responded in time. The problem for them was not the quantity of the intelligence at their disposal but, rather, their ability to separate the wheat from the chaff Washington deliberately provided them.

Like all eighteenth-century commanders, Washington worked as his own operations and intelligence officer, relying on the advice of several key advisors and using orderlies to assist him in writing the necessary inquiries and orders. The modern staff system dates only as far back as the second half of the nineteenth century. Sullivan, James Clinton, and Daniel Brodhead, the campaign's field commanders, participated very little in developing the operation and almost nothing to the intelligence work that underlay the plan. Washington granted both Sullivan and Brodhead considerable latitude in timing the campaign and choosing lines of advance, but little else.[11]

Selecting an appropriate objective became Washington's first step in planning for a western expedition. The British forts at Detroit and Niagara presented the two most prominent threats on the frontier. Detroit had been a particularly troublesome thorn in the side of Kentucky settlers, who found themselves constantly threatened by raiding parties operating from the Illinois and Ohio country. Washington considered the capture of Detroit a worthwhile goal as early as 1777; the following year he suggested it as a possible target for a mixed force of regulars and militia to operate from Fort Pitt in 1779. Any campaign against Detroit would require an elaborate logistical effort and the detachment of a sizable portion of the army's regulars to a target far from the main theater of operations. Should the fort fall, it required a permanent garrison to prevent its reoccupation by the British. In view of the strategic situation at the start of the 1779 campaign season, Detroit simply lacked the significance to warrant a major effort. Priorities had changed in the summer and fall of 1778, when Tory-Indian strikes against frontier settlements in Pennsylvania and New York pushed Detroit into the background.

Fort Niagara represented a more ominous threat. First, as the command center for British operations in the area, it was the primary source of trouble for the white settlements on the Pennsylvania and New York frontiers. It served as the conduit for supplies to both John Butler's Tories and his Iroquois allies. Furthermore, it functioned as the key link between Canada and British posts to the west, most notably Detroit. During the French and Indian War, Arthur Young, a British visitor to the post, stated clearly Niagara's importance:

> [Niagara is the] . . . chief and almost the only pass into the interior parts of North America, both from the north and south and from east to west, either from the French settlements or ours. In short, the importance of this place is almost inconceivable; it is the key to the whole continent; it awes and commands all the Indians of North America; it secures all the inland trade of that continent; it lays our colonies open to the inroads of the French and Indians—such is the consequence of this place!
>
> Niagara is even of much greater importance than the country on the Ohio, for this reason because it commands it. If we were possessed of Niagara, the French in Canada would be cut off from all communication with the Ohio, and from almost all their encroachments on us.[12]

Young undoubtedly overstated the importance of Fort Niagara, since control over the St. Lawrence Valley and Lake Ontario represented the real key to British power in the Great Lakes region. Nonetheless, the loss of Niagara would have damaged critically the British military situation in the West. American control of the post, situated as it was along the line of communications to Britain's western garrisons, rendered their continued retention difficult for the Crown. Furthermore, the Iroquois perceived Niagara as the most obvious evidence of British power. Its loss possibly might force the Iroquois to reconsider their participation in the conflict.

Niagara's military commanders had matched the post's defenses to its strategic importance. French leaders erected a rude stockade on the location in 1676. During the opening years of the French and Indian War, French military engineers expanded the stockade into a formidable Vauban-style pentagonal fortress.[13] Its ramparts sat on well-constructed earthen scarps to negate the impact of artillery. Heavy stone casements protected the powder magazines, and the angles formed by the fort's exterior walls gave the post's defenders the advantage of interlocking fields of fire against any attacker. Niagara was not impregnable, but any attacker desiring the prize had to be willing to commit to a Vauban-like siege.[14]

The British conducted such an undertaking against Niagara in the summer of 1759. Sir William Johnson, who assumed command of the siege following Brigadier John Prideaux's death, employed heavy siege artillery, including two eighteen-pound cannon, four twelve-pound guns, and a sizable contingent of smaller howitzers and coehorn mortars.[15] Under the fire of French guns his soldiers labored for several weeks digging the parallels and approach trenches in order to gain access to the fort's ramparts. Despite this combination of firepower and sweat, the French garrison of nearly six hundred soldiers still resisted for almost a month before surrendering.[16] Experience during the French and Indian War taught Washington and other colonials the necessity of appropriate artillery to reduce fortresses.[17] Washington demonstrated that he understood its importance from his first days in command of the army. Believing he might have to order an assault of Howe's positions in Boston, Washington sent Colonel Henry Knox off to Ticonderoga to bring its fortress artillery back to Boston.[18]

British commanders decreased the size of Niagara's garrison and permitted its defenses to fall into disrepair at the end of the French and Indian War. The coming of war in 1775 reversed this decline, although the effort to repair the fortifications progressed slowly. By 1778 Germain's plans for

British forces in North America underscored the importance of the western fortifications and the need to hasten their repair. Major General Frederick Haldimand directed his officers to give particular attention to preparing Niagara to withstand a siege. He supplemented the fort's battery with additional heavy artillery consisting of ten-and twelve-pound guns and ordered the building of a small naval fleet on Lake Ontario to secure the line of communications.[19] The personnel shortage represented a more difficult question. In May 1779 Niagara's garrison consisted of only six companies of infantry from the Eighth Regiment of Foot with a small artillery contingent to service the fort's guns.[20] With British regulars critically needed in the main theater of the war and German mercenaries considered unsuitable for frontier duty, Lieutenant Colonel Mason Bolton, Niagara's commander, believed his post to be badly undermanned. Haldimand agreed and reinforced Bolton with the Thirty-fourth Regiment of Foot, but the garrison's strength remained far from ideal.[21] Tory units and, to a lesser extent, the Iroquois might supplement the fort's defenses in the event a rebel army penetrated the New York backcountry. In addition, unless an attacking force possessed the ability to contest the British gunboats on Lake Ontario, British units from Canada could reinforce the garrison, if time permitted.

Washington initially hoped his western expedition could take Niagara. In February 1779 he ordered Brigadier General Lachlan McIntosh, then in command at Fort Pitt, to look into the possibility of building large canoes for a possible expedition up the Allegheny River then proceeding overland to Lake Erie.[22] Lest his intent be misunderstood, a month later he instructed Colonel Brodhead, Fort Pitt's new commander, to find guides with knowledge of the upper reaches of the Allegheny and the way to Niagara.[23] At this time Washington expected to send armies into the Iroquois heartland from two directions. Brodhead's men would strike from the south, while the main army approached from the east. The two forces would rendezvous and then proceed to Fort Niagara.

As the operation took form, however, Washington decided that Niagara fell beyond the operational reach of Sullivan's small army. Yet he still hoped that Sullivan might seize Niagara. The one scenario he believed possible anticipated that some of Britain's less enthusiastic Iroquois allies might sue for peace rather than risk the destruction of their villages. Should this happen, the friendly Oneida contingent accompanying the expedition, as well as the very influential Kirkland, might convince the Indians that, as an act of good faith, they should take Niagara by subterfuge. If the Iroquois expressed a willingness to do this, Washington authorized Sullivan to provide them with advisors and necessary supplies.[24] Neither man believed this scenario anything more than a long shot, but both understood, thanks to Schuyler's sources, that Iroquois support for the British remained tenuous. This necessitated planning to use any legitimate Iroquois plea for peace to best advantage. In his final instructions Washington made clear to Sullivan what to do with the prize if it fell into his hands but emphasized more strongly that waging a scorched-earth campaign against the Iroquois ranked as his primary mission:

> The expedition you are appointed to command is directed against the hostile tribes of the Six Nations of Indians, with their associates and adherents. The immediate objects are the total destruction and devastation of their settlements and the capture of as many prisoners of every age and sex as possible. It will be essential to ruin their crops now in the ground and preventing their planting more . . .
>
> Should Niagara fall into your hands in the manner I have mentioned, you will do everything in your power for preserving and maintaining it by establishing a chain of posts in such a manner as shall appear to you most safe and effectual and tending as little to reduce our general forces as possible.[25]

Intending to grant his subordinate sufficient latitude to deal with the unforeseen yet precise about his intentions, Washington's orders also outlined the general scheme of the operation. He notified Sullivan that Brigadier General James Clinton along with four regiments of infantry had been ordered to Canajoharie "subject to your orders either to form a junction with the main body on the Susquehanna, by way of Otsego—or to proceed up the Mohawk river and co-operate in the best manner circumstances will permit."[26] He instructed Sullivan to establish a post at Tioga and at as many other intermediate posts as needed to secure the line of communication. Fearing that an overemphasis on security might inhibit the expedition, he warned his subordinate to commit the smallest number of soldiers possible to this task so as "to diminish your operating force as little as possible."[27]

He lectured on the need to be vigilant to prevent surprise and included some advice on tactics. He stressed the need for an ongoing effort to gain intelligence concerning the enemy. Washington made only one noticeable omission from the orders. He neglected to give any specific time to begin, though he did make clear that he intended it to commence as soon as possible. Washington understood that problems with logistics made it difficult for him to dictate an exact time.[28] Wisely, he opted to allow his commander on the ground to make this decision.

Washington's orders suggest the growing sophistication of the Continental army at midwar with respect to operational planning. They clearly specified Washington's intentions, set priorities for campaign objectives, and outlined the general scheme of the campaign. The orders represented the product of considerable staff work and shed light on Washington's skills as a commander. Although unseen in the wording of the order, the operational concept rested on considerable intelligence and counterintelligence preparations brought together by a wide range of people.

Washington possessed some experience as an Indian fighter, but this had not been against the Iroquois. For advice in clarifying the objectives of the mission, he turned to Schuyler, who served as commander of the Northern Department and the Continental Congress's chief negotiator with the Iroquois. Schuyler possessed greater familiarity with the workings of the Iroquois Confederacy than any of Washington's other subordinates. The idea of launching a campaign against the Iroquois had not caught Schuyler unprepared. He had given considerable thought to the possibility and readily offered his advice. Any expedition focusing on the Iroquois had to give first priority to destroying the Seneca. They provided far more warriors to support the British than any other tribe, and their proximity to the Pennsylvania frontier made them a particular problem for settlers living along the north and west branches of the Susquehanna River or in the Allegheny Valley. Schuyler believed that the benefits of destroying the Seneca towns would be felt immediately on the frontier. "Destroy the Seneca towns and the Indians must fall back to Niagara," he wrote to Washington. "This is a long distance from the frontier. With no intermittent place to use as a supply base, no sizable body of Indians can raid the frontiers through the winter into the spring."[29]

After clarifying the objective of the operation, Washington began the process of gathering intelligence. Two interrelated concerns dominated this activity: evaluating possible avenues of approach into the Iroquois homelands and determining the size and strength of the enemy. Schuyler's experience as well as the spy network he had assembled proved invaluable. His agents doubted that the British and their Indian allies could put more than 2,050 men into the field to oppose the expedition.[30] Even this number rested on the assumption that British spies were able to provide their own superiors with sixty days' warning. The few British regulars they discovered led Schuyler's agents to predict that the Iroquois and their allied tribes would have to provide three-quarters of this number. The estimate also rested on their understanding of the ability of the British to keep their people properly supplied. Schuyler, with a better understanding of Britain's problems with logistics, doubted this presumption. Several Oneida who had visited Niagara in late winter informed the general that Niagara was short of supplies, and little evidence existed to suggest that Tory units such as Butler's Rangers were in any better circumstances.[31]

Schuyler's information about enemy forces directly affected the size and structure of the colonial expedition. The military situation in New York and New Jersey could become critical if the transfer of too many units to the frontier opened the way for Henry Clinton to strike Washington's weakened army. The six thousand soldiers Washington eventually allocated gave the Americans a three-to-one advantage over the most optimistic estimate of British strength. Yet the need for Sullivan and his subordinates to secure their line of communication required that significant numbers of soldiers be detached as the expedition penetrated deeper into the Iroquois country. As Sullivan's numbers decreased, other factors might combine to stop or even defeat the expedition, such as their foes' familiarity with the terrain. Aware of the manpower problem, Washington worked to minimize the diversion of soldiers to nonfighting purposes. A better understanding of all the avenues of approach into the Confederation could spell the difference.

Washington quickly developed four possible routes for the main army. The first three used Albany and Schenectady as a base of operations; the fourth used the Wyoming Valley. The first route envisioned a movement up the Mohawk River to Fort Stanwix then to Lake Oneida by way of Wood Creek. From there the army would take the Cayuga and Seneca Rivers to reach the Indian settlements. The British had used part of this route in their successful campaign against French-held Niagara during the Seven Years' War, making its risks and benefits the best understood of the four.

The second route called for an overland campaign striking west from Fort Stanwix; the third followed a southern route along the Mohawk River, Lake Otsego, and the Susquehanna River approach.[32] The fourth route would adhere to the Susquehanna-Chemung River route using the Great Warrior's Path. Washington continued to consider the Allegheny River approach but only for a small supporting attack. Logistical problems limited the viability of this route. Unless Washington made a concerted effort to build a large supply base at Fort Pitt, the river could not support more than a small detachment of men.

Even before Washington had a chance to ask him about the three New York–based options, Schuyler offered a plan using parts of the first two options. He proposed that three thousand men divided into two groups move up the Mohawk River from Albany at staggered times. The first would proceed to Fort Stanwix then on to Oswego, where it would build a fortified camp before attacking the Indian villages along Lake Ontario in the direction of Niagara. He intended this force as a diversion to convince both the British and the Indians that Niagara was the American target. A permanent rebel post at Oswego also threatened British communications to their western posts. With British attention fixed on Oswego, the second group would march from Fort Stanwix into the Iroquois homelands via an overland route, burning villages and seizing women and children to be held for ransom.[33] Schuyler hoped the Confederation's leadership might agree to resume its neutrality in exchange for the hostages.

Washington appreciated Schuyler's ideas and incorporated the idea of taking hostages into Sullivan's instructions, but he declined to settle on a plan without examining other options.[34] Taking the rejection in stride, Schuyler then recommended that Washington adopt the first option, arguing that an army moving along the overland route could not achieve surprise without the diversion he had suggested. He also believed that the difficulty of the terrain would force the army to take along a large number of packhorses, and it was uncertain whether the army's quartermasters could fill the expedition's needs. Schuyler considered the Lake Otsego–Susquehanna River route to require too extensive a portage to move boats and supplies from the Mohawk to Lake Otsego. Furthermore, he doubted that water levels would permit the use of bateaux below the lake, further complicating the army's supply problem.[35]

By March 1779 the operation had taken shape in Washington's mind. He decided to use the Susquehanna as either the main or a supporting avenue of approach. The Chemung River provided access to the Seneca homelands, making the fourth route an excellent option for at least part of the army. For the remainder of the expedition, either the first or third routes offered the best chance of success. The third route permitted a rendezvous at Tioga for the two segments of the army before they continued the operation. He finally rejected the second option due to its logistical constraints and worries over security. Still interested in using the Allegheny for a supporting attack, Washington concluded that a third detachment could attack Indian villages on the river's upper reaches before marching overland to join the main army in the Iroquois lands.

As early as December 1778, the commander-in-chief had begun gathering information on the main routes. He gave particular attention to the Susquehanna, clarifying his options by sending out detailed questionnaires to officers with knowledge of the river. He queried his chief quartermaster officers in Pennsylvania as well as Brigadier General Edward Hand. Having spent part of the preceding summer providing protection to the besieged residents of the Susquehanna Valley, Hand knew the Pennsylvania frontier better than any other general officer in the Continental army. Toward the end of 1778 Washington had asked Hand to look into the possibility of conducting a winter campaign against the Iroquois, using the Wyoming Valley as his base of operations. Hand complied, gathering considerable information on the river's upper reaches.[36] The impact of weather on movement and supply dissuaded Washington of the practicality of a winter campaign. Hand discovered little to suggest the river could not serve Washington's purposes. Zebulon Butler, commander of American forces at the Battle of Wyoming, also received a questionnaire. A resident of the valley, Butler had been one of Hand's key sources of information about the upper river. Aware of rumors that Pennsylvania had conducted surveys of the Susquehanna north of Wyoming, Washington asked President Joseph Reed to send him copies if they existed.[37]

Washington designed the questionnaire to obtain the precise kind of information he needed to plan the operational and logistical requirements of the campaign. Questions focused on distances between key points, the rate and depth of river flow by month, and the tribal affiliations of Indian villages along the route. He inquired about whether or not the terrain permitted the passage of wagons and field artillery. With the supporting attack up the Allegheny in mind, he asked for information on the trail systems connecting the Susquehanna and the Allegheny drainages. Taken as a composite, the answers afforded a fairly accurate picture of the terrain, particularly with respect to the river between Wyoming and Tioga. Based on this information, Washington concluded that the Susquehanna River was navigable at least as far as Tioga and probably some ways beyond for two- and three-ton bateaux. Ideal water for such an undertaking came in late April and early May, with the river's flow dropping markedly in summer. Transporting artillery presented some problems. Many of the respondents believed the broken terrain north of Wyoming meant the artillery would have to go by water.[38] The respondents became less certain of their answers beyond Tioga.

The breadth of the intelligence effort safeguarded the final product's reliability and validity. There is some evidence to suggest that the British, who had learned of American interests in the rivers leading into the Iroquois country, may have attempted to feed inaccurate information to Washington. In one case Pennsylvania's Executive Council approached Samuel Wallis for a map of the upper reaches of the north branch of the Susquehanna River. Unknown to the council, however, Wallis, a wealthy merchant with extensive tracts of land along the west branch of the Susquehanna, had remained loyal to the Crown, and evidence exists to suggest that he may have attempted to sabotage the expedition. Writing to Henry Clinton, Joseph Stansbury, one of Clinton's spies in Philadelphia, described Wallis's actions:

> Mr. Wallis is a gentleman of large estate in this province and better acquainted with the Indian country than almost any other person. As such he was applied to by the [Pennsylvania] council to furnish a drawing of the country and to assist them in their plan of the Indian expedition. To have refused would have exposed him to sufferings. His drawing was laid by Reed before Washington and the expedition formed on it. He leads them by it to 100 miles southwest of Tioga. A corrected copy of this drawing will be ready by return of your next. As it will be large it will require some address to get it through.[39]

Neither the copy of the map Wallis claimed he gave to Reed nor the corrected copy he promised Clinton has ever been found.[40] If Wallis did give a false map to Reed, it is unlikely it had much effect on the expedition. Washington's questionnaires had yielded a considerable body of substantiated information, making Wallis's attempt at deception openly suspect, if not obvious.

Aware of the gaps in his information, particularly concerning the country north of Tioga, Washington combed the Continental army for soldiers who might have knowledge of the area. This effort turned up a Lieutenant John Jenkins, who had lived in the Wyoming Valley since 1769. Taken prisoner early in the war, Jenkins was taken to Niagara by way of the Susquehanna and Chemung Rivers. After wintering at Niagara, he escaped and made his way back to Wyoming. Washington personally interviewed the young lieutenant, who gave a good account of the terrain and key villages along the route.[41] In addition, Washington also queried Indian prisoners (no record remains of how useful these interviews turned out to be).[42] The additional information only confirmed Washington's belief that the Susquehanna could serve his purposes.

Washington's inquiry also sought information on how best to move units westward from the Hudson Valley and from army outposts in northern New Jersey. In addition to Continental army units, Washington also planned to obtain assistance from New York militia drawn from east of the Hudson. He looked for and found a path connecting the upper waters of the Delaware with the Susquehanna.[43]

With the viability of three of the four routes finally established, Washington had to choose which would support the main effort. He also had to decide whether to bring the army into the Iroquois homelands as a unified force along a single line of advance or risk having his two detachments working along separate axes. Washington had already settled on sending Brodhead and his small force up the Allegheny if supplies could be found to support the effort.

In March 1779 Washington made a number of key decisions. Most important, he decided that the main body would follow the Susquehanna route, informing Schuyler that it should save time and expense. He hoped for the presence of the French fleet in northern waters sometime later in the summer and wanted to complete the Indian campaign as soon as possible to permit a combined operation against a British coastal garrison. Agreeing that the Seneca country would be the focus of the expedition, Washington told Schuyler that the Mohawk route seemed too "circuitous" to serve his purposes. The time and effort necessary to portage the army from the Mohawk River to Wood Creek concerned him, as did the number of posts and manpower needed to secure the line of communications along the route. But the main problem involved the question of risk. The expedition could deal with existing British-Tory-Indian strength in the theater but might be unable to repel any reinforcements rushed into the area. Washington feared that the Mohawk route's close proximity to the British line of communications between the St. Lawrence and Niagara rendered it too easy for the British to interdict the expedition. He was particularly concerned that the British might permit the expedition to penetrate to the Onondaga River then fall on the posts along its line of communication to Fort Stanwix and Albany. In such a scenario the army would have to choose between risking further advance with no link to its supply base or conduct a time-consuming withdrawal to reestablish the line of communication. Washington made it clear that he could not afford to risk losing such a sizable part of his main army. Under these circumstances, he told Schuyler, defeat "would be ruin."[44]

The Susquehanna appeared more direct and secure. In the event of defeat it seemed to offer the best opportunity for an orderly withdrawal because it flowed generally southward through hilly terrain that would frustrate a pursuing force. Furthermore, the distance separating the British line of communications on Lake Ontario from the headwaters of the Susquehanna made it difficult for the British to interfere with the expedition without mounting a major undertaking of their own. Washington also approved Schuyler's earlier suggestion that Onondaga, the Confederation's capital, be attacked in early spring, before Sullivan departed.[45] Schuyler entrusted this task to Colonel Peter Van Schaick, who departed Fort Stanwix on 19 April with five hundred men. Using the Wood Creek to Lake Oneida route, Van Schaick's men surprised the inhabitants of Onondaga two days later, reducing the village to ashes.

After selecting the routes, Washington outlined a tentative plan for three columns. The main body of three thousand men would penetrate the Seneca lands, using the Susquehanna-Chemung Rivers approach. A second force of a thousand men, consisting of three regiments from New York and one from Pennsylvania, would enter the Iroquois country using the Mohawk River to Lake Oneida route favored by Schuyler, while Brodhead and five hundred men marched to the headwaters of the Allegheny. Washington wanted these three columns "to cooperate as punctually as circumstances permit" and intended that they unite in the Seneca country.[46] He hoped that the Iroquois would defend their country and be brought to a decisive engagement, but the destruction of their villages and crops would signal success if the Indians chose not to fight.[47]

Preparations went forward to support this initial plan. Washington notified Governor Clinton in April of his decision to begin gathering men and materials at Canajoharie on the Mohawk.[48] The selection of Canajoharie indicated that Washington still had not settled on the final plan. Units gathered at Canajoharie either could move up the Mohawk to Fort Stanwix or portage overland to Lake Otsego on the headwaters of the Susquehanna.

Clearly, the wide separation of his two major detachments troubled Washington, who in another letter to Schuyler recounted the benefits and drawbacks of using separate axes. Columns advancing along separate routes would force the Iroquois to divide their attention and, given the localism of the tribes, might even split the Confederation. Washington believed that units moving along the Mohawk route could provide "cover" for the element operating along the Susquehanna by compelling any British reinforcements to come into the Iroquois country by way of Niagara or Oswego. If the reinforcements came by Oswego, units on the Mohawk could delay them long enough for the southern detachment to accomplish its mission. Washington also felt that separate routes permitted a more thorough destruction of the Confederacy. The drawbacks to this approach proved no less significant. Washington feared the distance separating the columns might undermine soldier confidence or, under the worst circumstances, subject one or both of the columns to defeat. Coordinating the two columns could prove difficult, and units marching along the Mohawk would have to move with "either too much caution or too much speed" for the maintenance of good security.[49] From the standpoint of logistics the army could least support an attack on separate axes.[50]

When he finished weighing the options, Washington decided to allow his subordinate commander to settle the question. Sullivan initially favored the use of the Mohawk as the main axis, with forces conducting a supporting attack or a feint operating along the Susquehanna. Sullivan pointed out that the Mohawk route conceivably permitted the cutting off and destruction of enemy forces falling back to Niagara; an army on the Susquehanna lacked this capability.[51] In the end logistics tipped the balance in favor of the Susquehanna. As the magnitude of the undertaking became clear to Schuyler, he informed Washington that available food supplies in the Hudson and Mohawk Valleys could not support the army. Pennsylvania's rich farms on the lower Susquehanna appeared better able to sustain the army, particularly in its need for flour.

Washington also gave additional thought to Brodhead's small army at Fort Pitt. Like their cohorts on the eastern rivers, the post's commanders had begun to gather information on the upper reaches of the Allegheny well before the end of winter 1779 to support the initial concept for Brodhead to join forces with the main army in the Iroquois country. Washington's questionnaire specifically addressed the feasibility of using Indian trails between the river drainages to permit the two armies to coordinate their actions. In April 1779 Washington decided this could not be done. He did not believe his quartermasters could keep everyone adequately supplied, Brodhead's situation being the most tenuous. Furthermore, he feared that Brodhead's departure would leave the frontier devoid of protection.[52] Abandoning the idea of a rendezvous, Washington instead instructed Brodhead to "chastise" the western tribes with a more limited operation into their homelands. Not content with his more limited mission, Brodhead took the initiative, stockpiling his own supplies and petitioning Washington to reconsider. Washington responded favorably to his subordinate's efforts, reversing his earlier decision. The presence of Brodhead's army at the western door to the Confederacy and close to the Seneca homelands, Washington believed, would serve as a "useful diversion" to keep pressure off Sullivan.[53] On 6 August Brodhead wrote Sullivan, outlining his plan:

> I have obtained leave from his Excellency, the Commander-in-Chief, to undertake an expedition against the Seneca Towns, on the waters of the Alleghany [sic], & he has directed me to open a correspondence with you, in order that our movements might operate in favor of each other.

... I shall set out for Cannawago in three or four days and expect to reach it about the 20th Inst. I do not intend to stop there, but expect to proceed nearer to the route I am informed you are going and will endeavour to write you again.[54]

Nowhere did Brodhead's letter state that the two armies would rendezvous, although that possibility certainly remained open. Because Brodhead's offensive began well after Sullivan's army departed for Tioga, Sullivan occupied the attention of most of the Tories and Indians mustered to defend the homelands, and Brodhead marched relatively unhindered up the Allegheny. This proved sound in the end; of the three detachments participating in the campaign, Brodhead's would have been most vulnerable, given its size and composition (fig. 3).

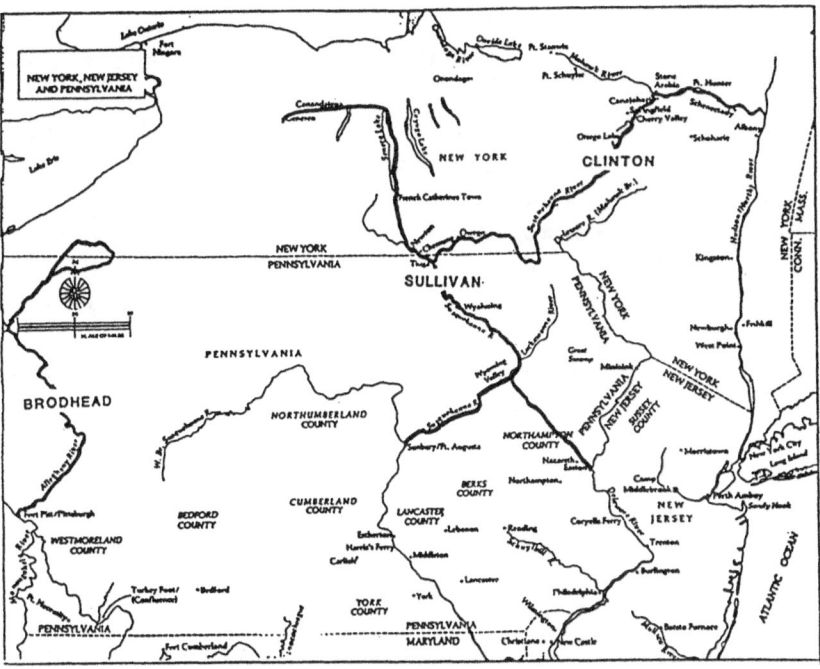

Fig. 3. Continental army's 1779 campaign against the Iroquois; adapted from *The Papers of General Nathanael Greene*, ed. Richard K. Showman, vols. 3–5 (Chapel Hill: University of North Carolina Press, 1986), 3: endpiece.

Concern for the security of his soldiers drove the commander-in-chief's actions in the East. Washington feared the British might build a new fort at Oswego, a move strongly backed by their Iroquois allies. This action would jeopardize Sullivan's operation because it rendered unusable the Mohawk River approach to the Iroquois country. To preclude this possibility, Washington decided to stage a demonstration on the Connecticut River. He knew the British saw this river valley as a natural invasion route to Canada and would watch it carefully for troop movements. In March 1779 he ordered Colonel Moses Hazen and his regiment to begin construction of a road northward along the Connecticut River, hoping to convince the British that they might face a rebel offensive in the spring or summer.[55] Anticipating a possible breach of security, Washington permitted Hazen to believe his efforts were preparatory for a real offensive rather than a demonstration.[56] He even requested that New Hampshire's chief executive, President Meshech Weare, move as many militia as possible to the river at Coos for three or four months beginning 1 June.[57]

Washington knew that Henry Clinton maintained a fairly proficient intelligence-gathering apparatus and expected the British to detect Hazen's road-building activities and the deployment of New Hampshire's militia. Both events, he hoped, would strengthen the enemy's perception of impending trouble in the Connecticut River Valley. The selection of Hazen and his regiment also served the commanding general's purposes. Hazen's desire to participate in a Canadian expedition was well-known, and the men of his regiment, many of them born in Canada, shared his enthusiasm.[58] Indeed, Hazen's diversion became the most successful part of Washington's counterintelligence effort, as both Haldimand and Clinton noted the road-building effort and concluded that another rebel invasion of Canada was in the works.[59]

The gathering of Sullivan's troops at Wyoming and at Canajoharie could not be hidden from the British for long. Sympathy for King George or greed for his money led many Americans to provide British officers with information. Lax security within the Continental army also posed a problem. Thomas Hughes, a British officer and prisoner-of-war on parole at Easton, noted in his journal the presence of Sullivan's army and the forthcoming campaign against the Indians.[60] It is unclear whether Hughes ever communicated this back to his superiors, but the loose limits on his captivity made it very possible that he did. Much of the British war correspondence of 1779 suggests that, if Hughes did not communicate what he saw, others did. In frontier towns such as Carlisle, Washington's commissary officers dutifully stocked the army's depot to levels not seen in years past. Few of the townspeople failed to guess the purpose, and many openly discussed the expedition's prospects.[61] British spies in Philadelphia reported the manufacture of large numbers of pack saddles and reported to Clinton that the Americans planned an Indian campaign for the summer.[62] Philadelphia newspapers printed a general recall of Continental officers still on furlough, a sure sign that Washington planned some kind of action.[63] Still other contacts reported the movement of Continental units westward from towns near the coast.[64] One correctly predicted a summer expedition under the command of Sullivan.[65] In early summer Butler's Rangers and Iroquois scouting parties operating on the Susquehanna River reported Hand's presence at Wyoming and the growing stockpile of supplies being assembled there.[66] Butler warned Bolton to expect Sullivan to attack up the Susquehanna. Unfortunately, none of the Tory or Indian patrols shadowing Sullivan's camp succeeded in taking a prisoner. As a result, the American army's objective remained in doubt. In June Clinton's contacts within the Continental army informed him of the composition of Sullivan's army. Benedict Arnold, now secretly in the employ of the British army, provided much of the operational information, including Sullivan's order of battle, troop strengths, expected routes, and operational objectives.[67] Arnold stated that Sullivan would conduct the campaign along two axes.[68] In nearly every facet, save that of operational objectives, the information Clinton received proved accurate.

Although possessing all the information necessary to construct an accurate picture of Washington's intentions, the British took no steps to block the American campaign. The British failure to act resulted primarily from possessing too much information and to a lesser extent from a reluctance to trust reports originating from Indian sources. Clinton and Haldimand simply proved unable to analyze and process the information they had obtained. Surviving British military correspondence indicates that Haldimand, the key figure in the defense of the Iroquois homelands, remained unsure of Sullivan's objective until it was too late to take effective steps to defend the Iroquois. Haldimand's failure rested squarely on his own shoulders. He steadfastly refused to recognize the accuracy of intelligence based on reports originating with the Iroquois, choosing instead to rely on Clinton's sources. Reports coming from Indian sources discounted any American move against Detroit. They argued, instead, that Sullivan would use the Susquehanna River to invade and destroy the Iroquois homelands.

Clinton controlled the largest body of potential reserves for Haldimand and performed with equal mediocrity. From the beginning of the campaigning season in April, Clinton told Haldimand the rebels would attack Detroit in the summer with a combined army of militia and Continentals. He also believed that a feint would be made on the Susquehanna to draw Butler's attention and prevent his redeployment to Detroit.[69] A month later Clinton's spies in Albany and Schenectady predicted an offensive up the Mohawk to Lake Ontario and reported the presence of one hundred and fifty bateaux at Albany, presumably for use against the Indians, since "none were fitted with cannon." But they vitiated this information by reporting that the Americans intended to invade Canada from the east by way of the Connecticut River.[70] A month later another source warned Clinton that "Joseph [Brant] and his bretheren [sic]" served as the expedition's objective, with the main invasion route being the Susquehanna.[71] Verifying Washington's intentions became Clinton's first priority, and he failed badly. Instead of clarity, Clinton continued to receive conflicting reports. Arnold's efforts to assist Clinton played a part in creating the confusion. With other sources confirming much of the information Arnold had passed, Clinton mistakenly assumed the probable accuracy of the rest. In June Arnold named Detroit, Niagara, and the Indian settlements as Sullivan's objectives.[72] A month later Arnold narrowed the list to Detroit, diverting British attention to the wrong objective.[73]

Regardless of how British commanders read or misread the intelligence picture, Haldimand faced a military threat against his position in Canada.[74] Had Haldimand been subordinate to Clinton, he might justly have expected his superior to either take the field to force Washington to reassemble the Continental army or send him the necessary reinforcements to block the expected American advances. The British command structure in North America, however, was divided into two coequal commands.[75] Haldimand depended on Whitehall for reinforcements. Failing this, he could only fall back on Clinton's good graces for assistance. As early as 10 November 1778, Haldimand had begun requesting reinforcements from Clinton.[76] Having detached soldiers to the southern colonies, Clinton could not satisfy the request.

The situation remained unresolved by the following spring. Clinton intended to take the field against Washington and informed Germain on 21 May 1779 that he would threaten American positions on both sides of the Hudson River once some of his detached units returned.[77] How Germain interpreted the word *threatened* remains unclear, but, when Clinton's men took Continental army positions at Stony Point and Verplank's Point and then failed to press on to test Washington's fortifications at West Point, it became clear that Clinton did not intend the word to signify the start of any major campaign capable of lifting pressure on Canada. Clinton had eighteen thousand men under his command in Rhode Island and New York; however, once he subtracted garrison forces from the totals, his field forces numbered only about eight thousand, a number he believed to be only slightly superior to Washington's field army.[78] The relative parity between the two armies made Clinton reluctant to test his offensive capabilities. Expecting reinforcements from England, Clinton decided to hold his gains and wait for his numbers to increase.

Believing he did not have the luxury of time, Haldimand continued to request reinforcements from both Whitehall and Clinton.[79] Finally, in July Clinton relented, promising to reinforce Haldimand with fifteen hundred to two thousand soldiers once a convoy could be assembled to move them to Canada. Clinton made the decision with great hesitation, informing Haldimand that the transfer would cripple his plans for an offensive in New York or New Jersey. "I have no doubt but you must have considered, sir, how severe a blow this must be to all my prospects, and I trust you will have weighed the exigencies that induces a measure so debilitating to my operations."[80] For Haldimand the delay meant that he would receive no reinforcements in time to move them into the Iroquois homelands. In the final analysis Clinton's contributions in rescuing Haldimand from the storm brewing against the Iroquois hurt rather than helped the British cause.[81]

While the British struggled to make sense out of the information they did have and pondered what to do with the forces at their disposal, Washington's own spies conducted a well-run intelligence operation of their own. Their efforts provided the commander-in-chief with a fairly accurate picture of British troop movements. The most important part of this effort concerned the size and movements of Clinton's main army in New York. They did not ignore British operations in Canada, since these directly threatened Sullivan's expedition. The British garrisons in Quebec and Montreal had been quiet during most of the winter. In the spring Washington's spies reported the presence of fifteen hundred British regulars and two regiments of Canadians in the two Canadian cities.[82] Haldimand intended to send some of these soldiers to strengthen the garrison at Detroit while using the rest to reinforce Tory-Indian efforts in New York, New Jersey, and Pennsylvania. In June Schuyler eased Washington's and Sullivan's fears when he reported that only four companies of these soldiers actually had passed up the St. Lawrence during the spring, mostly headed for Detroit, well beyond Sullivan's concern.[83] Fearing the possibility of a rebel offensive up the Connecticut, Haldimand grew reluctant to release large numbers of soldiers to his western posts.

By August Butler and his Tory Rangers and their Indian allies faced a rebel army that was too large to deal with without help. The preceding month, Butler had informed Bolton that Hand, with six hundred men plus artillery, occupied Wyoming and that Sullivan was expected soon with an additional nine regiments. Butler believed that he had to have reinforcements to defeat or delay Sullivan.[84] Haldimand doubted this appraisal. He lectured Bolton on Butler's tendency to relay exaggerated reports:

> It is impossible the Rebels can be in such force as has been represented by the Deserters to Major Butler, upon the Susquehanna. He would do well to send out intelligent white men to be satisfied of the truth of those reports if any thing is really intended against the upper Country. I am convinced that Detroit is the object. The rest is merely a diversion.[85]

When the reports did not change to reflect the rosier picture Haldimand believed existed, he decided that Butler should hear the message directly. He reassured the Tory leader that Sullivan's army could not be as large as reported and merely constituted a "feint."[86] Apparently certain that Washington would not risk a large force on an Indian campaign, he insisted that

Sullivan could not possibly have nine regiments and artillery.[87] With his patrols in daily contact with rebel patrols, Butler knew better what he faced. Before Sullivan departed the Wyoming Valley, Captain John McDonald gained the clearest picture yet of the threat he and Butler faced. He estimated Sullivan's combat strength at five thousand men, with "a long Train of Artillery, and a Brigade of Provision Boats" in support. At least a thousand packhorses and one hundred and seventy boats were being employed to move the army northward. The report was met with skepticism the farther it traveled from the Susquehanna Valley.[88]

By September Sullivan's "feint" of sixteen regiments had swept its Tory and Indian adversaries from the field at the Delaware village of Newtown and proceeded to torch the villages on Seneca Lake. Brodhead's men had done the same to villages on the upper reaches of the Allegheny before his supplies gave out and forced a withdrawal to Fort Pitt. Finally accepting the size and orientation of the attacking force, Haldimand now decided that Sullivan intended to seize Niagara. Rather than risk losing the post, Haldimand strengthened it to withstand a possible siege.[89] Only belatedly would Haldimand authorize John Johnson to come to Butler's aid. By then it was too late.

At one time earlier in the planning stage, Schuyler had believed that with sixty days' notice the British could put two thousand men into the field against Sullivan. This assumption was never really tested. British intelligence failed to provide two weeks, let alone two months, of lead time. Only after the Iroquois homelands lay in ashes did Haldimand finally realize what Sullivan had been after, and only slowly did he accept that Niagara was not the primary goal. His hesitation had left the Iroquois at the mercy of Sullivan. The following spring Haldimand attempted to cover his failure in a speech to the Iroquois, claiming he could not send help sooner because a rebel army on the Connecticut River had threatened Canada. The rebels, he assured them, would have cut the Iroquois off from their source of food and supplies if the invasion had been successful. He told them to take heart, however, as Sullivan's army had returned to the coast, where British soldiers had badly mauled it in battle, inflicting five thousand casualties.[90] Haldimand had stooped to lies to hold the Iroquois's loyalty.

From the first the British had seen the Iroquois as pawns to be manipulated for the Crown's benefit. The western theater figured as secondary to events farther east. British officers such as Haldimand complained continually about the cost of supporting the Iroquois and never proved willing to divert the manpower or materials necessary to defend their allies if threatened by an American counterattack. The Iroquois gave their loyalty to the Crown grudgingly, but they gave it nonetheless. They had faith that, if challenged, King George would send his redcoats to strengthen their defense. When Sullivan's army appeared at Tioga, the "southern door" to their tribal lands, the Iroquois found that their faith had been misplaced.

Washington did not envision Sullivan's expedition as anything more than a large-scale raid. His main objective was to bring "sure and fatal" destruction to the Iroquois tribes allied with the British, not a campaign to end the war.[91] He hoped his scorched-earth policy might bring peace to the frontiers. Should sizable numbers of captives fall into Sullivan's hands, the leverage they afforded would make it easier to keep the peace. At the very least the destruction of Iroquois villages and fields would force their war parties to operate at much greater distances from the frontier villages of Pennsylvania, New York, and New Jersey.

In the short run the expedition accomplished the destruction of the Indian lands. From a strategic perspective, however, the capture of Niagara offered a much better long-term solution to the problem of bringing peace to the frontiers. Practically speaking, this had never been a viable option. The logistical preparations required to lay siege to Niagara as well as Washington's reluctance to accept the risks associated with such an undertaking placed this beyond Sullivan's grasp. Under Bolton's direction Niagara's garrison had reconstructed much of the fort's formidable defenses. In addition, without a rebel naval presence on Lake Ontario, Haldimand could have mustered enough strength to break the siege. Laying siege to Niagara might have also prevented Washington from carrying out more strategically important operations. Had the French fleet appeared as Washington hoped, he would have been unable to take advantage of the opportunity, with so many of his veteran units tied down in western New York. Washington's failure to order Sullivan on to Niagara was a carefully considered decision and reasonable under the circumstances. It also represents the weakest element of the campaign planning. Washington assumed that, once the Iroquois homelands lay in ruins, the tribes could be forced back into neutrality. This was a dubious assumption at best. With winter approaching and their means of support destroyed, only the British could provide the food and shelter necessary for survival. Furthermore, given the parameters of the border war, an American victory could only spell disaster for Iroquois intentions to retain control over their homelands.

At the operational level Washington's ability to decide upon a line of advance and establish the intelligence network to make it succeed stands out as the most striking example of his talents as a commander. Although Sullivan's advance from Tioga represents a traditional single-axis advance, the army's operations prior to this proceeded along dual axes. This approach, along with the supporting attack up the Allegheny, made it extremely difficult for the disjointed array of Indian tribes, Tories, and British regulars to act in concert against any of the American elements. It also permitted Sullivan and his subordinates to inflict the widest possible damage on the Confederacy.

Washington accepted many risks as well. While Butler lacked the manpower to oppose the main body of the army working its way up the Susquehanna without large reinforcements, he probably could have challenged James Clinton's brigade during its move southward to Tioga. Brodhead's small army was even more vulnerable. The use of converging columns operating outside supporting distance violated eighteenth-century military doctrine, but a century later it became part of the U.S. Army's operational technique for Indian fighting on the western plains.[92] British regulars and Tories, soldiers well versed in the nuances of conventional combat, advised and supported the Iroquois, but, to lessen the risk, Washington took advantage of tribal localism. The multiple-route approach tended to make each village's warriors focus on their own homes rather than the overall good of the Confederation. At Newtown this served as a catalyst for a battle at a site that was favorable, but not optimum, for the Indians or their Tory allies. Lacking any other plans for defense, when Sullivan's soldiers flanked the ambuscade and forced its abandonment, Indian cohesion broke down. Warriors fled home to their villages, intent on removing their families from harm's way. In the meantime Sullivan advanced largely unopposed, burning his way up the east shore of Seneca Lake and then westward into the Genesee Valley.

Washington preyed on British localism as well. The demonstration on the Connecticut weakened and delayed the British response to the developing crisis. The different facets of the plan provided each of the rebel elements with a measure of security by limiting their opponents' ability to react.

The intelligence groundwork laid by Washington and his subordinates formed the foundation for the operational scheme. By the time Sullivan's army departed Wyoming, each of the key commanders had a generally accurate understanding of the terrain separating him from his objective. The wide-ranging effort to locate and interview reliable men with firsthand knowledge of the Iroquois lands paid dividends. The scope of the search enabled Washington to determine the reliability of his information before making it available to his subordinate commanders. Comparable effort went into monitoring British troop movements. Washington and his subordinates retained an edge in strategic intelligence until it was too late for the British to react expeditiously. As a result, Sullivan's army rampaged through the Iroquois lands then returned home largely untouched by their foes.

4

Tactics

The creation of an American army from the various militia and volunteer companies manning rebel positions outside Boston represented Washington's most pressing problem in 1775. The historical record of colonial soldiers in England's dynastic wars with France could not have offered him much hope that the process could be accomplished before the British Empire mustered its power to crush the rebellion. During the French and Indian War, General Jeffrey Amherst quickly came to the conclusion that American militias were nearly useless. "If left to themselves," he wrote, "[they] would eat fryed [sic] Pork and lay in their tents all day."[1] Brigadier General James Wolfe was no more flattering in his appraisal. "The Americans are in general the dirtiest most contemptible cowardly dogs that you can conceive. There is no depending on them in action. They fall down dead in their own dirt and desert by battalions, officers and all. Such rascals as those are rather an encumbrance than any real strength to an army."[2] Whatever use as British officers found for provincials, it was not in fighting. One British officer summarized their utility as being "sufficient to work our Boats, drive our Waggons [sic], to fell Trees, and do the Works that in inhabited Countrys [sic] are performed by Peasants."[3] In 1775 few British officers believed it possible for Washington to build a respectable army from the rabble at his command. By the time Sullivan and his army marched against the Iroquois in 1779, however, the qualitative gap that separated the Continental army from its British adversary had narrowed considerably, particularly in the area of tactical proficiency.

The transformation did not occur overnight, as the war's opening campaigns largely served to reinforce this opinion of American military prowess. Plagued by an utterly inadequate logistical system, the American invasion of Canada in 1775 had ground to a halt outside the gates of Quebec then been thrown back in a nearly disastrous retreat in 1776. Later the same year, at Long Island, Washington watched in anger and embarrassment as his largely untrained soldiers broke and ran in the face of Hessian and British regulars. Creating a well-trained army became a necessity, and by 1778 Washington and his subordinates had made significant strides toward this goal. In June 1778 the Continental line held its own at Monmouth in open-field linear combat against Henry Clinton's army, inflicting as much damage as it sustained. The process of development continued throughout the months leading up to Sullivan's expedition.

Sullivan's force represented a typical European-style army in its configuration for battle in the wilderness. It contained fifteen regiments of infantry and one of artillery organized into four brigades. The infantry contingent included at least one regiment of light infantry and the remnants of Colonel Daniel Morgan's now famous rifle corps, all of which were assigned to Hand's brigade. The artillery, under Colonel Thomas Proctor's command, included field guns up to six pounds, howitzers, and a coehorn mortar for a total of eleven crew served guns, giving Sullivan the capability to deal with any threat he might meet in the field short of siege operations against well-prepared fortifications.[4] In addition, Sullivan began the campaign with a small detachment of cavalry, probably not larger than a seventy-five-man troop. As had been the practice in past Indian campaigns, he employed Indian auxiliaries from the Oneida, Tuscarora, and Stockbridge Mohican tribes to act as guides and to enhance his long-range reconnaissance capability, although most of these men would not join his army until Clinton joined him at Tioga. His scouts also provided linguistic and cultural skills not available elsewhere.[5]

An indeterminate number of women and their children also accompanied the army. The term *camp followers* has all too frequently been attached to such women. Filled with sexual innuendo that suggests their primary role was that of prostitute, it represents an inaccurate portrayal of the duties they performed. In an army that was always cash poor, few women could make their keep through prostitution. Some of the women who accompanied Sullivan's army fell under the category of "women of the army." These were a recognized body of women, subject to military discipline, who drew both pay and rations. Many worked as nurses. A reorganization of the Continental army's medical staff in 1777 stipulated that one supervising matron and ten nurses were to be assigned to every one hundred patients.[6] A second group served in the gun crews of artillery batteries and may have been present in Proctor's regiment. The latter carried water to the men whose job it was to swab the cannon's barrel prior to loading a new charge. Although it is possible that a few of the remaining women served in line infantry regiments, most were the wives of soldiers whose primary job was to take care of their spouses. There had been considerable debate about how many of these women should be permitted to accompany Continental armies. Most officers, Washington included, believed that they slowed the army and placed a drain on the commissary; nevertheless, he decided to forgo any restriction on their numbers. "I was obliged to give Provisions to the extra women in these Regiments, or lose by Desertion, perhaps to the Enemy, some of the oldest and best Soldiers in the Service. . . . The latter with too much justice remarked. . . . 'Our wives could earn their Rations, but the Soldier, nay the Officer, for whom they Wash has naught to pay them.'"[7]

In addition to the women, Sullivan depended on boat crews, engineers, pioneers, chaplains, surveyors, and teamsters to support the needs of his army. The total number of men and women involved in the expedition came close to six thousand, although probably only a little over thirty-five hundred soldiers were available for combat on a daily basis.[8] Whether one examines the army's actions on the march, in camp, or during combat, the conclusions remain the same: the Sullivan expedition strongly suggests that, tactically, the Continental army had become a typical eighteenth-century European-style army.

The army accomplished the transition in a remarkably short time under wartime conditions. A dependence on drill and fire, technological innovation, and continuity with a military past stand out as the three characteristics most reflective of European armies in the eighteenth century.[9] Washington intended to build the Continental army along these lines. The process required hard work but not exceptional innovation. Russell F. Weigley contends in *A History of the American Army* that only the greater reliance placed on light infantry made the Continental army different in any significant way from its foes.[10]

Infantry dominated the eighteenth-century battlefield. Most European armies employed both heavy and light infantry. This division dates back to antiquity, when military commanders divided their infantry based on the weapons they carried and the roles they performed. Light infantry, carrying missile weapons such as the bow, were primarily employed to break up the cohesion of the enemy's formation. Heavy infantry, wearing armor and armed with thrusting weapons ranging from the Macedonian *sarissa* to the Roman short sword, engaged in close combat.

Infantry assumed a secondary role on the battlefield after the fall of Rome, when mounted cavalry displaced infantry as the dominant combat arm. Differences between light and heavy infantry continued throughout the Middle Ages. In the fifteenth century light infantry began to favor new technology employing gunpowder as a propellant. Known as an arquebus, this early version of the musket suffered from being slow to load and exceptionally inaccurate. The Spanish took the lead in developing the technology and tactics to accompany it, and in the years that followed most European armies followed their lead, arming their light infantry with the arquebus (and later the matchlock), while heavy infantry marched to battle in dense formations still carrying the pike. Light infantry took on the role of skirmishers with increasing frequency.

During the Thirty Years' War (1618–48) Sweden's King Gustavus Adolphus, improving on reforms made by the Dutchman Maurice de Nassau, created a new linear system of warfare employing both the pike and the arquebus. Each of his squadrons consisted of pikemen arrayed six deep and thirty-six across with ninety-six arquebusiers aligned in six ranks on the flanks to prepare the way for the decisive shock action of the pike.[11]

Gustavus's reforms revolutionized warfare and forced all European armies to find ways to combine fire with shock action while minimizing the vulnerability of the new linear formations to cavalry assault against their exposed flanks. Part of the answer to this problem appeared to be in finding a way to combine the roles of light and heavy infantry. This became possible in the latter years of the seventeenth century with two technological innovations: the flintlock mechanism for muskets and the socket bayonet. The combination gave heavy infantry the ability to deliver fire while retaining its basic function of engaging the enemy in close combat. Light infantry all but disappeared from the European battlefield as military leaders worked to develop tactics to maximize the effectiveness of the new technology.

A few military theorists such as Jean Charles de Folard and Maurice de Saxe argued that the new technology had brought too much concentration on fire over shock action. To correct the defect, Folard proposed using column formations to break through the thin lines of musketeers now common to most European armies, while Saxe suggested rearming some soldiers with pikes.[12] These advocates of shock failed to convince a military community increasingly enamored with the idea of fighting at a distance with muskets. Well-drilled infantry standing shoulder to shoulder in lines usually three rows deep offered the best way to achieve this while still allowing sufficient troop densities to allow the bayonet to decide the issue at close quarters. This method of forming soldiers for combat represented the European legacy to the American soldier.

Washington's problem was one of conveying this legacy to an American soldier not used to the discipline of military life. The solution to the problem arrived in the person of a former captain on Frederick the Great's general staff, Frederick William Baron von Steuben. The Prussian had shown considerable promise in Frederick's army, building his early reputation on his mastery of light infantry tactics and eventually becoming the deputy quartermaster general of Frederick's staff. Had he not insulted Frederick's son, his future in the king's army was assured. Instead, he found himself with neither army nor country. Willing to play the part of soldier of fortune, Steuben left Prussia and traveled to France, where he made contact with some of the military thinkers who would eventually transform the French army into the instrument Napoléon Bonaparte unleashed against the armies of Europe. It was through these French contacts that Steuben was eventually able to make his way to America. Misrepresenting himself as having held the rank of lieutenant general, Steuben managed to win an assignment to Washington's headquarters at Valley Forge in February 1778.

He immediately set himself to the task of condensing the drill regulations of the Prussian army into a body of easily learned standardized instructions while at the same time trying to incorporate some of the newer ideas he had acquired in France.[13] Using a model drill company of one hundred soldiers, he taught the business of soldiering to the rest of the army.[14] He worked on codifying the drills to insure that each officer and sergeant understood his responsibilities. Very much aware of the differences in outlook separating the Continental soldier from his European adversary, Steuben included instructions on leadership. Unlike European armies, he lectured his readers on the need to show compassion and concern for soldiers. "There is nothing which gains an officer the love of his soldiers more," he wrote, "than his care of them under the distress of sickness."[15] The Continental Congress accepted Steuben's *Regulations for the Order and Discipline of the Troops of the United States* as the army's standard for drill on 29 March 1779. With guidance on the loading and firing of muskets, battle tactics, movement techniques, encampments, and leadership, the pamphlet proved a godsend. Steuben's manual greatly shortened the time necessary to train an army of freemen possessing little or no military experience in the ways of linear warfare.[16]

Linear tactics required a great deal of the individual soldier, calling for him to perform almost as if he were an automaton, loading and firing to a series of shouted commands while facing a murderous fire from his foe. Uniformity based on unquestioning discipline became the order of the day. In the exchange of volleys that characterized battles of the period, the evolving theory held that the attacking army should methodically close the distance between itself and its foe. Commanders on each side could expect to sustain casualties during this process as the two sides traded volleys. The side capable of generating the greater number of volleys held an advantage in this attrition-driven exchange, but the final decision still rested on the outcome of combat with the bayonet. Frederick's soldiers became the standard for European armies to emulate. The Austrians credited the Prussian king's "walking batteries" of infantry with being capable of firing five volleys per minute for short periods.[17] Once the final push had begun, however, Frederick prohibited his infantry from firing their muskets, because it slowed the advance and damaged unit cohesion.[18]

In reality eighteenth-century battles seldom progressed to the point where the bayonet decided the issue. One of the opponents usually broke before this occurred. The volley fire that characterized battles of the period produced tremendous casualties, even victorious armies suffered 20 to 30 percent losses.[19] Most armies could ill afford such casualties and looked for ways to minimize them. A reemphasis on skirmishers offered one way to accomplish this, but heavy infantry trained in the mind-numbing drill of linear warfare and held in place by the harshest discipline proved ill suited to this role. To bring greater flexibility to the battlefield, military commanders, beginning with the Austrians, reintroduced light infantry to eighteenth-century armies.[20] The British followed suit during the French and Indian War, forming a distinct corps of light infantry to add to their expeditionary forces.

Colonel Henri Bouquet's Sixtieth Royal Americans became one of the first British light infantry regiments to see duty in North America. Bouquet pioneered changes in leadership and in the training of soldiers. Rather than motivate soldiers through fear, Bouquet inspired first with kindness and praise. He wanted self-reliant men capable of independent thinking. Bouquet demonstrated considerable selectivity in accepting soldiers into the Royal Americans. Physical conditioning and marksmanship skills ranked highest among the significant prerequisites for a recruit. Perhaps more telling for a war yet to come, Bouquet looked to the frontier to fill the ranks of the Royal Americans, believing that colonists made better light infantry material than that available in the mother country. In the French and Indian War and, later, during Pontiac's Rebellion the concept proved its worth, and many colonial leaders, Washington among them, took note incorporating a small corps of light infantry in August 1777.[21] Although designed to counter a European opponent, Washington's army possessed the flexibility necessary to deal with non-European opponents employing a completely different concept of tactics.

European tactics worked well against European armies. They required some modification when applied against non-European foes. The success of military endeavors into the wilderness rested almost entirely on the skill and fortitude of the infantryman. Emphasizing individual initiative, Native Americans had adopted an approach to war centered on stealth and surprise. Raids and ambushes characterized combat among tribes as well as their approach to warfare against Europeans. Not surprisingly, Indians seldom offered themselves up as the kind of target most vulnerable to volley fire. This so-called irregular warfare common on the frontier magnified a problem inherent to linear tactics, the inability to deliver aimed fire. For example, on a European-style battlefield the commander's ability to direct fire decreased markedly once the shooting began. When fired, an eighteenth-century flintlock musket gave off a jet of flame nine inches high from its pan and spewed a large cloud of gray-black smoke from its muzzle.[22] The command to aim seldom appeared among eighteenth-century drill commands because the volume of fire, not its accuracy, represented the key element in firepower.[23] Steuben included the command in the Continental army's drill manual, but it represented mostly wishful thinking.[24] The tight formations of soldiers insured that a cloud of gray smoke obscured the front of any unit after the first discharge. The limitations of the weapon further undermined the idea of delivering effective aimed fire. A typical smoothbore musket, such as the British Brown Bess, fired accurately to only eighty yards because of low muzzle velocity, a heavy bullet, and the lack of a sighting mechanism. The French Charleville, the most common musket found in the Continental army, could hit accurately at a little over one hundred yards, an improvement, to be sure, but not enough to change the relationship between musket and bayonet. Firepower primarily prepared the way for shock action.

The British soldier had shown a marked advantage over his American opponent in his ability to break American formations with the shock of the bayonet. In an attempt to take away this advantage, Steuben made a major modification in the tactical formations he incorporated into the American army by changing the British standard formation consisting of three lines to two. This allowed American battalions to maximize their firepower over a wider front. This modification had the effect Steuben hoped for on eastern battlefields, but, because frontier fighting rarely saw massed formations, Americans needed to explore new links between firepower and shock action.

Sullivan met the challenge by expanding the role of the riflemen in his light infantry brigade. The aura that had surrounded these soldier-frontiersmen outside Boston in 1775 had disappeared by midwar, as continuing problems with discipline damaged their reputation. Daniel Morgan's riflemen performed well at Saratoga under battle conditions particularly suited to their skills, but Washington increasingly doubted their usefulness as he and Steuben labored to develop a European-style army.[25] The rifle itself had several notable drawbacks limiting its usefulness in linear warfare. Its lack of a bayonet stud made it unsuitable for close combat. It took significantly longer to load. Additionally, it required a finer grain of powder than that of a smoothbore.[26] Only in the irregular warfare of the frontier did Washington still see a definite place for large bodies of riflemen, and he insured their presence in Sullivan's army.

Sullivan and his subordinates saw riflemen as one way to deliver effective fire against a dispersed, concealed foe. Hand's brigade contained the Eleventh Pennsylvania, a light infantry regiment, with several companies of Morgan's Rifle Corps attached to strengthen its ability to deliver aimed fire. The accuracy of the rifle, coupled with open formations that permitted each rifleman the freedom to find his own firing position, made the rifle ideal for frontier fighting.

A regiment of artillery augmented the fire of Sullivan's infantry. On European battlefields artillery had been growing in importance. During the Seven Years' War Frederick found himself increasingly dependent on his artillery, as the frightening casualties sustained by his infantry eroded their effectiveness. British commanders, on the other hand, still employed artillery primarily as a counterbattery weapon and only secondarily as an antipersonnel weapon. Knox patterned artillery employment in the Continental army according to the views of Frederick the Great, using it as a means to compensate for the Continental line's shortcomings with the bayonet.[27] For Sullivan artillery guaranteed him fire superiority over the most optimistic estimate of enemy forces, but this capability came at some expense. The price for firepower turned out to be speed. Limited to the Indian paths that linked the villages of the region, the rolling hills and densely forested terrain slowed the army's march speed. Proctor's gun crews poled their guns upriver from Wyoming by boat then pulled and cursed them forward once the army departed Tioga.

In European armies cavalry provided the mobility lacking in either of the other combat arms. On the march it screened an army's flanks and patrolled forward along its route. In combat it secured the flanks and, most important, made decision possible through its ability to pursue a broken opponent. A troop of cavalry accompanied Sullivan to Wyoming, but, after gaining a better understanding of the difficult terrain along his route of march, he decided to dismount his cavalrymen and employ them in other endeavors.[28]

With his army configured as a European army, Sullivan endeavored to have it operate as one. A sizable body of European military writings, some of it dating back to antiquity, guided the actions of Continental officers. Americans had been voracious consumers of this literature, and the war only served to spur this intellectual activity.[29] Starting with Washington, senior officers labored to assimilate what passed for military theory in the eighteenth century. The commander-in-chief carried an annotated copy of Vegetius's *Military Institutions of the Romans* along in his baggage. He read Humphrey Bland's *Treatise of Military Discipline* and Maurice De Saxe's *Reveries upon the Art of War*.[30] Frederick the Great's *Instructions for His Generals* as well as Henry Lloyd's *History of the Late War in Germany* provided more contemporary advice on war. Nor were the offerings limited to conventional conflict. Beginning in the late 1740s a new body of military literature dealing with partisan combat, or *la petite guerre,* began to appear. Both John Forbes and Henri Bouquet found Turpin de Crissé's *Essay on the Art of War* to be of use in their operations along Pennsylvania's frontier during the French and Indian War. At the same time, Robert Rogers's short list of instructions for British volunteers preparing to undergo ranger training offered similar tactical advice.[31] The Continental army's readership of these pieces was not limited to senior officers. Early in the war Captain Johann Ewald, a Hessian officer in the king's service, noted in his diary:

> I was sometimes astonished when American baggage fell into our hands . . . to see how every wretched knapsack, in which were only a few shirts and a pair of torn breeches, would be filled with such military works as "The Instruction of the King of Prussia to his Generals," Thielke's "Field Engineer," the partisans Jenny and Grandmaison. . . . This was a true indication that the officers of this army studied the art of war while in camp, which was not the case of the opponents of the Americans, whose portmanteaux were rather filled with bags of hair powder, boxes of sweet-smelling pamatum, cards (instead of maps), and then often, on top of all, novels or stage plays.[32]

Found among the pages of these books was advice on march security, encampments, and combat formations. Despite minor disagreements among the authors, enough consensus existed within these works to suggest that they provided the Continental army with a workable concept of military doctrine.[33] Though novices at war, American officers did not blindly accept European practices as suitable for every battlefield situation. Whenever New World demands ran against the grain of Old World military practices, they reshaped the doctrine as necessary. The American military past, particularly in the area of Indian fighting, certainly played a part in explaining the actions of Sullivan's expedition.

Washington's experience in Braddock's ill-fated campaign, for example, strongly influenced the guidance he gave to Sullivan. As the highest-ranking provincial officer accompanying Braddock, Washington had been in the thick of the disaster, having his clothes pierced by several musket balls, one horse shot dead from under him, and two later horses wounded.[34] He was certain that the event need not have occurred had Braddock and his men not been careless. The level of surprise achieved when the French and their Indian allies opened a flanking fire from some high ground to the right of the army produced first confusion then panic. Despite their best efforts, British officers never regained control over the situation. The enemy's occupation of this low ridge dominating the army's line of advance violated established European military practice of the day and indicated a breakdown in Braddock's security arrangements.[35] Washington faulted British arrogance for part of this problem, noting he had warned Braddock to fashion his operation around "the mode of attack which more than probably he would experience from the Canadian French and their Indians on his march through the mountains and covered country."[36] Braddock was no stranger to combat and understood the procedures necessary to insure the safety of his army. His problem was one of execution rather than ignorance. He understood the need for Indians to guide and screen the army's movements then yielded to those who advised that he cut costs by releasing all but eight of these men. He dedicated one-third of his infantry to flank security and yet lived long enough to see his army broken by a successful flank attack. Neither Braddock nor his staff had kept their edge as the army closed on Fort Duquesne, but they had retained all their rigidity in thought. Washington related that the British were so "in favor of regularity and discipline and in such absolute contempt" of the enemy that they could find no value in the advice he had to offer.[37] As a result, a decidedly inferior force maximized their advantage of terrain and the element of surprise to defeat a force with superior numbers. Washington also blamed British officers for not adapting their tactics to the environment.[38] Several groups of British regulars attempted to deliver volley fire only to have their efforts fail entirely against a foe that refused to show himself but for a few brief moments. However familiar British officers were with partisan warfare, British soldiers demonstrated no such adaptability. Faced with the realization that they had not been prepared for this kind of warfare, discipline gave way to panic.

When it became time for his own army to attempt an undertaking closely akin to Braddock's, Washington took every precaution to insure its success. He stressed the importance of maintaining an offensive spirit. "I beg leave to suggest as general rules that ought to govern your operations," he advised Sullivan in May 1779, "to make rather than receive attacks, attended with as much impetuousness, shouting, and noise as possible; and to make the troops out in as loose and dispersed a way as is consistent with a proper consent and mutual support."[39] Remembering the panic set off among British regulars when their foes opened a deadly fire against their flank, Washington stressed the need to slavishly adhere to the precautions necessary to secure the army on its march.

Military writers had given considerable thought to marches and related security precautions. Vegetius, for example, argued that "an army is exposed to more danger on marches than in battles" because "on a march the soldier is less on his guard . . . and is thrown into disorder by a sudden attack or ambuscade."[40] He suggested that a direct relationship existed between an army's size and its security: the larger the army, the greater its vulnerability during the march.[41] Commanders could minimize their risk to ambush through diligent patrolling and a flexible march formation. To keep order in the event the unexpected occurred, Saxe advocated that generals adopt what he referred to as "standard combat procedures" to govern the action of subordinates when time or circumstances made it difficult for superior officers to control events.[42]

In nearly every aspect of the campaign that followed, Sullivan adhered to the dictates of these theorists and the wishes of his commander regarding security. The army already had what passed for a set of standard combat procedures. Sullivan augmented them to fit the needs of the mission then had them disseminated to the rest of the army. To give himself a better feel for the terrain, he initiated an aggressive reconnaissance plan. Even before the main body of the army had assembled at Easton, Sullivan had his light infantry scouting the line of march to Wyoming. Once the army had moved to Wyoming he extended his patrols northward to Tioga. A similar process occurred with James Clinton's brigade camped on the shores of Lake Otsego.

While his scouts conducted reconnaissance patrols of the upper river, Sullivan and his generals developed plans for the army's movement and for its actions on contact with the enemy. Sullivan envisioned the army moving in a hollow square with artillery and pack trains at the center of the formation (fig. 4).[43] In the plans Hand's brigade, containing three regiments of infantry and Morgan's rifle companies formed the lead unit on the march. The rifle companies, under the command of Major James Parr, provided the army's advanced guard moving as much as a mile in front of the army's main body. Musket-bearing light infantry elements followed several hundred yards behind the advanced guard, where they could reinforce the advanced guard or maneuver to the flanks of small enemy detachments. These lead elements served primarily as the army's eyes and ears. While at Easton, Sullivan ordered them drilled in security measures, such as the crossing of defiles, necessary to protect the army during movement.[44] If these units were taken under fire, Hand's brigade had sufficient firepower to hold their ground until the remaining brigades of line infantry could be brought to bear. Furthermore, the distance between the lead brigade and the remainder of the army insured that, even if the enemy did execute the perfect ambush, it would catch only a small part of the army in the trap. In the meantime the enemy's flank or rear stood vulnerable to attack by one or all of the remaining three brigades. To lend additional support to Hand's brigade, Sullivan assigned several light artillery pieces to Hand.[45]

Maxwell's and Poor's brigades of four regiments each of infantry followed in column formation behind Hand. Each of these brigades provided one hundred soldiers to patrol the army's flanks, the light infantry company in each regiment furnishing the manpower.[46] One of the brigades drew the additional assignment of securing the far shore of the river. The Susquehanna River is shallow during most of the summer months and easy to ford in many places. Sullivan feared that his foes might slip past him on the opposite bank then cross downstream to attack his rear. To minimize this threat,

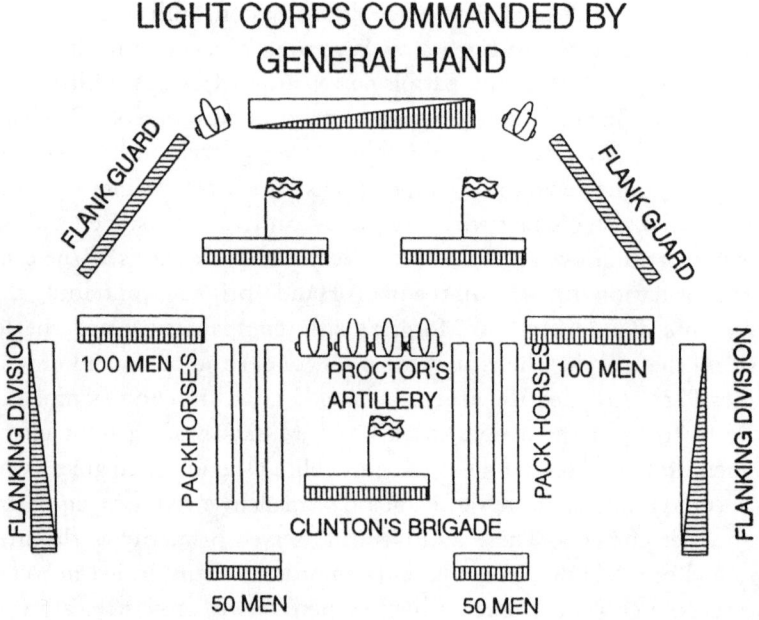

Fig. 4. Sullivan's movement formation; adapted from *Journals of the Military Expedition of Major General John Sullivan against the Six Nations of the Indians in 1779*, ed. Frederick Cook (Auburn, N.Y.: Knapp, Peck, and Thomson, 1887), 66. (courtesy of Pennsylvania History and Museum Commission).

a company of light infantry patrolled the river's opposite shore. To cover these soldiers, Proctor arranged his sizable fleet of bateaux to support the infantry with small grasshopper cannons and a howitzer. In addition, he allocated some boats to evacuate the men if they took fire.[47]

Successful flank security required an understanding of terrain and a good eye for distances. Officers charged with this responsibility had to recognize and clear potential points of contact. They had to operate far enough from the main body to provide protection against an ambush, but they also needed to stay close enough to the main force to permit quick reinforcement. When an attack occurred, the parent brigades supported the engaged patrol, while Hand's men doubled back to attack the enemy's flank. Sullivan planned for Clinton's four regiment brigade to provide rear security following the rendezvous at Tioga. He also assigned to Clinton the task of serving as the army's reserve.

The formation represented a trade-off between speed and security. Hand's brigade had to march in line formation with individual platoons in column spread across the army's front (fig. 5).[48] The broad front insured the army's security while at the same time positioning the lead brigade to support the maneuver of one or both of the follow-on brigades. The precautions should have made movement of a less-well-trained army tedious and slow, and both the security-conscious formations and the artillery and supply trains did impede the army's march. Nonetheless, the army still averaged from twelve to sixteen miles a day when it did not stop to destroy villages. Even complicated operations such as river crossings failed to hinder the army's rate of march appreciably.

Sullivan's army conducted one major crossing of the Susquehanna on the way upriver and made several crossings of the Chemung beyond Tioga. Sullivan began preparations for the first crossing on 10 August 1779 while his army camped on a large flat of ground about five miles south of Tioga. He took several regiments from the New Jersey brigade and conducted a thorough reconnaissance for a suitable crossing site.[49] Following the doctrine of the day, several factors influenced his decision. The most important considerations concerned the river's depth and speed. The entrance and exit points on the river needed to be secured easily and not dominated by high ground. The crossing should occur at a bend in a river or near islands capable of obstructing the enemy's view.[50] The exact location Sullivan selected is difficult to determine, but diaries point to a place one and a half miles south of Tioga on a river plain known as Queen Esther's Flats. The river there broadens slightly to a width of approximately two hundred yards, mitigating the effects of a stiff current. Smooth stones line the riverbed, and the water depth seldom exceeds four to five feet on an average August day. The banks vary in height from three to six feet. The sediment-rich soils probably presented few problems for army pioneers to cut through to provide the wagons and artillery easy access to and from the river. No high ground on either side commanded the crossing. The only thing missing from Sullivan's selection of a crossing site was the lack of islands or bends in the river to conceal the movement.

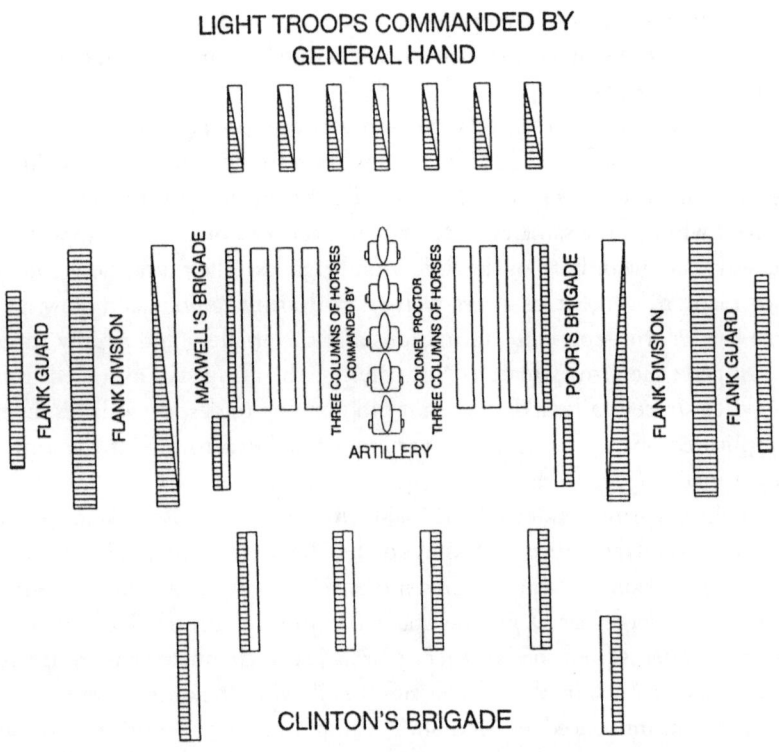

Fig. 5. Sullivan's formation for combat; adapted from Cook, *Journals of the Military Expedition*, 67.

The following day Sullivan moved to the crossing. He first secured the near side of the river with the soldiers from the reconnaissance party. Then he ordered several six-pound artillery pieces to bombard the woods across the river to chase away any opposition.[51] Soldiers of the Second New York and the Second New Jersey then waded the river to seize the far shore.[52] These regiments came from different brigades. Brigadier General Enoch Poor commanded Lieutenant Colonel Philip Van Cortland's Second New York, while Brigadier General William Maxwell commanded Colonel Israel Shreve's Second New Jersey.[53] These regiments acted as the flank elements of the two brigades and would resume those positions once their units cleared the river. With near and far shore security in place and a variety of artillery pieces on shore and in the bateaux positioned to provide support fire, Sullivan brought the army across. The entire operation took approximately thirty minutes and did not cause the loss of a single soldier or pack animal.[54]

The army reached Tioga the same day and began building its first fortified camp, complete with a four-blockhouse fort Sullivan permitted to be named after himself. During the march from Wyoming the army's nightly encampments had been strictly conducted according to European doctrine. Pickets and an active system of patrols secured the army's perimeter. This attention to detail continued in the securing of the army's encampment at Tioga. Sullivan's men built Fort Sullivan at "the carrying place," a canoe portage linking the Susquehanna River with the Chemung River. The location at the narrowest piece of land along Tioga's peninsula provided a water obstacle on two of the fort's four sides (fig. 6). To provide the fort's defenders with an unobstructed view of the surrounding ground, Sullivan gave detailed instructions to Colonel Israel Shreve, the post's commander:

> When I mentioned your removing every obstruction that might possibly prevent the free operation of your cannon, I did not confine myself to the Peninsula on which the Fort is founded, but had reference to the Island likewise, and now desire you to have all the Timber thereon cut down and burnt or removed.[55]

To strengthen the position further, Sullivan left behind several six-pound artillery pieces from Proctor's artillery.[56] With palisaded walls stretching across the narrow piece of land between the two streams, the fort commanded the river plain to the south, protecting livestock the commissary pastured there.

The efforts of Shreve and his men did not go unnoticed. Tory and Iroquois patrols watched the fort go up. Its size convinced them that the Continental army meant to use it as a permanent post. Understanding its importance to the expedition, they hoped to seize it either by storm or deception after the army departed. Without artillery they realized the futility of the former. Unless the security-conscious garrison provided an unexpected opportunity, they also recognized the unlikelihood of the latter.[57]

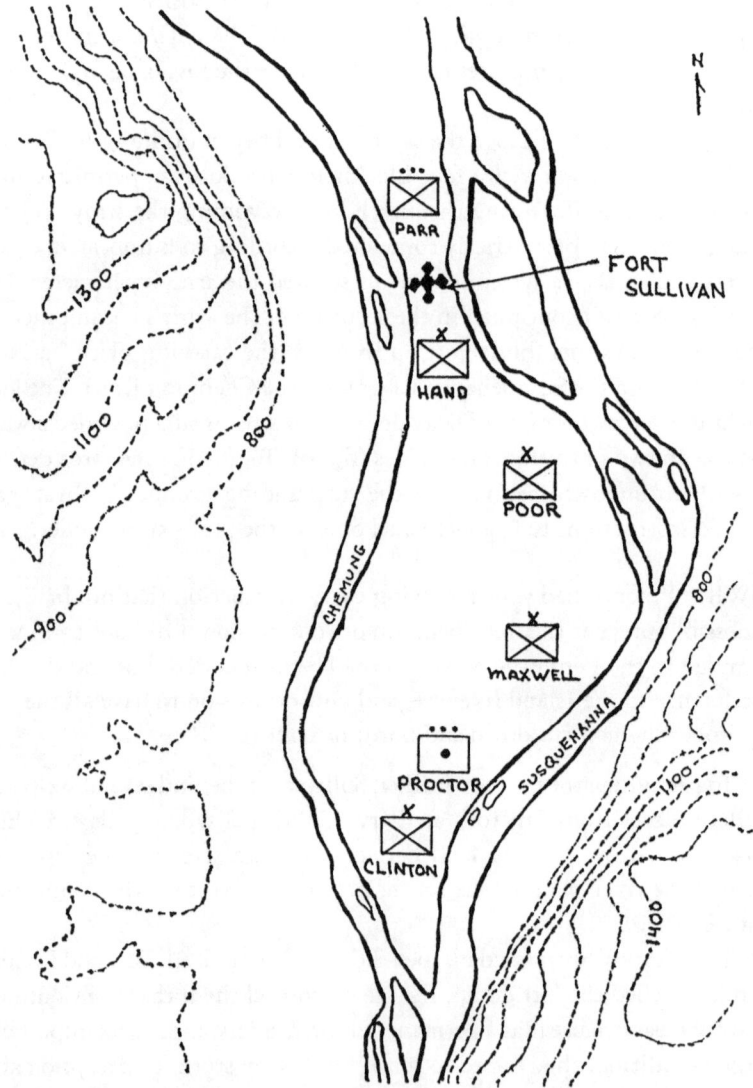

Fig. 6. Army's encampment at Tioga (scale: 3.38 in. equals 1 mi.)

Whether on the march or in camp, Sullivan's concern for security continued throughout the campaign. The techniques he adopted centered on active measures: patrolling, a challenge and password system, and well-thought-out movement formations. Passive measures such as a concern for minimizing noise appear at first glance to have been largely ignored. By today's standards it was a noisy army. Judged against the norms of the eighteenth century, however, the army performed much like any other European army. Sullivan relied on audible signals to control movement and pass commands. Cannons started or stopped the army's march.[58] At the regimental level infantry commanders used drum ruffles.[59] On the river, boat crews reacted to horn signals.[60] The army undoubtedly made noise but not without a purpose. Command and control of an army several miles long during the march required a recognizable set of signals. The dense forests and broken terrain limited the usefulness of visual signals. The army actually sacrificed little for its dependence on audible signals. Sentry reports made it clear that Butler's and Brant's men had stalked the army every step of the way since it left Wyoming. The Iroquois realized long before Haldimand or Henry Clinton did that Sullivan meant to destroy their homelands and intended to use the Susquehanna and Chemung Rivers to accomplish his aims. From the moment Hand's riflemen began the march upriver, operational security had ceased being a factor. Furthermore, part of the psychological impact of Sullivan's army was its sheer boldness. It never made any pretense after leaving Wyoming of concealing its objective. The very openness with which it marched warned its foes that they could do little to stop it. Some officers even went so far as to try to convince their wives that the army's size made it too large to challenge. Peter Gansevoort wrote reassuringly to his wife, "the General Opinion of all the officers is that not a Shott [*sic*] will be fired on us."[61] Size represented the most important component of military force in an age of low technology, and Sullivan deliberately worked to make the army appear as large and powerful as possible to intimidate his foes.[62]

The army arrived at Tioga largely untouched, thanks in equal measure to the skill of Sullivan's soldiers and the disarray of his opponents. Somewhere among the pine and oak forests that covered the hills upriver from their encampment, the army expected its luck to end and the test of its prowess in battle to begin. During the six weeks that followed, Sullivan's men fought two skirmishes and one small battle with their foes. Tactically, the army gave a good account of itself, brushing its adversaries aside as it swept into the Indian homelands and burned them to the ground. Sullivan and his subordinates displayed a mixed record in their ability to react to the tactical situation, exhibiting exceptional speed in designing and carrying out a raid against Chemung while taking altogether too much time to bring their power to bear at Newtown. Minor problems also existed among junior-grade officers who were still working to master their responsibilities.

The first real glimpse of the army's combat skills came soon after its arrival at Tioga, with Sullivan's decision to raid the village of Chemung. The army had no sooner begun the process of setting up camp at Tioga on 11 August 1779, before Sullivan sent an eight-man reconnaissance patrol under Captain John Cummings up the Chemung River to scout the village.[63] The patrol consisted mostly of soldiers from the Second New Jersey, although Sullivan sent along his guides, Captain John Franklin and Lieutenant John Jenkins. The latter had been captured early in November 1777 and transported upriver by way of the Chemung to Fort Niagara. During his journey into captivity Jenkins had passed through the village of Chemung.[64]

Cummings's patrol pressed slowly forward throughout the night, arriving in the vicinity of Chemung early the following morning. Taking a position on some high ground overlooking the village, Cummings and his men watched the village below. Chemung saw a flurry of activity that morning, but Cummings could not determine whether the Tory and Indian parties he saw in the village were readying themselves for offensive action or preparing to abandon the site.[65] Around midday Cummings withdrew undetected from the vantage point and hurried back to Tioga, some twelve miles downriver.[66]

Cummings arrived late in the afternoon. Sullivan called a hasty council of his key subordinates. Still lacking Clinton's brigade, Sullivan felt that the gathering at Chemung threatened his position at Tioga. After a brief discussion the council decided to raid Chemung the following morning. Leaving two regiments behind to secure camp, the army departed the same evening for Chemung. Night attacks seldom occurred in the eighteenth century, because the normal command and control measures built on drums and horns made surprise nearly impossible. Small units might successfully attempt such undertakings, but Cummings's information indicated the need for a major effort, given the number of Tories and Indians in the village. Only experienced units could execute this kind of operation, and such endeavors carried tremendous risks. Planned in a very short time and executed across difficult and unknown terrain at night, Sullivan's undertaking stands out for its boldness.

The plan required precise timing and considerable skill from his subordinates. In its design it bore some similarity to what in the modern era would be referred to as "hammer and anvil" tactics. Sullivan ordered Hand to pass around the village to cut the escape routes to the north. To frustrate any attempt to escape west across the river, he instructed that Colonel George Reid take two regiments, ford the Chemung, and establish a position opposite the village. With the three New Jersey regiments and some artillery, Sullivan intended to seal the last remaining way out of the village to the south. Poor drew the mission of sweeping the village from the east.[67] Neither Sullivan nor any of his primary subordinates possessed firsthand knowledge of the terrain around the objective. In addition, the need to strike quickly precluded any rehearsals. The plan rested solely on the information gained by Cummings.

Sullivan's attempt failed, but it did come close to succeeding, despite its shaky preparations and complexity. Darkness and difficult terrain slowed the march to the village. In addition, the activity Cummings had spotted was in fact the early stages of abandoning the village. Hand's light infantry departed Tioga around 6:30 in the evening, with the final regiments moving out as late as 10:00 p.m.[68] Only the men from Cummings's patrol had experience with the route, and they had traversed most of it during darkness. The march did not go well. "On our march we passed several very difficult defiles and as the night was very dark and the path but little us'd we found great difficulty in proceeding," wrote Lieutenant Colonel Henry Dearborn.[69] Instead of arriving at Chemung before dawn, the army reached the village just after sunrise. The route had roughly followed the north side of the Chemung River. West of the present-day town of Waverly, New York, the terrain becomes very steep, with high precipices overlooking the river. Soldiers moved slowly, only one and two abreast, across these areas. For a small group of artillery men the march proved exceptionally difficult. They had to leave the horses behind and hand-carry a small coehorn mortar mounted on an improvised carriage the twelve miles to Chemung.[70]

Hubley's advanced units arrived first at Chemung. A dense early-morning fog rising from the river obscured their visibility while at the same time concealing their presence. The village turned out to be deserted, although still-burning cooking fires and the presence of a sleeping dog indicated that the enemy had not long departed the scene. Quickly modifying the original plan, Hand had Hubley's soldiers sweep through the village. Though they found no one, the sound of cowbells convinced Hand that his foe was just ahead on one of the trails leading from the village, and Hubley's men took off in pursuit. This decision proved to be a mistake. About two miles beyond the village the trail crossed over a small hill at an oblique angle. In the tangled underbrush Captain Rowland Montour of Butler's rangers had improvised an ambuscade with twenty Delaware warriors. Caught in the open when Montour's men opened fire from their concealed positions, Hubley lost six dead and nine wounded.[71] Montour's ambush could have been even more destructive if he had had more men or if Hubley's men had been less dispersed. Those detachments not caught in the ambush Hubley posted to flank Montour's position. Realizing that the Americans were on the verge of running down the long axis of his flank, Montour withdrew his men.

The army completed the destruction of Chemung and its surrounding fields before returning to Tioga by nightfall, a round-trip of twenty-four miles. Sullivan had mixed feelings about the operation. He bragged to Washington about the "exceedingly praiseworthy" conduct of his soldiers. If anything, they had been too eager to rush the enemy when engaged.[72] The plan of attack had been sound, and, despite the difficult march, most of the units arrived at their proper pre-attack positions simultaneously. Most important, the burnt houses and blackened fields around Chemung could no longer support a force large enough to threaten Sullivan's camp at Tioga.

The army's performance had not entirely pleased Sullivan, and he took steps to correct the problems. Though happy with the exuberance of his soldiers, Sullivan believed that some of his regiments had not performed up to standard during the engagement. Rather than blame his soldiers, he laid the responsibility squarely on the shoulders of his junior officers:

> The officers of Regiments are positively ordered not to be absent from their respective command, whenever their Regiments are ordered to a place where there is a possibility of an attack from the

enemy, and the soldiers are cautioned against wantonly throwing away their fire when they have no object to level it at. How exceedingly pleasant it must be to four or five cowardly lurking savages to see one fire from them to produce a wanton discharge of the muskets in a number of Regiments without any kind of aim, meaning or order, and levelled at no object but endangering those officers who are endeavoring to restore them to order, and spreading carnage among themselves. Painful as it is, the General must say that much of the mischief done yesterday to our troops, was done by ourselves, by an unguarded and unjustifiable conduct by troops to whom every part of their conduct proved that they had sufficient bravery to engage and conquer ten times the number of their dastardly foes.[73]

Montour's resistance at Chemung convinced Sullivan and his officers that the enemy still hoped to stop them. Concerned for the safety of James Clinton, Sullivan dispatched Poor with nine hundred men and eight days' provisions to move up the Susquehanna River in search of his missing brigade. Sullivan expected Poor to clear the river downstream from Clinton, thereby denying Butler or Brant any opportunity to ambush the northern wing of the army before it reached Tioga. After Poor's rendezvous with Clinton's army, the combined force would proceed back to Tioga.

Poor found Clinton on 19 August, and the two brigades rejoined the main army on 22 August. Sullivan wasted no time in preparing his men for their move toward the Finger Lakes. Small bands of Indians continued to harass his sentries, the supply situation had gone from bad to worse, and the cooler evenings left no doubt that little remained of the campaign season. Four days after the rendezvous, the army moved northward along the Chemung toward Catherine's Town. The march formation adhered to Sullivan's previous instructions. Hand's brigade led the formation with Poor's and Maxwell's brigades on the flanks and Clinton's in the rear. Hand divided his brigade into six columns then spread them across the army's front, with two to three hundred yards separating each column. Parr's light infantry worked the woods in front of Hand's columns.

Difficult terrain and rainy weather combined to slow the march. Pioneer teams labored from sunrise to sunset, the sound of axes marking the progress of the wagons and artillery. Major Jeremiah Fogg remarked in his diary that "the transport of which [the artillery and supporting wagons], to the Genesee, appears to the army in general, as impracticable and absurd as an attempt to level the Alleghany [*sic*] mountains."[74] The following day's march went even less smoothly. At one point an entire regiment of infantry had to be dedicated to the chore of cutting a passable road through a nearly perpendicular twenty-foot bank. The process took seven hours and required the use of drag lines to pass the guns and their caissons. Fogg noted that for officers and their men alike, "a universal cry against the artillery" had gone up.[75] Seeking the flattest ground for his wagons, Sullivan held close to the river, crossing it as necessary to avoid traversing the nearby hills. Recent rains made this practice difficult as well. During a crossing on 28 August the current swept several soldiers and three packhorses downstream. The men managed to swim to safety. The overburdened packhorses were not so fortunate, costing the army the supplies they carried.[76] If the pace could not be quickened, many officers knew that the supply situation threatened to bring an end to the campaign.

Butler, Brant, and the rest of the Indian leadership realized something had to be done to stop the Americans but found themselves increasingly plagued by problems of their own which hindered their efforts at defense. Over the course of the summer supplies of food and ammunition in the Iroquois homelands had all but dried up. Whitehall had never seen the border war as anything more than a sideshow. Regardless of their pledges to the Iroquois, British priorities for supplies did not begin with the Iroquois.

In 1778 Butler had been able to subsist his men as well as his Iroquois and Delaware allies off the land of his opponents. His operations also had succeeded in securing considerable numbers of cattle, which his raiding parties carefully herded back to the Iroquois homelands. The raids had been so successful, however, that they had succeeded in driving the frontier eastward and thereby made it increasingly difficult to rely on foraging for food. Depending on the farmlands surrounding Iroquois villages to make up the difference also had its problems. The Iroquois had focused their attention on fighting in 1778, and their farming had suffered as a result. The cattle herded to the Iroquois homelands had helped sustain them through the winter when their food supplies ran short.[77] With the coming of spring, neither the rangers nor their Indian allies had adequate food for the campaigning season without additional help from the Crown. Butler made this situation clear very early, telling Bolton on 3 June 1779 that provisions collected across the winter and in the early spring were almost expended and further operations depended on a speedy response from Niagara.[78] After two frustrating weeks in which his pleas appeared to fall on deaf ears, Butler wrote again: "I have made every effort to support myself as long as I could without troubling you for Provisions, as I know how precious an article they are, but I can no longer avoid it, and unless you send us some speedily, we cannot support ourselves in the Country, or even get enough to carry us out of it."[79] Butler had in the past been able to procure some of his beef from the Indians, but the supply had dwindled, and the price had risen. To complicate matters, rumors had spread among the Iroquois that Butler had been underpaying for his beef. As a result, he found the Iroquois unwilling to sell their few cattle for the rate offered.[80]

Butler's pleas did find their way to Haldimand in Quebec, but relief still did not come. Haldimand expected thirteen ships from England with badly needed supplies for his soldiers as well as for the Iroquois and Butler's rangers.[81] By the end of August ten of the ships had docked in the St. Lawrence. Three ships had not yet arrived. Eventually, word came that one of the ships had fallen into the hands of John Paul Jones.[82] Haldimand understood that the shortages were crippling the efforts of his subordinates and complained to Henry Clinton that, without the lost supplies, he could not hope to keep all his forces properly supplied.[83]

By late summer green corn had become a staple in the diet of both rangers and Indians. The situation had its effect on their ability to defend the Iroquois homelands. McDonald's successful raid on Fort Freeland (near present-day Muncy, Pa.) in July might have been even more devastating had McDonald been able to convince his Iroquois allies to accompany him downriver to Fort Augusta and the magazine at William Maclay's house. Instead, the Iroquois proved far more interested in the 116 cattle they had captured in the farms around the fort than they were in pressing their advantage against the fort and magazine at Sunbury. Of the cattle taken at Freeland, McDonald found himself able to shepherd only 62 of these back to the Iroquois homelands, owing to thefts by his own Indians.[84]

Food shortages among the raiding parties helped aggravate an already difficult problem with ammunition. Short of cattle and corn in the early summer, the Indians turned to hunting. Disgusted with what he considered a lack of discipline, Butler noted that "the Indians fire at every little bird they see," with the result that what little powder and ball as remained among the Iroquois had largely been used.[85] With Sullivan's army now poised to penetrate the Iroquois lands, both the Iroquois and their Tory allies faced the prospects of doing battle on empty stomachs and with little ammunition to spare.

Growing distrust inherent in the coalition of Tories and Indians complicated matters for Butler and Brant. The conspicuous absence of more than a handful of British regulars along the Chemung did not escape the notice of the Indians. The British had portrayed themselves as both powerful and rich. Now, in the face of adversity, they appeared just the opposite. The Iroquois began to suspect that the British had either lied to them about their power or cared little for the plight of the Iroquois.[86]

The Iroquois were not the only ones feeling frustrated with an ally. British officers as well as Butler and his rangers had developed an equally dim view of the Iroquois will to oppose the invasion. With their homelands under attack, neither Butler nor his superiors could understand why the Iroquois and their Delaware allies seemed so hesitant to engage in combat. Just before the American raid on Chemung, Butler appealed to Bolton to have however many Iroquois warriors as might be assembled at Niagara join him on the upper Susquehanna.[87] Bolton tried to help his subordinate but found only forty-four of the two hundred warriors camped near the fort willing to go to Butler's aid.[88]

Outnumbered better than four to one, Butler, Brant, and the rest of the Iroquois and Delaware leadership sought a way to compensate for their numerical inferiority. Seeking to repeat on a larger scale their successful ambush at Chemung, they found a suitable position near the Delaware village of Newtown. Better positions existed upstream and along the trail to Catherine's Town. Butler and Brant wanted to use Newtown as the first in a series of delay positions designed to sap Sullivan's strength. They hoped to use the high ground on either side of the river as positions from which they could attack Sullivan's flanks and rear.[89] Their views, however, counted for little as the assembled chiefs discussed the plan. The Delaware chiefs present were accorded the right to make the final decision on the site of the ambuscade because the American army most directly threatened their villages and crops.[90] No attempts were made to prepare additional positions beyond Newtown.

Located just west of a small stream known today as Baldwin's Creek (fig. 7), the heart of the ambush ran along the top of a glacial esker to the left of and at an oblique angle from the main trail. Constructed of logs taken from village homes and concealed with freshly cut pine and oak branches, the works were formidable. On the right of the trail the ground rose toward the top of a nearby ridge. To catch Sullivan's soldiers in a crossfire, the plan required Indian and Tory forces to conceal themselves along the lower levels of the ridge facing the trail. On the ridge crest, and on several of the surrounding hilltops, scouts guarded against the possibility that Sullivan's soldiers might attempt to flank the position and kept alert for opportunities to fall on Sullivan's flank and rear. The plan also called for a few warriors to conceal themselves in the brush along Baldwin's Creek. The effective length of the ambuscade measured only a little over a half-mile, insufficient to attack more than a fraction of Sullivan's army. Its architects apparently hoped to spring the ambush on Sullivan's lead elements, while the two wings of the Indian-Tory formation fell on the American flank and rear. Under attack from three sides the American army might buckle, exposing the supply train and livestock to destruction. The restrictive terrain east of the river would make it difficult for Sullivan to attempt to rescue his trapped men, and, with his supply train decimated, his only remaining option would be to withdraw. The configuration of the ambuscade conformed, within the limits of the terrain, to the half-moon formation frequently employed by Indians of the eastern woodlands of North America.[91]

Working quickly, the combined force of Indians, Tories, and a detachment of British regulars finished their preparations several days before Sullivan's arrival. Most of the Iroquois and Delaware warriors present occupied the left side of the ambuscade, while McDonald, with sixty rangers, and Brant, with an additional thirty warriors, took positions on the right. The rest of the rangers along with the small detachment from the British Eighth under Butler's command held the center.[92]

Neither the Iroquois nor their Tory allies understood how much the terrain had slowed Sullivan's army and no doubt expected it to arrive sooner. They waited in their position all through the daylight hours of 28 August and then withdrew to their camp at nightfall. For most of the men it was a sleepless night. Little but green corn was available to eat, and few of the

Fig. 7. Battle of Newtown (scale: 3.19 in. equals 1 mi.)

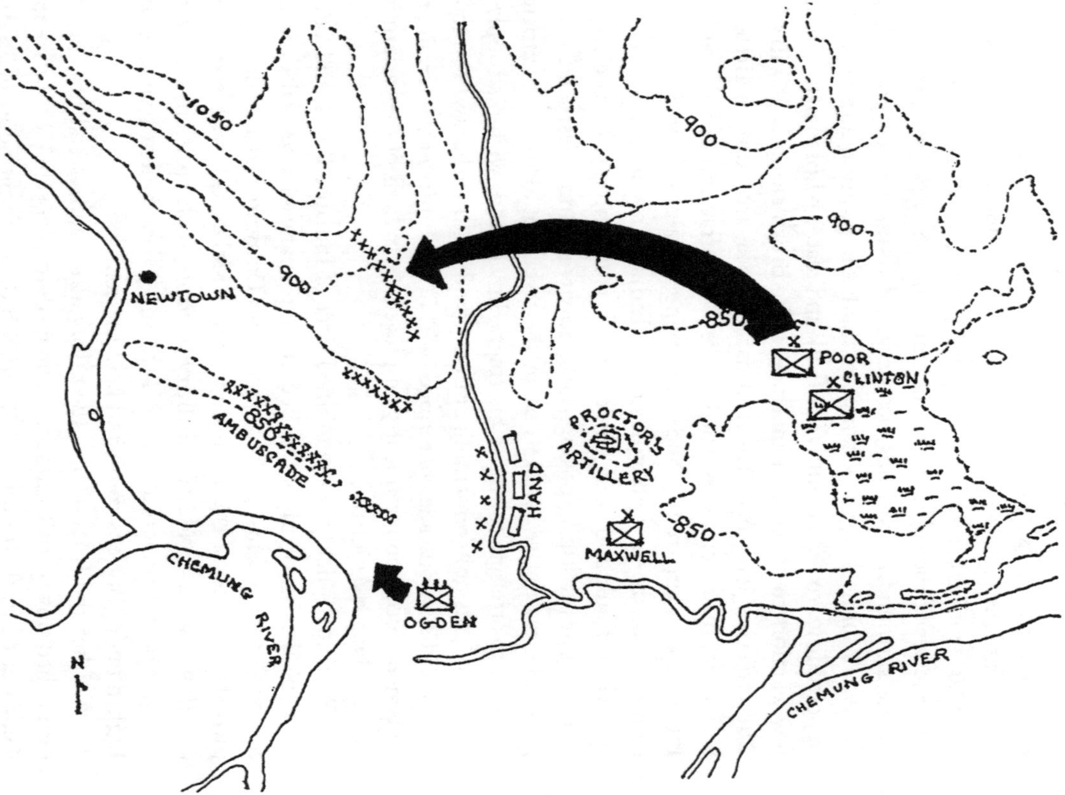

men had blankets, as Butler had already ordered camp gear be loaded on packhorses and removed from the area to prevent its capture should the ambush fail. The next morning the men returned to the ambuscade to resume their wait. Instead of occupying the same trace as the previous day, at least one warrior on the left elected to change his position. Butler protested the move to the assembled chiefs, arguing that the new position made it easier for the Americans to flank the whole ambuscade. As things would turn out, Butler's judgment was sound, but his arguments failed to sway anyone.[93] The morning hours passed slowly. Boredom set in, and with it came carelessness. One Indian fired on a deer that wandered past his position.[94] Cooking fires produced a noticeable haze over the encampment. Most devastating of all, a small group of Indians engaged in shadowing the Americans could not resist the opportunity to fire on several soldiers who had crossed the Chemung to burn a house.[95] The engagement produced no casualties and only served to further heighten alertness in the already security-conscious American army.

Sullivan increased his patrols as the army made camp 28 August near the ruins of Chemung. One of the patrols, under Captain Jason Wait, climbed a nearby hill to gain a better view of the valley beyond. Wait spotted the smoke from the cooking fires at Newtown. Comparing its density with the smoke coming from the fires of his own army, he estimated the enemy's strength as half that of his own army.[96] Other patrols had even more luck, reporting that the Indians appeared to have built some fortifications six miles north along the trail.[97] As morning dawned on 29 August, every soldier in Sullivan's army expected he would find himself in a fight before the end of the day.

The initial contact between the two forces occurred late in the morning about one and a half miles in front of the ambuscade, nearer to the ruins of Chemung than Newtown. The Indians withdrew up the trail after a brief exchange of musketry with the Americans. This meeting probably occurred by accident, a chance contact by a party of Indians searching for their overdue foe.

Hand found himself unwilling to permit his men to give chase. The chance contact suggested the possibility of another ambush. With his light infantry spread across his front, Hand cautiously resumed his march. Near Newtown the woods gave way to fields of head-high grass. Rather than push blindly ahead, Major James Parr, commanding the rifle companies, signaled the brigade to halt. One of his men climbed a nearby tree for a better look at the ground to the front. In the distance he spotted the ambuscade, its camouflage now noticeably withered against the backdrop of live trees and brush.[98] In addition, one of Brant's warriors, painted red with war paint, had positioned himself where gaps in the camouflage failed to conceal him.[99] Hand passed this information to Sullivan then quietly deployed his soldiers into a loose line and held his position.

Each side detected the other's presence at the same time in the early afternoon. Realizing they had been discovered, a party of about four hundred warriors ventured out of the ambuscade and engaged Hand's soldiers.[100] Several times these Indians feigned a panicked retreat, with the hope of causing the type of careless pursuit so costly to Hand at Chemung. Parr's riflemen would not be fooled by the ploy, choosing instead to seek cover and return fire. Hand reinforced Parr with a company of infantry from the Fourth Pennsylvania, while the rest of the brigade formed to the rear in line for battle.

For two hours the fighting centered around Parr's reinforced riflemen and the Indians and Tories holding the forward positions of the bulwark. With a heavier contingent of riflemen than any of the other brigades, Hand's unit proved well suited to the demands of this kind of decentralized combat. The distances separating the two sides still exceeded one hundred yards. Only rifle-equipped soldiers had any capability of accurately engaging targets in the ambuscade at that distance. Hand therefore made his riflemen the backbone of the brigade's fire support.[101] He did not, however, leave them there alone to hold the army's front. With Sullivan's approval, Hand had Proctor bring coehorns and three pieces of field artillery forward. A small knoll four hundred yards from the Indian's position offered a good position for supporting artillery. Located well back in the formation, Proctor's crews laboriously fought to get their fieldpieces into position. Samuel McNeill, a member of one of the crews, remembered the move:

> General Hand Continued Transmitting his Discoveries to General Sullivan from time to time, while the Artillery was Crossing an Exceeding bad Defile, and the men had to hitch Dragropes to the wagons, and with the help of Horses, it took one hundred and

Twenty men to each wagon to draw it up the Hill. At 12 o'clock the artillery was brought before the enemy's works. The Riflemen kept up a slow fire, amusing the Enemy and in order to keep them from Turning out of their works to make Discoveries, the artillery was planted in the most advantageous Place at about 400 yards Distance.[102]

After a hasty council of war, Sullivan ordered Hand to move his men forward toward the ambuscade under the cover of the artillery positioned on the knoll. While they fixed the enemy in position, Poor's and Clinton's brigades circled around to the right, intending to pass over the high ground and descend on the enemy's left flank and rear. Sullivan dispatched Colonel Matthias Ogden's First New Jersey regiment to the army's left flank with instructions to move upriver and attack the enemy's right flank after the engagement had begun. He held the rest of Brigadier General William Maxwell's brigade in reserve. Noting the presence of a chain of hills within two miles of the army's right flank, Sullivan speculated that his foes might have positioned men there to fall on his flank or rear during the battle. To prevent this, he dispatched several small reconnaissance patrols to clear the hills.[103] Taken in its entirety, the plan Sullivan outlined to his subordinates amounted to a double envelopment. To make it work required timing and considerable luck. Both proved beyond the army's grasp.

Sullivan intended to delay any frontal assault until his flank elements could get into position. At three o'clock in the afternoon Poor's brigade began the flank march but did not go far before encountering a swamp. Unable to go around it, they found themselves forced to wade into the lily pad–covered waters. The soft bottom and lush vegetation slowed the movement to a crawl and made control difficult. Innocent of his flank element's problems and believing the two brigades to be nearing the top of the ridge overlooking the ambuscade, Sullivan ordered Proctor to open fire. Poor's men had just begun to make the steep ascent, with Clinton's brigade still being at the bottom of the hill. Aware that he was out of position, Poor attempted to make up time. He had his men fix bayonets and press forward. With officers yelling to hurry and men attempting to pull themselves up the tree-covered hill, the brigade closed on the top of the ridge. Poor's men encountered no opposition until they reached the crest of the ridge, where a large number of Indians and Tories opened fire on the fatigued Americans. Momentarily surprised at the intensity of fire, which one soldier described as being thick as "hale," Poor managed to regain control.[104] He ordered his riflemen forward to act as skirmishers, while he gathered his regiments for a bayonet charge.[105] The attack that followed quickly shattered the enemy center. One group of warriors and rangers attempted to flank Lieutenant Colonel George Reid's Second New Hampshire, Poor's right-most regiment. Seeing the threat develop, Lieutenant Colonel Henry Dearborn, commanding the Second New Hampshire and operating without orders, changed front to reinforce Reid and successfully drove back the attackers.[106] Reeling under the momentum of Poor's attack, all opposition on the ridge fell silent as his opponents fled the scene. However successful the engagement had been for the Americans, it had cost time and made the Indians and Tories in the valley below aware of the danger to their flank.

The two flank brigades had not been gone a half-hour before the guns on the knoll opened fire. At first the artillery fire was slow and sustained, as Sullivan had wanted. As the gunners adjusted fire and began hitting their marks, the rate of fire quickened markedly.[107] While solid shot from the American cannons smashed into the ambuscade, Hand's light infantry with Parr's riflemen leading the way maintained a steady and increasingly accurate fire on the Indians and Tories. The occupants of the ambuscade responded in kind and a brisk fire ensued lasting a half hour.

When Poor's and Clinton's men won the contest for the ridge, the Indians realized they faced being cut off from their avenue of withdrawal. None of the chiefs proved willing to stop the precipitous withdrawal that followed. Iroquois and Delaware alike fled the field, leaving their dead where they had fallen. Butler's 250 rangers and 15 British regulars found themselves left behind to face 5,000 Continental regulars. He and his men pulled out of the position and made their way to the top of the hill behind the original ambuscade. There they found themselves locked in a nearly mile-long running skirmish with soldiers from Poor's brigade before breaking contact and making their escape.[108] In disgust Butler wrote, "the shells bursting beyond us made the Indians imagine the enemy had got their artillery around us and so startled and confused them that a great part of them ran off . . . many made no halt, but proceeded immediately to their villages."[109]

As mentioned previously, Sullivan had intended that Hand's brigade and Proctor's artillery keep up a sustained fire to pin the enemy down until the flank units arrived to seal the victory. Some evidence suggests that both Hand and Proctor may have had a hand in bringing about the premature abandonment of the ambuscade. Nathan Davis blamed Hand for being too eager to decide the issue himself, recalling that Sullivan had to intervene personally to insure that Hand did not lead an assault onto the ambuscade before the flank elements moved into position. Hand already had ordered his musketeers to fix bayonets when Sullivan moved to stop the attack. Proctor's artillery crews suffered from a similar lack of control. McNeill stated that, once the gun crews found their mark, they proceeded to pour a combination of solid shot, iron spikes, grape, and exploding shells into the ambuscade which proved so intense that the Indians chose to abandon their positions long before Poor could reasonably be expected to be in position.[110] Given Butler's own contention that Proctor's artillery demoralized the Indians, McNeill's criticism appears accurate and undoubtedly undermined the execution of Sullivan's plan.

Sullivan narrowly missed achieving a decisive victory over his foes. The army had to settle for a more limited tactical victory that granted them the field of battle but made it possible for their foes to fight again another day. Newtown temporarily shattered whatever unity had existed between the Iroquois and their Tory allies and rendered any immediate opposition to Sullivan impossible, despite the presence of very defensible terrain between Newtown and Seneca Lake.

The battle did not measurably cut into either side's strength. Sullivan lost at Newtown three dead and thirty-nine wounded, with all but four of the casualties coming from Poor's brigade.[111] Butler claimed he lost only five killed and three wounded.[112] His toll should have been much higher. These numbers probably do not include Indian losses, as Sullivan's soldiers found twelve dead Indians, including one female, on the battlefield and took two prisoners.[113]

Several factors combined to defeat Sullivan's plan. First, and most important, Sullivan had been the victim of the "fog of war" when Poor's and Clinton's units undertook their flank march. With little time for preparation, no one could have foreseen the swampy nature of the terrain along that approach to the ambuscade. Second, the execution of the plan took too long to develop. Sullivan felt he needed a council of war to insure that everyone understood their role. The emphasis on caution when the moment demanded audacity hindered the timing of the operation. Finally, Proctor and his officers failed to control their gun crew's rate of fire. These soldiers understood the psychological impact of artillery against Native Americans. Not surprisingly, too much shot and shell tended to discourage continued Indian resistance.

One key factor beyond Sullivan's control accounting for the final outcome at Newtown was the different cultural perspective the Iroquois brought to the practice of war. The Iroquois decision to withdraw from the battlefield at Newtown did not represent cowardice. Prior to the arrival of whites, war in Iroquois culture had been steeped as much in social demands as in the kinds of external disputes common to European nations. Among the former, the Iroquois had frequently waged "mourning wars" to make up for population losses. In these conflicts capturing prisoners took priority over killing the other side's combatants. The Iroquois marched their captives to their villages, where a chieftain awarded them to families that had suffered deaths among their ranks during recent months. The family's matron held the power of life or death over the prisoner. If accepted, the prisoner underwent a ceremonial adoption prior to acceptance into the family. Rejection meant death following torture and mutilation.[114]

The practice of mourning war had fallen in significance when whites came into the Iroquois homelands. European diseases, firearms, and the intensified fur trade all combined to drive up casualties to a point at which such engagements often took more lives than could be made through the capture and adoption of prisoners.[115] Beginning in the second decade of the eighteenth century, the Iroquois again began to practice limited mourning wars. During the French and Indian War as well as the Revolution, Iroquois war parties did make a practice of carrying women and children into captivity if circumstances permitted. Mary Jemison, the "white woman of the Genesee" who was originally captured by a Shawnee raiding party and subsequently sold to the Seneca, provides a good example of this practice. The Iroquois concern for maintaining their population also explains their fighting practices. Their tactics centered on ambushes and raids in which surprise worked to minimize their own casualties. Costly frontal attacks or even hazarding an engagement when significantly outnumbered represented two situations that violated the precepts of the Iroquois way of war. Iroquois religious practices also reinforced their selectivity in choosing the circumstances for combat. Iroquois warriors killed in battle were buried near where they fell or along the journey home and therefore away from the burial grounds of their family and village. The isolated burial meant that the dead warrior's spirit had to spend the afterlife separated from the spirits of his clan.[116] Butler's account of Newtown leaves one with the impression that the Iroquois had lost their nerve and fled. A closer reading of his own correspondence, however, reveals that Butler himself had recommended abandoning the position before Proctor's artillery began to splinter the logs and cut brush that made up the ambuscade. He had been overruled by the Indian leadership present, who apparently still believed that the day could be saved.[117] Most of the Iroquois withdrew from their positions at Newtown only after it became clear that the Americans had nearly enveloped the ambuscade. To the Iroquois way of thinking, further opposition seemed futile, if not needlessly sacrificial.

Despite the incomplete success at Newtown, the engagement illustrated two notable strengths in Sullivan's army. First, Hand's light infantry performed exceptionally well as the army's advanced guard. They detected the enemy position long before it could in any way endanger the following brigades. Second, the reliance on riflemen to provide supporting fire for the maneuver elements stands out as a noteworthy American adaptation to the problem of woodland warfare. Daniel Morgan had admitted that in linear warfare riflemen required the support of bayonet-equipped line infantry.[118] On the frontier the opposite proved true.

Newtown became the last major engagement of the campaign. The defeat broke the morale of the Iroquois and rendered useless Butler's and Brant's plan to fight a delaying action back through the passes that led to the Finger Lakes. Their plan had merit, for very defensible terrain existed along Sullivan's expected route. The passage from the Chemung River to Seneca Lake runs through a deep valley over fourteen miles long. A small stream called Catherine's Creek meanders along the valley. It was a place of deep pine and hardwood forest interspersed with cattail-filled swamps. Had Sullivan faced an enemy capable of dropping timber in his path and able to harass his pioneer crews from the bluffs on either side of the valley, the expedition might have ground to a halt. The Tory-Indian defeat at Newtown provided Sullivan the opportunity to move through the valley unopposed. Even without opposition the move proved a nightmare. Supply wagons sunk to their axles and horses to their chests. Soldiers manhandled the loads through the quagmire crossing the stream seventeen times during a journey that lasted well into the night and was described by one officer as a "disagreeable scene of confusion."[119]

Despite the best efforts of Brant and Butler, however, there would be no more attempts to stop Sullivan until his army had burned its way into the Iroquois homelands around Seneca Lake. When Sullivan turned his army westward at the head of Seneca Lake and headed toward the Genesee River Valley, Butler redoubled his efforts to oppose the American advance. Fearing that Niagara might be the final objective, he persuaded his Iroquois allies to risk another attack on Sullivan among the low rolling hills just west of Conesus Lake. The trail Sullivan had been following crossed one of the lake's tributaries on a small bridge before proceeding into the hills. Butler burned the bridge to buy time, then he set about preparing another ambuscade.

Sullivan, cautious as ever, proved to be in no hurry. When his lead units came upon the destroyed bridge, Sullivan stopped the army and rebuilt the structure. In the meantime he dispatched another patrol under Lieutenant Thomas Boyd to find the village of Chenussio. Sullivan instructed the young officer to take only four or five men, scout the path to the town, and report back to headquarters by the next morning.[120] Boyd exceeded his instructions. He assembled a force of twenty-three men, far more than specified.[121] Most of the men came from Parr's rifle companies, although the Second and Third New York regiments as well as the Fourth and Eleventh Pennsylvania also were represented.[122] Several Indians accompanied the patrol to include Hanyost Thaosagwat, one of the Oneida chiefs. The larger force turned out to be too large for security and too small to fight its way out of a major engagement.

Boyd set out for Chenussio unaware that the Seneca had moved the village a few years earlier to the western side of the Genesee River. The patrol managed to miss Butler's ambush on its departure and by luck followed the right trail to the new village of Chenussio. Finding the village abandoned, he had his men hide nearby to watch for enemy activity. Once in position he sent four men back to report back to Sullivan.

Shortly after the messengers departed, four Indians on horseback rode into the village. At this point Boyd committed his second violation of orders. Not content to observe, Boyd had his men attempt to kill the four. Among Boyd's patrol was Timothy Murphy, perhaps the best-known marksman in the American army.[123] His first shot pitched one of mounted men to the ground dead. Unfortunately, Murphy's fellow riflemen failed to match his skill. They managed to wound only one, but not seriously enough to prevent his escape. Boyd had chosen to risk the success of his mission and the safety of his soldiers on an opportunity to take a few scalps.

After revealing the presence of their patrol, Boyd and his men started back to Conesus Lake and the safety of camp. His failed ambush should have produced a greater sense of caution. Instead, Boyd chose to move at a leisurely pace along the same route he had followed to Chenussio. After moving along the trail for several miles, the young lieutenant decided to take yet another liberty with Sullivan's orders and called a halt to the day's march. Instead of returning to camp before daybreak, as instructed, Boyd instead decided to await the arrival of Sullivan. He sent two more messengers to Sullivan with information he had collected. The two men had not been gone long before they returned to report several Indians on the trail ahead of them. Boyd took the bait and had his men start out in pursuit. The warriors managed to stay ahead of the soldiers as the two groups raced down the trail toward the main American army. Boyd's Indian scouts warned him of a potential trap, but he refused to listen. He led his men into the center of Butler's ambush in a small draw facing an open field. A small grove of trees stood in the field, and Boyd moved his besieged patrol into it, attempting to hold off his attackers until help arrived. Nearly four hundred Indians and Tories overwhelmed the surrounded patrol (fig. 8). Only the first messengers Boyd had dispatched and a few of the soldiers securing the patrol's right flank had managed to escape. Murphy was in the latter group.[124] Hand's soldiers responded to the sounds of battle covering the half-mile that separated them from Boyd's beleaguered patrol but arrived after Butler's men had departed. Boyd and Private Michael Parker had been captured alive, only to be tortured and killed the following day.[125] The relief party discovered fourteen corpses among the trees. The powder burns around their wounds indicated that most had been killed in close combat. Thaosagwat's body was found nearly dismembered.[126]

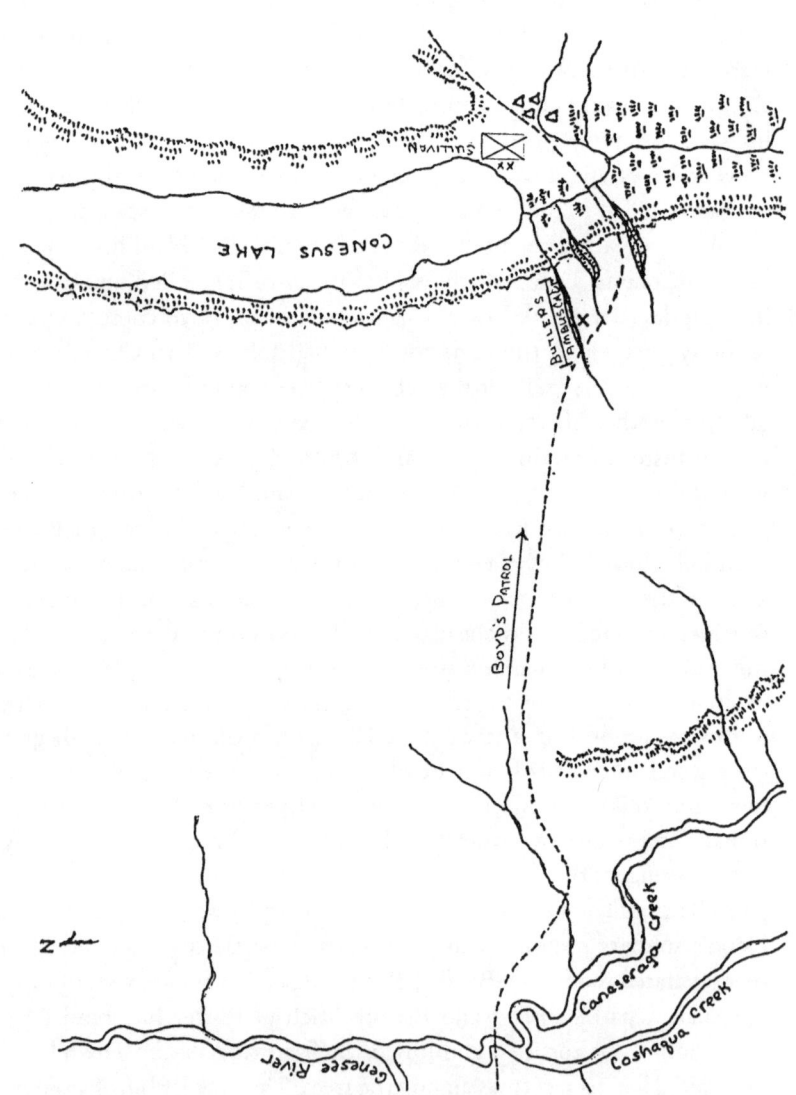

Fig. 8. Boyd ambush (the remains of fourteen members of the patrol found at x).

Tactics

The destruction of Boyd's patrol produced the largest single group of casualties of the campaign. Boyd was young but not inexperienced. His violation of orders as well as his careless disregard for security cost him and most of his patrol their lives. His failure to follow such established principles as varying his departure and return routes suggests how much training remained to be done at the lower levels of command. At the army level, however, Sullivan's insistence on an active patrolling program again paid dividends. Whether or not the army could have been lured into Butler's ambush became problematic because Boyd's patrol encountered it too soon.

Tactics involve the planning, training, and control of organized formations of soldiers when contact with an enemy is either imminent or under way.[127] The topic entails two major concerns. The first requires an understanding of weapons and ways in which to employ them to best advantage. Human factors, such as the interplay between courage and fear, forms the second element. It is difficult to say much about the army's nerve under fire, because Sullivan's opponents failed to execute successfully any of their plans for defending the Iroquois homelands. This failure, however, came not so much from ineptitude on the part of Tory soldier or Indian warrior as it did from the growing tactical prowess of the Continental soldier. Outnumbered and outgunned, Sullivan's adversaries depended on their ability to surprise the Americans. Sullivan's Continentals never provided them the opportunity. The army still had faults, to be sure, but these tended to come from too much exuberance and, at times, too little regard for their foe. Casualties sustained on the raid of Chemung and from the destruction of Boyd's patrol resulted from failures on the part of company-grade officers to follow recognized practices for security.

Sullivan and his chief subordinates grasped effectively the accepted tactics of the day and their combat experience rendered them no longer novices. The army's marches, for example, demonstrated exceptional concern for tactical security, and Sullivan's elaborate list of standardized procedures provided the kind of direction necessary in the event that the army encountered the unexpected. They executed complicated operations such as river crossings according to recognized doctrine and in a timely fashion. Order and discipline had found a place in the Continental army by midwar.

On the battlefield Sullivan's army conceptually set the standard for the U.S. Army's later Indian campaigns. Firepower and maneuver characterized the battle plans at Newtown and the standardized procedures regarding chance contacts. Even in an age of smoothbore muskets, the Continental army preferred to find the enemy's flank rather than suffer casualties from frontal assaults. The problem for Sullivan (as well as later commanders of Indian campaigns) became the need for mobility to maneuver successfully against Native Americans. A century later the plains of the American West would give cavalry a premier role in this facet of tactics. For Sullivan and later commanders who had to fight Indians in the woodlands of the East, mobility depended on the speed of infantry, and this often proved inadequate to execute sound plans.

Like most eighteenth-century armies, the Continental army depended on well-drilled formations of smoothbore infantry supported by a select group of riflemen. Sullivan's dependence on the latter as his only source of aimed fire stands out as a logical extension of their more conventional role as skirmishers. The difficulty of the terrain required new tactics and forced Sullivan and his officers to adjust. Newtown represents the most noteworthy example of the greater reliance being placed on rifles. Even in matters as small as the composition of patrols, evidence suggests that officers attempted to insure that patrols contained at least equal numbers of riflemen and musketeers.[128] Looked at as part of the overall developmental picture, British and French officers began to reappraise the role of the rifle and the importance of light infantry tactics because of the example provided by the Continental army.[129]

Artillery proved important to the army's wilderness tactics, and Sullivan went to considerable trouble to insure its presence. The effort Proctor expended on mounting a howitzer as well as some small grasshoppers on his bateaux provided the first indication of its high priority. With an ability to fire all the standard ordnance of the day, Proctor's river fleet could provide covering fire to the infantry company clearing the river's opposite shore. Though the artillery left Wyoming by boat, only muscle and sweat could move the pieces beyond Tioga. Sullivan ordered one coehorn hand carried along on the raid on Chemung. At Newtown the artillery played a key role in driving the enemy from its positions. Sullivan had most of his heavy artillery taken back to Tioga after Newtown but proceeded to carry several small cannons all the way to the Genesee River. A reliance on overwhelming fire support has characterized the U.S. Army during the wars of the twentieth century. Sullivan's fixation on keeping artillery with him even at the expense of speed indicates a similar attribute in the eighteenth century.

The most important assessment of the growing proficiency of the American army came from its foes. Despite numerous promises to harass and impede Sullivan's march, Tory and Indian leaders failed miserably, blaming their lack of performance on the army's regularity and order during the march. McDonald boasted that he would "hang upon the Rear of the Enemy, and harass them as much as possible on their March, with a few of the most active of the Rangers and about 100 of the Indians."[130] Many factors delayed Sullivan's move to Tioga, but the efforts of McDonald and his men could not be counted among them. When pressed by Lieutenant Colonel Mason Bolton, Niagara's commander, for a better showing against the army, Butler responded, "You certainly must be misinformed in regard of these People, for from the accounts of every Prisoner that has been taken, they are some of the best of the Continental Troops commanded by the most active of the Rebel Generals, and not a Regiment of Militia among the whole."[131] Following his defeat at Newtown, Butler again emphasized the prowess of his foe. "They move with the greatest caution and regularity & are more formidable than you seem to apprehend. We have not been able to get a Prisoner, tho our Scouts have been constantly about their Camp."[132] In no uncertain terms Butler made his message clear: his foes were "regulars" in every sense of the word.

5

LOGISTICS

"History knows many armies ruined by want and disorder than by the efforts of their enemies, and I have witnessed how all the enterprises which were embarked on in my day were lacking for that reason alone."[1] Cardinal Richelieu's observations of seventeenth-century warfare certainly applied to the Sullivan expedition a century later. Until Sullivan's army reached the Iroquois homelands, it would depend on the tenuous nature of the Continental supply system for support. This system had failed its soldiers more than once in the past, Valley Forge being the most memorable example. Thanks largely to the efforts of Quartermaster General Nathanael Greene, the situation had improved in 1778, but, as the war began yet another year, the army found itself still short of both supplies and transport. Geography complicated Sullivan's endeavor. Unlike any other campaign launched by Washington during the war, this one required a supply system capable of supporting soldiers operating on the frontiers. Devoid of roads and with only the broad shallow Susquehanna River to use for transport, this wilderness threatened to strain the support structure beyond its limits.

Nor could Sullivan count on much help from the local areas in which he planned to bivouac his army. Butler's raiding party had ravaged the Wyoming Valley in 1778, precipitating a mass exodus of settlers from the region. Many of the farms that had not been destroyed outright lay untended the following spring. The central regions of the Susquehanna River down to Sunbury were in only slightly better condition. A series of smaller raids had terrorized the lower valley and up the west branch of the Susquehanna. For those settlers who remained, providing security for their families took precedence over all other matters, resulting in less cropland under tillage. Sullivan would have to rely on whatever supplies Greene's subordinates could bring upriver from Wright's Ferry and Estherton until he could join Clinton. Brodhead faced an even more precarious situation. Washington planned for most of his supplies to come from Virginia because farmers near Fort Pitt had suffered through the same ravages of guerrilla war as the Susquehanna Valley settlements.[2]

The Continental army's supply situation had been an ongoing nightmare for Washington from the war's opening days. France's entry into the war in the summer of 1778 eased the problem somewhat, but shortages still plagued the army and limited its effectiveness. Even with Britain's commanders now focused on the demands of a wider war in the West Indies, Washington still feared his army's supply problems might cost him an opportunity to resume the offensive. Greene reassured his superior that sufficient supplies existed in the farmlands of Pennsylvania and New York to sustain an expedition against the Iroquois if everything went according to plan. In war, plans seldom survive intact the beginning pangs of execution. Sullivan's expedition and Brodhead's supporting attack succeeded to the extent that they did despite the logistics system, not because of it. There was certainly a lack of sophistication in the army's administration and inefficiencies built into its logistics, yet several hard years of campaigning had developed in its soldiers a resiliency that made it possible to muddle through despite the odds. As it turned out, the timing of the campaign also helped. Sullivan's small army entered the Iroquois homelands when the summer crops were ripe and ready for the harvest. Faced with food shortages that could not be made good from his downriver base at Wyoming, Sullivan chose to live off the lands of his foe. The fact that Sullivan moved against the Iroquois nearly two months later than Washington had hoped came as a result of the breakdown of the supply system. This was clearly not the intent of the commander or his quartermaster general.

Washington and Greene had hoped to create a modern army patterned after the best armies of Europe, but the process was not complete by 1779, particularly concerning logistics. Both men understood the importance of services and support to the operational success of the army and wanted to structure their logistics according to prevailing military theory. Ideally, eighteenth-century commanders hoped to wage war at their enemy's expense. In Europe this meant moving one's army quickly into an opponent's territory then drawing food and fodder from the surrounding countryside until battle or negotiations decided the dispute. The problem for Washington, however, was that he hoped to accomplish much more than simply pacifying the Iroquois during the coming campaign season. He could not permit Sullivan the luxury of a long campaign in the enemy's homelands because he had hopes for more decisive operations against British forces at New York City or Newport, Rhode Island. Furthermore, living off the bounty of one's enemy included a number of inherent dangers if not done correctly. Past experience demonstrated that armies lacking a base of operations must keep moving. Any extended delay might compel an army to consume the food in its immediate vicinity, forcing a withdrawal to avoid starvation. The safer and preferred method for waging war was to build a series of depots beginning inside friendly territory along the line of advance. Once in place these could sustain the force throughout the campaign. Quartermasters and commissary agents charged with building the depots could more systematically draw supplies from the populace, where depots existed in conquered territory while bringing additional supplies from the home nation. When working correctly, this system was more resilient to changes in the operational situation and allowed the army to concentrate its efforts on the waging of war rather than on feeding and clothing itself. Washington could ill afford to lose one-third of his army in a Braddock-like disaster and so set the wheels in motion to support Sullivan properly.

The reliance eighteenth-century armies placed on magazines and depots had its drawbacks. This system required that a government possess the fiscal means to pay for the materials of war and a transportation system adequate for moving supplies to the point of need. In the latter case most armies moved their supplies by wagon or, preferably, by boat. Assuming a navigable waterway and comparable numbers, boats could move supplies faster and more efficiently than wagons. Where practical, commanders relied on boats to move supplies to depots and on wagons to service armies in the field.

The size of an army's wagon train was the most important factor limiting its operational reach. Eighteenth-century commanders generally found themselves unable to operate more than fifty to sixty miles from their base. The need for fodder was the problem. Hay, grain, and straw, the most common forms of horse feed, were heavy commodities. A European army possessing twenty-five hundred horses required fifty wagons for carrying fodder just to sustain its livestock for two days.[3] Using pasture in the surrounding area was one stop-gap measure, but it made feeding livestock a time-consuming process.

In exceptional cases some European commanders working off of a depot system managed to extend their operational reach to one hundred miles.[4] These efforts required additional manpower as well as wagons and teams to keep supplies moving between the army and its depots. Insuring the security of these trains demanded even more men, particularly cavalry units, who could be better used nearer to a battlefield. This loss of personnel to noncombat duties meant that the commander had fewer available soldiers as his army moved farther and farther from the last depot. Eventually, the army would reach a "culminating point" at which the need to maintain supply lines had so depleted manpower as to make further offensive operations impossible.[5] The trick for commanders was to succeed in their mission before this occurred.

Washington understood the concept and sought to allocate the bulk of his logistic assets to support Sullivan so his subordinate could execute the operation in the shortest possible time and with the least loss of soldiers to supply-related missions. In this Washington would fail. Sullivan eventually found himself forced to divert at least twenty percent of his available strength to service support. This failure did not come about from oversight or a lack of planning. From the very beginning logistics shared equal weight with operational considerations. In the early discussions among Washington, Greene, and Schuyler concerning the best approach to the Iroquois homelands, Schuyler argued for the old Mohawk River to Oswego route, as it had the advantage of a deep-water river for much of the distance and required only one major portage to move supplies from the Mohawk to Wood Creek. Washington disagreed, making clear his preference for the Susquehanna River because it offered the most direct route into the Seneca homelands and linked his army with the lower Susquehanna's abundant supplies of flour.[6] Greene sided with Washington for a number of reasons, noting that the Susquehanna route was more direct and lessened support requirements. Greene believed that the portage into Wood Creek and subsequent movement of supplies downstream to Lake Oneida would be too costly and tedious to make the Mohawk route viable.[7] Furthermore, Greene's subordinates in Pennsylvania sold him on the idea that the necessary boats could be more easily built at Wright's Ferry.[8]

Washington understood that the shallow Susquehanna had its drawbacks. Shallow-draft small boats such as bateaux performed best on this river; even the Durham boats that worked the Delaware and lower reaches of the Susquehanna would have trouble navigating some of the shallow rapids in the upper river.[9] For this reason Washington planned to have Sullivan accumulate his supplies in May, when the spring runoff raised water levels, then attack northward from Wyoming in June. Had everything worked according to plan, Sullivan should have been able to raid the Iroquois homelands and rejoin the main army at Middlebrook by the end of August.

Problems woven into the structure of the operation at its earliest conception virtually guaranteed that the plans would not go smoothly. Most obvious was the financial situation facing the army in 1779. Greene began planning for the spring campaign season as early as January but found his financial resources depleted by March. His purchasing agents lacked the money to contract for goods and services because the Continental Congress had failed to appropriate the funds. Still begging for money as late as April, Greene warned Washington that he could not continue working to sustain Sullivan unless money arrived soon.[10] The nation's deepening fiscal crisis compounded the problem. The Continental Congress had begun issuing paper money in 1776 to compensate for a lack of hard currency. The program initially had called for increased taxes to retire the money expeditiously and control inflation.[11] In 1776 one paper dollar equaled slightly less than one dollar in specie, but by the summer 1779 the ratio had soared to better than twenty to one.[12] Farmers and merchants accepted paper money reluctantly, knowing that the longer they held it the faster its value depreciated.

A second problem grew out of Washington's desire to keep his plans secret until the last possible moment. He did not settle on a preliminary plan of attack until March.[13] Despite the best efforts of Greene to anticipate his superior's needs, Washington's emphasis on operational security placed a burden on the quartermaster and commissary officers. Supplies had to be contracted for, produced, and moved to depots close to the area of operations. Although work began as early as January, the accumulation of supplies went badly, their movement even worse.

Throughout the closing months of 1778 and into early January 1779, while the commander-in-chief mulled over several different plans for the coming spring campaign, Greene nimbly tried to anticipate his superior's desires and lay the groundwork to support them. In these early plans the operation against the Iroquois did not stand out as the preferred choice.[14] Another expedition against Canada using the Hudson River–Lake Champlain line of advance seemed far more likely; therefore, Greene had his deputy quartermaster in New York, Colonel Morgan Lewis, begin preparing a depot in Albany.[15] Lewis was one of Greene's better deputies and promptly began the task of preparing for the expedition. By 12 February he had accumulated hay magazines totalling three hundred tons and had set shipwrights at work building the necessary river craft, even though he had not yet received authorization to spend money on the project. In early February Greene wrote to Lewis that Washington's ideas for the campaign season had changed, leaving it unclear what the army would do come spring. Intent on providing his subordinate with at least some guidance, Greene suggested that an Indian expedition now appeared most likely.[16] The change did not present Lewis with any major problems. His preparations would benefit an Indian expedition as well, because Albany's location made it an appropriate base to support a move up the Mohawk into the Iroquois homelands.

Military options are truly options only if staff officers take the steps necessary to make them usable in advance of the commander's decision. Greene understood this and attempted to plan for all contingencies. Despite an early focus on New York and the possibility of a move against Canada, Greene also ordered his deputies in Pennsylvania to begin accumulating supplies along the Delaware at Easton, the Susquehanna at Wright's Ferry, and the Allegheny at Fort Pitt. Any expedition sent northward against the Iroquois required the establishment of depots at Easton and at Wright's Ferry. Fort Pitt's depot could sustain operations against either the Indian villages on the northern reaches of the Allegheny or against the British post at Detroit. Much of the focus on overland transportation centered on the developing depot at Easton, while supplies headed to the Susquehanna and Allegheny required packing for water transport.

Washington chose Easton as the eastern staging point for Sullivan because of its proximity to the army's winter quarters at Middlebrook and its location along the Delaware River. Greene's deputy quartermaster in Pennsylvania, Colonel Robert L. Hooper, coordinated the construction of this depot. Hooper faced a more daunting task than any of his peers building the Susquehanna depots. His most important problem was the Continental army's lack of sufficient wagons to meet its transportation needs. In the past the solution had been to contract the services of private wagon owners.[17] That system had not been adequate because farmers preferred not to take depreciated Continental currency and seldom received their wagons and the teams back in the same condition in which they were lent. Abusive wagoners, inadequate forage, and the difficult nature of the terrain combined to damage wagons and wear out teams. When private contracting failed, impressment became the alternative. This involuntary draft of wagons and teams was even more unpopular with farmers.[18] During the French and Indian War colonists found impressment to be a thorn in their side, believing it to be an unjust imposition of the state on the rights of the individual. Their opinions had not changed over the intervening years. Understanding its unpopularity, Washington made it clear to his quartermasters that they were to use it only as a last resort. In the Continental army, however, courses of last resort occurred all too frequently.

Greene diligently worked to fix the army's transportation shortages before the start of the campaign, instructing his officers to cannibalize those wagons believed to be too badly damaged to repair.[19] Neither Greene's planning nor Hooper's efforts to contract wagons in Easton bore much fruit. By April it was clear that impressment of wagons and teams would be necessary, with the onus falling on Pennsylvania.

Impressment triggered a controversy that helped sabotage Greene's plan to support Sullivan. In an early example of state versus national rights, Pennsylvania's Supreme Executive Council had created its own administrative system to procure wagons for the army in January 1778. Under this system the army's quartermaster general applied for transport to a state-appointed wagon master general, for wagons, specifying the type and number required. The state's wagon master general would then issue warrants to county wagon masters. The council designed the system to protect citizens from army quartermasters and to spread the burden equally across the affected counties. The council could grant blank impressment warrants under emergency circumstances, but army quartermasters and commissary officers were subject to legal action for abusing their impressment privileges. To add teeth to the law, the council prescribed a fifty-pound penalty for army officers who failed to follow the procedures.[20] This law grew out of the perception that quartermaster officers had misused impressed material to move private property.[21] The fact that Pennsylvania's laws limiting impressment powers were not well understood within the army complicated the situation. Sullivan realized that the law hindered his quartermasters from securing horses or wagons, and on 11 May he requested that Joseph Reed, president of the council, "procure an order from the Executive Council Empowering the Quarter Masters to Impress in this County such Wagons, horses, &c., as may be found necessary for forwarding the Stores, &c., over to Susquehannah."[22] By this time the shortage of wagons was crippling preparations. Greene's subordinates had accumulated supplies in Philadelphia but could not move them.[23] Quartermaster agents operating at the army's western depot at Carlisle faced the same situation. The shortage of wagons thwarted Sullivan's plan to march his army from Easton to Wyoming as early as 20 May.

With apparent disregard for the need to fix the problem expeditiously, Reed first suggested to the Board of War that Sullivan's requests bordered on being excessive and suggested that "a stricter economy" was necessary in the army's management of material.[24] Adopting a different approach with Sullivan, he wrote that difficulty with the term *impressing* had prevented the council's responding more quickly.[25] After informing Sullivan of how the state's wagon service worked, Reed granted a limited number of warrants permitting the general to impress wagons in the neighboring counties. The delays could have been prevented by informing the council of the upcoming expedition, added Reed, who also lectured Sullivan on why the law had been put in place:

> We are sensible that cases may happen when the sending to us for powers will be attended with inconvenience, but this is one of the consequences which have flowed from former abuses of confidence,

and can now only be remedied by foresight and care in the application, and dispatch in the execution.[26]

Reed ended with a request that Sullivan avoid pleas for excessive support, lest he stand guilty of "distressing the country too much."[27]

Pennsylvania's frontiers had been aflame for nearly a year. Tory and Indian raids had depopulated much of the upper Susquehanna, and frontier settlers from most of Pennsylvania's western counties had sent appeals for protection to the Executive Council. With a six thousand–man detachment of Washington's army poised to carry the war back into the Iroquois homeland, Reed's concern that Sullivan not burden eastern farmers appears provincial. The distance between Easton and Philadelphia was fifty miles, or two days' ride. Given the problems facing the army, Reed's delay in explaining the situation suggests the council either did not understand Sullivan's plight or was less than enthusiastic in its support. Sullivan answered Reed's letter on 26 May, expressing a willingness to work with Reed and regret that he had used the word *impressment* in his earlier correspondence.[28] The same day he informed Washington that he believed his problems with wagons were over.[29] But within a month he again found himself dependent on the council for impressment warrants. Pennsylvania's efforts to protect its citizens from the excesses of the army had imposed an additional layer of bureaucracy upon an already inefficient system, further complicating the procurement process. The system could work only when the army provided early notification of the extent of its needs. This threatened operational security.[30] The council reluctantly bent itself to meeting Sullivan's needs by the end of May, but the state's cumbersome machinery for impressment cost valuable time.

Apart from wagons Hooper contended with an array of needs. Livestock accumulating around Easton lacked forage. The process of securing feed had not begun until 27 April, and Hooper anticipated meeting opposition from local farmers reluctant to rent pasture or sell forage. He instructed his subordinate, Major William Hart, to take the problem directly to county magistrates if problems arose.[31] Shortages of pack saddles and wagons rendered his stock of horses largely unusable. Hooper's contacts in Philadelphia provided the pack saddles after the usual delays; the shortages of wagoners proved more tenacious. In April the Continental Congress had authorized Washington to enlist competent wagoners for nine months or the duration of the campaign at a pay of up to forty dollars a month. As an enlistment bonus, recruiters could offer interested men a suit of clothes.[32] Adjusted for inflation, these wages failed to entice enlistments. By May Hooper increased the wages to one hundred dollars a month but to no avail.[33] Again, Hooper had to rely on Pennsylvania's wagon master to make up the difference. When this failed, Sullivan resorted to using soldiers from his infantry regiments to act as drivers. Aside from its unpopularity with many of the soldiers now turned drivers, this expedient forced Sullivan to dissipate his manpower further to noncombat jobs.

Many of those pushed into service as wagoners abused wagons and teams impressed from farmers. As early as 28 May 1779, Sullivan found himself forced to issue the following directive: "Public horses being much injured by wagoners and others of a like class riding and driving them hard, officers are desired to endeavor to prevent any further abuse of the kind by immediately punishing or confining every offender in that way."[34] Poor treatment and overuse of the teams supporting Sullivan's army accounted for part of the difficulties with ground transport. Shortages in teams and packhorses eventually forced Sullivan to dismount first his cavalry and then, as the situation grew worse, his officers.[35] Although suffering from gout, Sullivan did not exempt himself from the dismounting of the officer corps.[36] Despite his best efforts, the situation worsened as the terrain took its toll.

Between Easton and the Wyoming Valley lay the Pocono Mountains, a forbidding area of dark hardwoods, hemlocks, and dense laurel thickets. The region consisted of mountains ground down by the last ice age and an extensive drainage system of numerous swamps and small streams which made crossing the region a nightmare. One poorly traveled path connected Easton and Wyoming. Washington believed that with a little work it could be made passable to wagons. As early as 18 April, he dispatched Colonel William Malcolm and his regiment to Easton to begin widening the trail.[37] Knowing the weakened condition of this unit, Washington later ordered the regiments of Colonel Phillip Van Cortlandt and Colonel Oliver Spencer to join Malcon. Soon after their arrival Sullivan requested additional clothing to outfit these men. Cortlandt's men lacked shirts, while Sullivan described Spencer's men as "almost naked."[38] Most had no tents and relied on bush shelters to cover them during their construction project. As the men set themselves to the job, it became clear that Washington's early failure to instruct someone to reconnoiter the route would cost Sullivan time.[39] The existing path proved inadequate; a new road would have to be constructed. In late May Sullivan described the situation to Washington:

> The Indian Path was no kind of advantage nor does the Road now Cut follow it half a mile in the whole way—the Road is now Cut the whole Distance & through a Country the most Difficult I ever Saw—it is not possible for a Country to be Thicker with wood among which the Laurels are so thick that a man cannot get through them but on his hands & Knees. The number of Sloughs & Creeks are almost Incredible.[40]

Slightly more than a month later Sullivan's men had cut and cleared forty miles of new road. The broken terrain had necessitated considerable additional work, almost all of it done by hand, as horses sank up to their chests in the bogs.[41] In areas where the route passed through swamps, crews painstakingly corduroyed the road. In other places the streams and rivulets forced the construction of extensive wooden bridges.[42] The Reverend William Rogers, Hand's chaplain, recorded in his diary that cutting the road wore on the men, so much so that he did not preach to them during the period because fatigue rendered most of them too tired to listen.[43] The finished product stood as one of the best examples of American military engineering during the war. Although impressive, this project had not figured in the original plans for the operation and was completed nearer to mid-June than early May.

While Hooper wrestled with the problems of building Sullivan's base of supply in Easton, a number of Greene's subordinates worked in the Susquehanna Valley to lay the groundwork for the campaign's primary system of depots. As in Easton, here too there were problems.

The process of building the Susquehanna depots began early, indicating Washington's and Greene's understanding that no course of action was viable unless resources existed to carry it out. In February Washington secretly ordered that four months of supplies capable of sustaining a thousand men be deposited at Sunbury.[44] In April, as the concept of the operation became clear, he directed that supplies in all the Susquehanna depots be increased to a level capable of sustaining three thousand to forty-five hundred soldiers.[45] Greene did everything in his power to make the plan work, including the assignment of Major Richard Claiborne to the project as his special deputy quartermaster. Answerable only to Greene, Claiborne was to act as a troubleshooter for the other quartermaster and commissary agents working in the valley.

Claiborne's presence did little to change the growing confusion in the valley. Colonel Ephraim Blaine, the ranking commissary officer in the lower Susquehanna Valley, had already begun the process of gathering food from Pennsylvania's southeastern counties and moving it westward to Esthertown. Stockpiling and moving the stores required transport, and again the shortage of wagons hindered the work. While Blaine struggled to get supplies to the river, a new problem presented itself—a lack of boats. As with wagons, the desire to maintain the campaign's operational security brought inevitable delays in contracting for bateaux. Although sufficient resources existed near the river, the contracting process began too late. Benjamin Eyre, the Middle Department's coordinator of shipbuilding, set up shop at Middletown and Wright's Ferry, where he and his shipwrights began building small bateaux in the two-ton range.[46] The presence of a number of sawmills near Estherton insured a ready supply of lumber; what Eyre lacked was time. Though their shipbuilding commenced in April, late May found them still short of the necessary boats.

Blaine began shuttling provisions upriver to Sunbury, then on to Wyoming, the moment he had boats operational; however, the limited numbers of craft at his disposal hindered his efforts. By 18 May he had just twelve boats working the river. To complicate the situation, the first boats turned out by Eyre's people proved inadequate for handling the rapids found upstream. Eyre adjusted his design by adding keels and round futtocks to provide the boats with better strength and to prevent them from sticking on rocks.[47] While Eyre worked to correct the problems with boat design, Blaine diligently continued to build the depots on the lower river. The last week of May he told Sullivan that the depots at Middletown and Harris Ferry stood well stocked with flour, salt, provisions, and whiskey. Spring rains had raised water levels, making the river ideal for navigation. Unfortunately, Eyre still could not offer more than fifty boats, many lacking crews, for the journey upriver.[48]

Quartermaster officers found few men in the Susquehanna Valley willing to work as boatmen for the campaign. Again the problem was wages.

The spring planting season rendered an already tight labor market even tighter. Few farmers or their sons could afford to accept duty as boatmen, given the depreciation of Continental currency. Once again the solution involved detailing soldiers as boatmen.[49] Hand sent Lieutenant Colonel Adam Hubley, commander of the Eleventh Pennsylvania, to Fort Augusta to organize and conduct the movement of supplies upriver. Hubley and his men labored from May until well into July moving most of the supplies that Sullivan eventually had on hand when he arrived in Wyoming.

At Middleton, Blaine claimed he had three thousand barrels and seven hundred bags of flour, fifteen hundred barrels of salt provisions, fifteen thousand gallons of rum and whiskey, and one thousand cattle.[50] In addition to the food and spirits, Greene managed to get clothing and other accoutrements sent to the threadbare army. Many of the soldiers assigned to the expedition possessed only the clothes on their backs. Blankets and tents remained scarce. For Washington this problem went beyond making soldiers more comfortable. Sullivan faced difficulties that would require detailing sizable numbers of combat soldiers to support duties, and he could ill afford the loss of additional soldiers to sickness. Realizing that Greene could not make good the shortages from Pennsylvania or New York, Washington ordered shirts, overalls, hunting shirts, shoes, and stockings moved to Pennsylvania from depots as far away as Boston.[51] Some of these supplies found their way upriver or overland to Wyoming. Few of them reached Brodhead's garrison at Fort Pitt, despite Washington's best intentions.

Washington took steps to lay the logistics groundwork for Brodhead's participation very early. In February he instructed Jeremiah Wadesworth, his commissary general, to stock four months' supplies for twelve hundred men at Fort Pitt over and above the garrison's normal allocations. He wanted these provisions available no later than 1 May 1779.[52] In March he revised this to four months' rations for eight hundred men.[53] His quartermasters in western Pennsylvania went to work at the task of satisfying Washington's desires. As in the eastern portion of the state, material and personnel shortages as well as the ordinances of Pennsylvania frustrated their efforts. Deputy Quartermaster John Davis, working out of Carlisle, reported difficulty in moving supplies to Fort Pitt because local county magistrates imposed militia fines on his wagoners. Davis had issued his men Continental army certificates of service in an effort to exempt his wagoners from militia duty, but the local magistrates refused to accept the certificates. Pennsylvania's Executive Council had taken steps the preceding year to clarify its militia ordinances by ruling army certificates of service valid exemptions for militia duty within the state.[54] The local magistrates of western Pennsylvania either had not received word of the ruling or chose to ignore it. Either way, their actions caused more delay, particularly for Brodhead.

Because the Allegheny River formed Brodhead's primary line of operations, Eyre ordered his shipwrights at Fort Pitt to begin building bateaux. Washington's early consideration of Fort Niagara as a possible objective had led the commander-in-chief to toy with the idea of building pettiauger canoes at Fort Pitt.[55] These large, sturdy canoes had a sizable carrying capacity and could withstand the buffeting of Lake Erie. As it became clear that Niagara was beyond the logistics reach of the Continental army in 1779, the focus shifted to bateaux.

Eyre's men worked into the summer building the small craft and completed work well before Brodhead moved out. The same cannot be said of Wadsworth's commissary agents, who scoured the countryside for food while pleading to superiors for more supplies. Brodhead's expedition got under way more poorly supplied than Sullivan's force on the Susquehanna and, therefore, capable of making only a token contribution to the campaign. Instead of four months' provisions, Brodhead departed Fort Pitt with a month's supply of food and critical shortages in shoes and clothing.[56] He returned a month later to find that Greene's quartermasters had been unable to replenish the fort's stores. Many of his soldiers came back barefoot and some nearly naked, Brodhead complained in his after-action report. "I have neither Shoes, Shirts, Blankets, Hats, Stockings nor Leggins to relieve their necessities."[57]

Only in New York did preparations go according to plan. Unlike the case in Pennsylvania, there were real shortages of supplies, especially flour, facing the Continental army. Yet, when Clinton's force moved up the Mohawk and overland to Lake Otsego, they did not plague his force. For the most part Clinton moved with adequate land and water transportation, even though quartermasters in New York appear to have had less time to prepare than their peers in Pennsylvania. A number of reasons account for Clinton's success, the most important being that Governor George Clinton, James's brother, stood solidly behind the expedition. The governor had good reasons to back the plan. Clinton's political support came from the more rural regions of the state, and his constituents had suffered through two years of devastation at the hands of raiding parties from the Iroquois country. The governor probably also hoped eventually to open much of the Iroquois homelands to white settlement. A successful military operation against the Iroquois would help make this vision a reality. As a result, Clinton insured that his country magistrates facilitated rather than inhibited the war effort.

Governor Clinton was not the only reason logistics preparations went so well in New York. James Clinton benefited from the earlier preparations for the abortive Canadian campaign. Much of this material existed at Albany, and, by April, Greene's quartermasters had begun moving it westward. With none of the urgency present in Sullivan's letters of the same period, Clinton reported to Washington in late May that a sizable depot as well as a small fleet of bateaux existed at Schenectady ready for the operation.[58] In June, when Sullivan sent Clinton's men to the headwaters of the Susquehanna at Lake Otsego, they lacked only wagons. Clinton's quartermasters subsequently secured the required number through county magistrates.

Clinton accumulated his forces at Lake Otsego during June and early July. As the troops gathered, Clinton's men dammed the outlet from Lake Otsego to raise the lake's water level. Narrow and shallow, the lake's outlet would not permit the passage of even light bateaux. Clinton depended on the dam to produce a surge of water capable of sweeping his bateaux to deeper water downstream. Success was crucial because, clearly, Sullivan relied on Clinton's supplies to compensate for his own deficiencies.

Things had not worked out as planned by the key officers involved in supplying the main army. Hubley's men had been shuttling supplies upriver since early May, but the shortages in boats and crews had limited the effort. Many of the civilian boatmen had deserted, forcing even more soldiers into moving supplies. The weather exacerbated Hand's problems. With the passing of spring, the Susquehanna dropped sharply, adding time to the upriver journey from Esthertown. In frustration Hand informed Sullivan about shortages of food, clothing, and powder at the Wyoming depot. Sullivan could do little to help because the road between Easton and Wyoming remained unfinished. Once complete, Sullivan could move supplies overland from Easton.

The shortages disrupted the timing of the campaign. Washington grew increasingly eager to get the expedition under way despite the logistical situation. But Sullivan reported reluctantly to his commander in mid-June: "I should have moved from this post before now, but the stores not having got up the Susquehannah [*sic*] I thought it imprudent to throw the whole army on to consume the provisions before we were in readiness to move on."[59]

Sullivan's caution proved justified. Situated on a navigable river in a settled region largely untouched by the raids, Easton surpassed Wyoming as a source of supplies. Easton figured more prominently in the support plans, as material arrived at Wyoming from downriver, and Hand's inspectors found that much of the packed meat as well as other food was spoiled. Alexander Steele, Sullivan's commissary of issues, reported twenty bad barrels out of a hundred in one shipment. He further complained that the army had not had liquor for ten days and that much of the bread had molded.[60] Subsequent shipments of packed meat arrived at Wyoming during the remaining summer months. Though the quality varied, the problem persisted. Sullivan estimated that as much as one-third of his packed meat was tainted. Though some of the spoilage may have come from deliberate attempts on the part of teamsters to lessen their loads by draining brine from the barrels, inspectors placed most of the blame on coopers using green wood for the kegs. Warm temperatures dried the kegs and caused the seals to break.

Sullivan informed Washington of the problem, castigating the Continental army's commissary officers for incompetence that had delayed his expedition. The commissaries may have deserved such criticism. Steele himself expressed surprise at the amount of spoiled food found among the army's stores, suggesting that Blaine had not been diligent in checking the packing at Wright's Ferry.[61] It is more likely, however, that coopers in southern Pennsylvania were forced to use green wood because Washington kept his supply officers in the dark about the campaign until February.[62] The winter months are not conducive to drying wood for barrels, and any wood cut in the spring contained considerable sap. Clinton's commissary officers found little spoilage among the barrels accompanying his expedition. These stores had been set aside the previous fall in anticipation of a spring campaign against Canada. As a result, the coopers in New York had used properly dried wood.

Sullivan pressed Greene and Washington for a solution while taking measures to correct the problem himself. His first step tightened inspection to detect spoiled meat at the earliest possible time. By doing this, Sullivan hoped to avoid wasting precious carrying capacity. Inspectors examined barrels at Wright's Ferry and Estherton before shipment upriver; however, Hubley employed his own inspector to perform this key examination at Fort Augusta.[63] An ideal point for inspection, located fifty miles above Wright's Ferry, Fort Augusta received supplies already subjected to several days of summer temperatures on their trip upriver. Many green kegs would be leaking by the time they arrived at the fort.

Sullivan also attempted to salvage unspoiled meat from barrels with broken seals. Under instructions from his superior to recure, repickle, and repack this meat, Hand built a number of smokehouses at Wyoming. As a further precaution, Sullivan ordered the reinspection of all meat before the troops received it.[64] It turned out that much of the repacked meat remained unfit for consumption. Despite orders from Sullivan to the contrary, commissary officers issued it to soldiers with predictable results: many soldiers fell sick. Ensign Daniel Gookin of the Second New Hampshire noted in his diary that he had drawn some of the resmoked meat. The smoking process had killed the smell, but Gookin cautioned that it had done little for the taste, which resembled "the juice of the grape" and sickened officers and men.[65]

A third part of Sullivan's program sought subsistence to the greatest degree possible off the local economy. Though Wyoming could offer little in the way of additional agricultural produce, the valley held abundant fish and game. Soldiers fished the river or hunted the local woods to supplement the meat supply. Many surviving diaries mention plentiful fish in the Susquehanna, but neither fishing nor hunting offered more than temporary relief.

As the fourth and most important part of the solution, Sullivan hoped to increase the number of cattle at his disposal. Most armies of the day relied on their own herd of cattle as their primary source of fresh meat. Greene had always planned to provide Sullivan with a sizable herd. In May Blaine boasted to Sullivan that he planned to have a thousand head of cattle heading upriver before the end of the month.[66] Instead of a thousand cattle, only a few more than two hundred left Estherton. Many of these got only as far as the grassy river plain outside the palisaded gates of Fort Augusta, where Hubley's inspection led him to question whether most of these beasts would survive the last leg of their journey to Wyoming. Rather than risk losing those too weak to move farther, Hubley sent most of the herd to pasture in an attempt to rest them. These could be moved later. Only fifty cattle continued upriver.[67]

Subsequent attempts to increase the size of Sullivan's herd met with some success but in the end served only to further delay movement. Under pressure from Washington, Commissary General Jeremiah Wadsworth ordered one hundred cattle delivered to Sullivan from Morristown, New Jersey.[68] Although his commissaries eventually sent two hundred and seventy, this proved only a partial remedy to the problem.[69] Regardless of their condition at the start of the journey, most of the cattle lost weight passing through the Poconos, because of limited forage.

Sullivan welcomed the additional cattle but knew he lacked sufficient food to achieve his objective. He would have to rely on foraging off the Iroquois lands and on the provisions that Clinton could bring downriver from Lake Otsego. Other shortages also plagued the expedition. Much of the promised clothing had not arrived, and few of the soldiers possessed blankets. With summer wearing on, it had become clear to many that the expedition, if it went forward, would not finish its work until late September or early October.[70] Sullivan's concern over supply clearly was justified, and no solution sufficient to correct the problem presented itself before leaving Wyoming.

Despite his efforts to make the supply system work in Sullivan's favor, Washington never really understood the scope of the problem. By early July Sullivan counted on the supplies Clinton had stockpiled at Otsego to help carry the expedition into the Iroquois lands and see it safely downriver on completion. As a result, Sullivan encouraged Clinton to take as much food and other supplies as possible. This course of action carried risks. A sizable enemy force had been reported on the upper Susquehanna between Otsego and the proposed rendezvous at Tioga. In addition, a shortage of bateaumen plagued Clinton. Like Sullivan, he detailed his infantrymen to serve as boatmen and accepted the decrease in size and effectiveness this decision meant for his regimental commanders. Clinton's extensive supply train, however, contradicted Washington's guidance that the northern wing of the expedition travel as lightly as possible. The commander-in-chief had assumed that Sullivan would supply Clinton after the two linked up, not the other way around. Upon finding out about Clinton's abundance of supplies, Washington sent a heated letter to Sullivan:

> I have received a letter from General Clinton of the 30th of June by which I find that his taking so large a quantity of provisions & stores with him was in obedience to your orders—I cannot but be extremely apprehensive that this party will be exposed to the most imminent hazard from so great an incumbrance of stores, especially under the intelligence you communicate of the enemy's assembling at Chonowataline. We may expect that their whole force will be bent against General Clinton—Notwithstanding my apprehensions I would not undertake to interfere with your arrangements but I shall leave him to act as you direct; at the same time, I must entreat you to consider whether he may not still disembarrass himself of a part of his stores.[71]

Sullivan attempted again to explain the situation and to place the blame where he believed it belonged in a letter dated 10 July:

> I thought my former Letters had fully Shown that I was far from having a prospect of Supplying General Clinton's Detachment with provisions that I have not Even now the most Distant prospect of keeping that part of the Army which is with me from Starving Long Enough to Compleat the Expedition. This I early foresaw & Endeavored to Guard against—Notwithstanding the flattering Accounts given by those Employed by QuarterMasters & Commissaries which they are fond of giving when near your person.[72]

Washington took Sullivan's comments seriously and had Greene look into them. An exchange of accusations by the Board of War, Greene, his subordinates, and Sullivan followed.[73] Sullivan's opponents claimed that he had not provided an accurate count of the number of soldiers under his command.[74] Sullivan responded that he had been assured at the time Washington gave him command of the expedition that the necessary arrangements would be made to provision his soldiers and therefore saw no need to tell the Board of War or the Commissary Department how many men were under his command. Neither explanation proved adequate. With Greene's proximity to Washington, the quartermaster general should have been able to estimate the number of soldiers from muster rosters of units assigned to Sullivan. Furthermore, Washington's initial guidance for preparing depots on the Susquehanna and the Allegheny came close to anticipating the actual number of troops Sullivan and Brodhead took upriver.

The real problem for Greene and his subordinates lay in their failure to keep abreast of the logistical situation in Sullivan's army. Numerous references to men without shoes or adequate clothing before the campaign got under way indicated that key officers lacked accurate information about the status of regimental supplies. The Quartermaster and Commissary Departments could estimate the army's needs, assuming adequate supplies at the start of the campaign. Greene knew that some of Sullivan's men lacked adequate clothing and shoes but failed to understand the extent of the problem. As a result, Greene and his officers found themselves working to meet Sullivan's repeated requests for more shirts, overalls, shoes, and blankets. They unfairly criticized Sullivan behind his back for seeking more supplies than he would need. Sullivan made the requests after reviewing the conditions in his small army. That his units emerged from the winter in such poor condition to face a new campaign season cannot be attributed to Sullivan. Almost all of the regiments were new to his command, as Sullivan had spent the winter with his old division in Rhode Island.

Sullivan did deserve part of the blame for his logistics. No newcomer to the army, he had seen it through some of its leanest years and should have monitored more closely quartermaster and commissary preparations. His complaints and accusations demonstrate a complete lack of understanding of the problems facing these officers. Regardless of who deserved the lion's share of blame, it was clear as July drew to a close that Sullivan's men would have to execute their mission ill clad and ill fed.

Washington grudgingly accepted the problem as intractable, given the lateness of the season. He even suggested to Sullivan that he might be oversupplied in some areas and urged his lieutenant to lighten his load to expedite the expedition. In a letter just two days before Sullivan's move from Wyoming, Washington directed:

I cannot but repeat my intreaties, that you will hasten your operations with all possible dispatch; and that you will disencumber yourself of every article of baggage and stores which is not necessary to the expedition. Not only its success but its execution at all depends on this. Tis a kind of service in which both officers and men must expect to dispense with conveniences and endure hardships—They must not and I trust will not expect to carry the same apparatus which is customary in other operations.[75]

Sullivan had not received this dispatch by the time his army departed Wyoming. It is doubtful that he needed the reminder. His supply train included 120 boats, 1,200 packhorses, and 700 cattle. Bateaux transported most of the barreled meat upriver, while packhorses and the soldiers themselves carried the flour. Because no commissary returns from August have survived, it is impossible to determine the supply of rations in Sullivan's army. The cattle alone should have provided eighteen days of meat for an army of four thousand men; however, this number is misleading because, as noted, several hundred women and children accompanying the army drew rations.[76] The much anticipated rendezvous with Clinton added approximately sixteen hundred soldiers to the burden of an already overextended supply system but brought no large infusion of additional rations. During their wait at Lake Otsego while Sullivan gathered supplies at Wyoming, Clinton's men had consumed much of their food. Furthermore, Sullivan had misjudged Clinton's carrying capacity.[77] He incorrectly assumed Clinton's two hundred bateaux to be two-to three-ton craft similar to his own. The Susquehanna's outlet from Lake Otsego was shallow and only thirty feet wide. Below the lake the river narrowed even more before widening again several miles downstream. Adapted to the constricted nature of the upper river, Clinton's boats generally had a capacity of less than two tons.

Disappointed that Clinton could not alleviate his difficulties, Sullivan realized the need for an internal solution to the problem. Washington sought to restock the depot at Wyoming in anticipation of Sullivan's return, but for the moment Sullivan's army lay beyond Washington's ability to help. The breakdown of the Continental army's logistics had converted an operation originally scheduled for spring into a late-summer effort. Washington's plan for Sullivan to destroy quickly the Iroquois homeland had failed. Now

Sullivan found himself at Tioga at peak harvest season. Indian corn filled the fields, contending for space with a bountiful assortment of squash, beans, and pumpkins. Foraging presented an obvious though incomplete remedy to Sullivan's problem. Washington remained concerned about the division of the Continental army and continued to press Sullivan to complete the mission. The more circumstances forced Sullivan to rely on the Iroquois lands for food, the slower the expedition could move. In addition, foraging could not satisfy the army's need for meat, its primary source of protein.[78]

Problems of supply weighed heavily on Sullivan's officers and men, who blamed the quartermasters and commissaries. Major John Burrowes of the Fifth New Jersey remarked in his diary on 25 August that only twenty-seven days' provisions remained, with one hundred and twenty miles of unknown country still between the army and Chenussio. Fodder presented a similar situation. Eighteenth-century armies preferred to transport their own fodder by wagon to enhance mobility. If Sullivan chose to rely entirely on his depots for fodder, his packhorses and teams would require quartermaster officers to provide at least twenty-five wagons for feed. The lack of wagons, difficulty of terrain, and distances involved rendered this an unworkable option. Sullivan decided to sacrifice mobility in the interests of extending his army's reach. He took every opportunity to let his packhorses and livestock graze the fields of Indian villages and Tory farms on the upper river, but this was not sufficient, given the demands of the journey. Even before departing Tioga, he knew that his pack animals had begun to give out.[79] Getting his army and its supplies into the Iroquois homelands would be a problem; pulling them out might be impossible.

Sullivan believed his supplies and pack animals could sustain the army through to the Seneca settlements located along the Genesee River. Unsure of the return trip, he left Shreve and his men at Tioga with instructions to build a new depot to support the army on its withdrawal.[80] Sullivan anticipated an overland march for the rest of the expedition. The small fleet of bateaux that had supported the two wings of the army on the march to Tioga now could be employed in moving supplies upriver from Wyoming. While some of his men began the return trip to Wyoming, Shreve turned his attention to gathering food from sources closer at hand. He had the remainder of the regiment gather crops from nearby fields and comb the woods for cattle that had strayed from the main army's herd.

Shreve's efforts to improve the ration situation proved necessary, for Sullivan had badly misjudged the ration shortage. Five days beyond Tioga, Sullivan asked his soldiers to accept half-rations for the duration of the campaign. He promised to reimburse them in pay for the missed meals and hoped they accepted this offer. Sullivan's soldiers willingly acquiesced in their commander's request.[81]

Two sets of undated commissary returns from September indicate that Sullivan probably deferred too long in making his request. The first specifies that the army had meat for 15.4 days at half-rations. The second return shows meat for 9 days, indicating that the returns were made a week apart.[82] Both stipulate that the numbers included rations found at both Fort Augusta and Wyoming, none of which would be immediately available to Sullivan. Furthermore, as mentioned previously, an indeterminate number of women and children subsisted on these rations. Though Sullivan ordered most of the women and children back to Wyoming after he and the main army departed Tioga, he nonetheless continued to feed them from his supplies.

Sullivan and his soldiers considered their ration situation precarious by the start of the second week of September. Corn increasingly became the mainstay of the army's diet. When the corn became too hard to boil or roast, soldiers grated it into meal, mixed it with squash and pumpkin, then baked it.[83] Prior to taking a small Indian village on 7 September, Major Jeremiah Fogg, Poor's aide-de-camp, noted that some of his men had spent their waiting moments scavenging the vegetable gardens near the village. With disgust he described the scene: "But whatever might have been the cause, the whole party from the monkey to the rat, had armed themselves with almost every species of the vegetable creation, each man with three pompions on his bayonet and staggering under the weight of a bosom filled with corn and beans."[84] Fogg berated his men and the officers who condoned this breach in discipline, calling them a "damned unmilitary set of rascals" and asking if they planned to "storm the village with pompions."[85] The barrage of abuse had the intended effect, as the soldiers dropped their prizes in an attempt to avoid the major's further wrath. Fogg alerted Poor and the rest of the brigade's officers that soldier concerns over the army's food shortages had grown to a point that they threatened to undermine the mission.

Sullivan called a council of his chief subordinates on 8 September to discuss the problem. The group debated whether the situation had become so critical as to warrant turning back. Many of the officers present supported withdrawal. A few enlisted men, discouraged by the lack of food, caught wind of the debate and conveyed their views. One proved so obnoxious in condemning the expedition that the sentries at the council received orders to chase the man off and shoot him if he returned. Sullivan wanted to continue and carried his point. The army would march the final sixty miles to the Genesee and hope it could return to Tioga before exhausting its supplies.[86]

Sullivan had begun to plan for a further deterioration in his ration situation before the army departed Tioga. Recognizing that at least part of his army would have to return along the route out, Sullivan left some fields of corn and vegetables untouched. To guarantee the widest possible destruction as well as insure them sufficient food, a few detached units would take alternate routes back to Tioga. Another would return by way of Fort Stanwyx, using that post's supplies as its springboard to the Hudson River and safety. He quickly realized that foraging might well be his primary means of support for the return march. As further insurance, he had Shreve build a small depot along the Chemung River (near present-day Elmira, N.Y.), several days' march from Tioga. Fort Reed, as the depot came to be called, sustained the army on its withdrawal south from Seneca Lake.[87]

Only minor problems plagued the withdrawal. Many supply animals did give out, forcing Sullivan to order their destruction just short of Fort Reed. Sullivan collected his army at the small depot and prepared it for the trip to Tioga. Shreve's regiment had improved the situation with rations both at Fort Reed and at Tioga. The army arrived at Tioga on 30 September, remained a day, then moved downriver. The men reached Wyoming in six days and Easton in another week. Logistics had haunted the expedition almost from its inception, threatening the army with ruin and causing more delays than Sullivan's human foes. Happily for Sullivan, the trip home suffered from minimal disruption on this front.

The Sullivan campaign marked the U.S. Army's first Indian expedition. From the standpoint of logistics it failed at the strategic level. Despite considerable effort, Washington's commissaries and quartermasters proved largely ineffective in providing a base of supply capable of sustaining the army. At the operational level Sullivan managed to support his soldiers, albeit at less than the preferred levels, while accomplishing his assigned mission.

Any army is limited by the degree to which it can marshal, transport, and distribute supplies. The strategic failure that threatened Sullivan's army derived from a combination of internal and external factors that could not be overcome in the short time set aside for the expedition's planning and preparation. The two crucial external factors working against Sullivan were the decrepit state of the new nation's financial system and the need to maintain popular support for the war. With Continental currency dropping rapidly in value by the week, Continental quartermasters and commissaries experienced difficulty contracting for transport and supplies. Frustration with reluctant farmers and merchants led Washington down the road to impressment. He understood that impressment angered civilians and consequently tried, with partial success, to limit its use. State governments found themselves called upon to fill the breech, by acting as honest brokers between the power of the army and that of affected civilians. Citizens welcomed this; the army did not. For farmers living on the frontier, Sullivan's success could spell an end to their Indian troubles. Inhabitants of more settled areas to the east, far distant from the problem of midnight raids, exhibited less enthusiasm for Sullivan's army. Primarily concerned with their own economic well-being, they resented the army's intrusions. Localism dominated concerns, and state governments sought to mediate between military and local priorities. In New York government dutifully performed its role, while in Pennsylvania memories of past slights and perceived lapses in integrity on the part of quartermaster agents combined to make the Executive Council less than accommodating.

Internally, the Continental army had not developed a working system of supply. What existed better served the army in settled areas than campaigning on the frontier. One of the most glaring shortcomings was the lack of a system to provide Greene and Wadsworth with up-to-date returns on the supply situation facing the army. As for long-term planning, expertise existed within the Quartermaster and Commissary Departments, but the lack of an organic transportation capability made execution difficult. Terrain along Sullivan's single line of supply complicated this problem. The shallow Susquehanna proved a difficult waterway, and the Great

Warrior's Path that Sullivan built into a crude road wreaked havoc on his wagons. Finally, the existing correspondence indicates that the whole supply structure lacked coordination. With the possible exception of operations in the Susquehanna Valley, a jumbled chain of command produced a time-consuming and inefficient logistical effort in support of Sullivan's army.

Yet Sullivan did get to the Genesee and back without subjecting his soldiers to undue want, let alone starvation. The operation certainly took a toll on the soldiers. Regiments assigned to Sullivan's command began the campaign in better health than the army as a whole. In July Sullivan had 7.6 percent of his force unavailable for duty because of illness, as opposed to 9.4 percent for the Continental army as a whole. Following the campaign, Sullivan's returns indicate a sickness rate of 16 percent, compared to 10 percent for the army as a whole. It nonetheless seems evident that few men lost their lives as a result of disease.[88] As Martin Van Creveld points out in *Supplying War,* most eighteenth-century armies, relying on a depot system, limited their operations to fifty to sixty miles beyond the depot.[89] These European armies operated for the most part in settled areas with better-developed road and water transportation. Sullivan's men marched some one hundred and twenty miles from Tioga to the Genesee and nearly two hundred miles from his major upriver depot at Wyoming. Brodhead's small force accomplished similar feats of endurance on the Allegheny. Certainly, the time of the year helped make this possible. Indian crops provided needed supplements to the diet of these soldiers, but a reliance on foraging alone would have proved time consuming. Sullivan's ability to manage the meager resources he did have allowed him to press on when many of his subordinates argued to turn back.

Whether the credit belongs to Sullivan or to his subordinates, the logistical system that evolved during the expedition demonstrated the resiliency of a seasoned force. Its ability to adapt resembled a Napoleonic army more than any eighteenth-century peer. For example, when the quartermasters found themselves unable to man the wagons and boats that eventually found their way to Easton and Esthertown, Sullivan assigned his soldiers to grab the reins or pick up the poles. Lacking an adequate road between Easton and Wyoming, his men cut one through virgin wilderness in a little more than a month's time. When the outlet at Lake Otsego proved too shallow for passage of loaded bateaux, the soldiers dammed the lake then destroyed the dam with gunpowder to float their boats through the shallows. Sullivan and his officers consistently demonstrated mental agility and an ability to improvise. Officers set up smokehouses for repacking meat, an inspection system to discover tainted meat before it took up valuable cargo space, and encouraged foraging to minimize the drain on an inadequate stock of food. When pack animals grew weak, Sullivan employed officers' horses, including his own mount, and pressed captured Iroquois horses into service. The men who worked the army's supply system maintained a continuous effort to be responsive to Sullivan's needs. On days when the army rested, these men did not. They built additional depots, scoured the surrounding hills for stray cattle, repaired boats and wagons, and forwarded supplies.

Sullivan paid a price for this adaptability. His need to assign soldiers to supply and transportation missions diminished his operational strength. By early July Washington believed that Sullivan planned to use a thousand men to move and secure supplies and cautioned his lieutenant to reconsider the size of his support detachments. Whether Sullivan took the advice is unclear, but he later dedicated Shreve's entire regiment to building the depot at Tioga. Though impossible to determine exactly, it appears that at least a thousand soldiers served as support personnel, while about forty-five hundred (including Clinton's men) filled the combat units. Was the detachment of 20 percent of his army to support duties excessive? These men permitted the army to march 255 miles from their base at Easton into the heart of the Iroquois nation. The fact that Sullivan reached his objective and accomplished Washington's orders underscores the logistical adaptability of the army at the operational level.

6

LEADERSHIP

Washington realized shortly after assuming command of American forces outside Boston in 1775 that much needed to be done to turn his new charges into a force resembling an army. The quality of his officer corps particularly concerned him, because the rebellion's future appeared dim without leaders capable of transforming his vision for the army into reality.

Problems appeared among New England's militia officers almost from the opening volley at Lexington. Following the Battle of Bunker Hill, Washington court-martialed one colonel and five captains for cowardice.[1] He lectured other officers on basic leadership responsibilities. In one instance he had to remind his officers that it was difficult to expect enlisted men to remain on duty when they themselves made a practice of departing camp without authorization.[2] The frequency with which officers appeared before courts-martial for ethical problems provided an even more damning indictment. On 2 August 1775 a military tribunal tried and convicted Captain Oliver Parker for "defrauding the men of their advance pay, and drawing more rations than he had men in his company, and for selling the provisions he by that means obtained."[3] Parker would not be the only officer to face such charges. The frequency with which similar violations occurred greatly concerned the commander-in-chief. In the army's general orders for 10 August 1775 Washington expressed his disgust for such behavior:

> It is a matter of exceeding Concern to the General, to find, that at a time when the united efforts of America are exerting in defense of the common Rights and Liberties of mankind, that there should be in an Army constituted for so noble a purpose, such repeated Instances of Officers who lost to every sense of honor and virtue, are seeking by dirty and base means, the promotion of their own dishonest Gain, the eternal Disgrace of themselves and Dishonor of their Country.[4]

Frustrated with what he found in his new command, Washington lamented to his brother Lund that his "officers generally speaking are the most indifferent kind of People I ever saw."[5] The army consisted largely of New England units at this time, and Washington blamed his leadership problem on what he believed to be the peculiarities of New England's cultural background. Egalitarianism and excessive individualism represented two characteristics of New England troops which ran counter to his need to build discipline and cohesion in the army. He hoped that a healthy leavening of battalions drawn from the other colonies would provide some immediate relief to the problem. Any long-term solution rested on developing an officer corps that understood how to lead.

By midwar Washington had made considerable strides toward promoting a distinctive style of leadership in the army. It was an evolutionary model of leadership for a revolutionary army. Built on British roots, it focused on positive motivation rather than reliance on fear of punishment to motivate men. It asked officers to set an example of technical competence, ethical behavior, and, most important, a willingness to share the hardships of war with their soldiers. He demanded that his officers impart a sense of discipline and order within the army. Washington never fully rid his army of incompetent leaders; nonetheless, the formation of a competent officer corps was well advanced by the time of Sullivan's expedition.

Washington found himself handicapped by having little influence over who entered the officer corps. The states provided battalions complete with their complement of officers for service in the Continental army. The leadership skills of these officers varied widely, and few easy options existed to correct shortcomings. Experience in battle stood as one of the surest ways to achieve competency, but it could be a most unforgiving teacher. Though considerable literature existed in colonial society dealing with military issues, little of it dealt with the question of how to lead soldiers in combat. Most addressed the science of war (i.e., the building of fortifications, layouts of camps, drill, and related matters), leaving the question of leadership to experimentation and chance.[6] The problem crippled the army's performance during the early years and threatened the continuing existence of the new nation. Yet over time, largely because of Washington's vision, officer performance and the capabilities of the army markedly improved.

The subject of leadership and the climate of command in the Continental army poses problems. On one hand, this army of "rag, tag, and bobtail," as the British laughingly referred to it early in the war, managed not to lose the war across the seven long years that followed the first shots exchanged on Lexington's green. In contrast, numerous mutinies by parts of the Continental line during the latter years of the war darkened the army's reputation. Rhode Island regiments mutinied in 1779. Connecticut units followed suit the following year.[7] In January 1781 both the Pennsylvania and New Jersey lines, after yet another campaign season of short rations and inadequate clothing, staged the war's best-known uprising. Only Washington's adept maneuvering held these mutinies in check and kept the army to its course.[8] The nation's failure to support its soldiers underlay these revolts. The fact they occurred late in the war and that Washington settled them with little bloodshed stands out as significant.[9] The army's leadership not only prevented the British from breaking the army on the field of battle but also kept it from destroying itself from within when starvation, sickness, and inadequate pay combined to devastate morale.

The survival and success of the army proved no small feat, particularly considering that Washington built a proficient eighteenth-century army in a short time, under the stress of war, and on a societal base very different from that of his opponents.[10] No examination of leadership can ignore the challenge that a changing colonial society presented to Washington and his officers.

Historians differ on some points concerning the nature of power relations in colonial society before the war. John Shy, in *A People Numerous and Armed*, argues that, unlike Europe, the power of America's ruling classes rested primarily on accumulated wealth. Their positions were precarious, however, because they could rule only with the consent of the governed, and voting requirements were lenient enough to allow an expanded electorate capable of removing them from power.[11] Although not denying the importance of wealth, Gordon Wood in *The Radicalism of the American Revolution* finds colonial society remarkably similar to that of England and contends it was monarchical in nature. Common people paid deference to their more educated and more affluent betters in affairs of government and social life. Ties of patronage and kinship determined the upper echelons of colonial government. War shattered this social structure and replaced it with a republican one.[12] Although many of the old elites retained their places, merit and talent came to displace patronage and kinship as the foundation of power.[13] This social leveling spilled into the newly formed Continental army as well. Performance could not be coerced. It had to be brought voluntarily from soldiers.

When the war began, a *rage militaire* swept colonial society, producing a popular outpouring of support for the cause and spurring enlistments in the army.[14] Unlike armies in Europe which regularly impressed the lower classes into service, an army professing to represent a free people sought to rely mostly on voluntary enlistments.[15] The passing of time and setbacks in Canada and New York quickly brought this initial enthusiasm to an end and cast doubt on the army's ability to maintain itself throughout the war. Colonial society's reluctance to bend itself to the discipline of military life further complicated matters. With the exception of the period following the Seven Years' War, the colonies had been prosperous. Britain's thirteen colonies had been lands of opportunity in which making a living required less effort than had been the case in the Old World. These civilians-turned-soldiers believed that the war would be brief, their sacrifices transitory, and a return to peace and prosperity a near thing. Washington and his officers had to shift the focus away from the end of the war to the present. An officer corps building an army must develop in soldiers the strength of spirit to sustain the rigors of military life, to suffer and fight, to kill and, if need be, die for the good of the cause. These were not the strengths or the skills of the average farmer who stood on the green at Lexington in 1775.

Historians disagree about why civilians enlisted in the army during the opening years and then stayed as the war dragged on.[16] The average soldier was young, probably less than twenty-three years of age, and owned little property. Promises of land and bonuses rather than patriotic fervor may account for their desire to enlist, particularly later in the war, but this fails to explain why many of the soldiers stayed on when promises went unfulfilled and the nation provided inadequate food, shelter, and clothing.[17] Winters at Valley Forge and Morristown produced in the army a growing sense of cynicism, the product of too many broken promises and a realization that the army lived in poverty while the society it defended enjoyed comparative plenty. When bad conditions reached a certain level, soldiers mutinied or deserted. They may have been disappointed in their officers, but, with the exception of the mutiny in the Pennsylvania line, the men had other targets for their anger.[18] Perceived incompetency and inefficiency in the Continental Congress clearly disgusted them, but, rather than directly threaten the legitimacy of that body, they asked only that it hear and redress their grievances. A hard core of Washington's army neither mutinied nor deserted. In May 1783 nearly twelve thousand soldiers remained under arms at Newburgh, New York.[19] With little to indicate that Congress would honor promises for pay and allowances still owed the army, Washington furloughed many of the men, realizing that most would begin the trek back to their homes and never return. These soldiers had stayed until the final hour. Whatever their economic motivations at the time of enlistment, it had long since been clear that most would not be satisfied during the war. Furthermore, no Congressional action suggested that their efforts would long be remembered in peace.[20] What explains the motivation of the soldiers who trudged homeward from Newburgh?

Sullivan's expedition provides interesting insights into the climate of leadership and command in Washington's army at midwar, suggesting that these factors may account for the development of military spirit that the Continentals carried into the latter years of the war. By this time the officer corps had made marked improvements in their performance and had developed into an experienced and competent group of leaders. Neither experience nor competency existed uniformly throughout the corps. General and field grade officers tended to be better at their jobs than company grade subordinates, yet all ranks had made progress. The differences that separated general and field grades from company-level officers partly reflected experience. Many senior officers benefited from the limited military exposure they had received during the French and Indian War. The most important explanation for the differences, however, was the former's proximity to Washington, whose vision drove the officer corps' development. By midwar he had succeeded in imparting his concept of leadership on senior officers, and they in turn labored to pass his vision down to company level.

Washington kept his concept of leadership simple. He desired his officers to set the example. He expected his officers to exhibit a number of attributes, not the least of which was tactical competence. Sullivan's army proceeded upriver in a methodical and expeditious way, given the logistical situation. European-style armies operating in the backcountry enjoyed a mixed reputation for success. Braddock's disastrous showing in 1755 did not linger far from the minds of Washington or Sullivan. Butler and Brant could have played the part of Daniel Beaujeau and Jean Dumas at Fort Duquesne. They possessed the military power and made several attempts to impede or halt their opponents yet failed to accomplish anything of note in defending the Iroquois homelands. They failed largely because Sullivan and his officers meticulously adhered to proper security precautions during the march to their objective, providing their foes no opportunity to strike the kind of blow that Braddock received. Butler and Brant attempted two large-scale ambushes in an attempt to recreate Braddock's defeat but found themselves foiled in each attempt by Sullivan's soldiers.

Luck had little to do with Sullivan's tactical success. From the earliest days of the campaign, when Sullivan and Clinton assembled their forces at Easton and Otsego, the army trained by practicing those tasks it could most expect to do in combat. Units honed their movement techniques and modified them as necessary to the dictates of the rough terrain. Of particular importance was the need to practice crossing defiles.[21] In the language of modern tactics these danger areas represented places where constricted terrain made ambush possible. James Clinton, who had most of the light infantry at Otsego, required that his soldiers "prove their marks" prior to beginning the march to join Sullivan.[22] Boat crews worked to perfect drills designed to support and evacuate the infantry company assigned the mission of securing the far side of the river. The army's officers executed a training program designed to rob the enemy of their one tactical advantage, surprise—succeeding only because they understood the mission and its requisite tactics.

No army schools existed to teach junior officers their trade. The American army would have to wait until the establishment of the United States Military Academy at West Point in 1802 for any system of formal education. Experience in battle had instructed many of Sullivan's officers, who, with responsibilities of command or staff by 1779, were survivors in the literal sense of the word. In a day when command and control made it necessary for leaders to lead from the front, good officers presented inviting targets.

Although experience played a crucial role, Baron von Steuben also contributed significantly to the army's growing proficiency. He provided administrative order and a uniform set of drill instructions.[23] Perhaps more important, though less emphasized, Steuben changed the relationship between officers and men. Patriot officers previously followed the best tradition of European armies, yielding responsibility for drill to their sergeants. Professional European armies, with a more highly developed noncommissioned officer corps, could afford this; the Continental army could not. Lacking knowledge of drill and tactics themselves, the sergeants did their best but produced soldiers unable or unwilling to stand up to British or Hessian regulars in the open field. Steuben's personal example on the drill field taught officers that participation in the mundane aspects of training brought results and strengthened the tie between leaders and led, a relationship critical to the performance of units in combat. Steuben encountered some difficulty in transmitting his ideas, but, with Washington's backing, his concept of an officer's role became the American model.

The fact that many officers exhibited a genuine curiosity about their trade abetted Washington's work. Regardless of rank, many officers avidly read military literature, including tracts on the ancients as well as more recent works by Frederick the Great and Maurice de Saxe.[24] Washington certainly welcomed this intellectual curiosity but understood that knowledge alone did not constitute leadership. He stressed time and again the need to set an example for soldiers by willingly sharing their hardships and showing concern for their welfare. Soldiers giving battle in defense of liberty and equality would not long countenance an officer corps of aristocrats perceived to be set above the everyday hardships of army life.

Washington's officers found themselves caught between two very different sets of expectations. On the one hand, many company grade officers had known their soldiers during peacetime and recruited them into the army. This system acted as a brake on aristocratic pretensions but also bred the kind of familiarity that tainted judgment. But older officers whose military experience dated from the French and Indian War looked to the British model, with its aristocratic overtones so repugnant to American soldiers.

Americans had come to regard British officers as belonging to a corrupt aristocracy, one that demanded and all too frequently received deference from a democratic society it held in contempt.[25] Washington's problem became one of finding a way to create a distinctive officer corps free to exercise independent judgment on how best to use the army while at the same time insuring that these officers recognized and took seriously their responsibilities to their men.

Washington worked to communicate this to his subordinates, a process under way but still incomplete by 1779. Very early in the planning of Sullivan's expedition, Washington warned his officers that he expected the summer's undertaking to be difficult. It had been comparatively easy for officers, particularly field grades and above, to take large quantities of baggage along on earlier campaigns. The difficulties that quartermaster officers were experiencing securing horses and the rough terrain over which Sullivan's small army would operate rendered this practice counterproductive. Washington strongly encouraged Sullivan and his officers to travel light. Rather than use the horse shortage as justification for having the officers disencumber themselves of their baggage, Washington saw the situation as ideal for teaching leadership. "Sensible to the force of good examples on the minds of the Soldiers, it ought to be the pride of an officer to share the fatigue, as well as the dangers, to which his men are exposed," he wrote to Sullivan. "On foot, marching by their sides, by sharing he will lessen every inconvenience and excite in them a Spirit of patience and perseverance."[26]

Many officers ignored Washington's guidance. Even Sullivan seemed determined to take superfluous baggage, including large marquee tents for his headquarters which struck both Washington and Greene as unnecessary. Brigade and regimental officers resisted as well. To pull or carry the baggage required horses, and officers vied to insure themselves the use of a mount. Most senior officers believed it absolutely necessary to have a horse at their disposal. Valid reasons supporting this contention had nothing to do with transporting baggage. The need to control troop movements meant that general officers and some field grades had to have horses available to position themselves where they could control events as well as motivate soldiers. For the most part, however, this requirement went no lower than regimental level. Sullivan began by ordering company grade officers to surrender their mounts to the quartermaster before the army departed Wyoming. As the transportation shortage grew acute later in the campaign, he had the rest of his officers, including himself, follow suit.[27]

As Washington predicted, soldiers noticed when their officers chose to accompany them on foot. During the river crossing Sullivan conducted on 11 August 1779, soldiers suspended their cartridge boxes from the ends of fixed bayonets and filed into the river, "each man holding on to the man in front of him."[28] Field grade officers on horseback could easily cross the stream with little risk. Most did so, and in one case Sullivan's adjutant, Colonel Francis Barber, saved a soldier swept away by the current. What caught the attention of Thomas Grant, a member of the army's surveying team, was that Hand elected to dismount his horse and wade the river along side his men.[29]

Enlisted soldiers seldom mentioned junior officers in their diaries, and existing entries say little about their quality. Some evidence, however, suggests that problems existed at this level. Sullivan discovered that many of his junior officers did not understand their responsibilities. He partly blamed the disappointing results of the Chemung raid on junior officers absent from their units at the beginning of the engagement and made clear his expectation that this not occur again.[30] The army fought a major engagement at Newtown and one skirmish with its elusive foe as the campaign progressed toward the Genesee River. Because the orderly books contain no additional mention of poor behavior, Sullivan's efforts to correct problems among junior officers appear to have been successful.

In addition to tactical competence, Washington reminded his officers that responsibilities of command extended to concern for their soldiers' well-being. In an army constantly short of basic supplies, this difficult subject frustrated the commander-in-chief and his lieutenants. Washington encouraged his officers to overcome the inefficiencies in the system and supported them even when their actions embarrassed him. Sullivan's ongoing battle with the army's quartermasters and commissaries, the Executive Council of Pennsylvania, and anyone else capable of positively influencing his supply situation represented the combativeness Washington expected.

Below Sullivan regimental officers sometimes found themselves arguing with their state legislatures concerning logistical support. As the army congregated around Easton in the spring of 1779, the New Jersey line suffered greatly from a lack of clothing and other basic supplies. Realizing that politicians in Trenton seemed reluctant to correct the problem, Maxwell scathingly reminded them of their responsibilities, explaining that his soldiers had "been so shamefully neglected by the Legislature of the state that I am at a loss to know how to address the subject." He went on to accuse the legislature of treating the men as not "worthy of their notice or care."[31] At the same time, Maxwell's officers petitioned the legislature for assistance, claiming that "our pay is now only minimal, not real, . . . that four months pay of a private will not procure his wretched wife and children a single bushel of wheat."[32] In desperation, officers of the First New Jersey filed a second petition to Trenton threatening to resign en masse within three days unless the state addressed grievances regarding pay and allowances.[33]

Two points are important relating to these petitions. First, Washington knew of Maxwell's letter and of the officers' threats of resignation. He tolerated the letter. The general had been in trouble with New Jersey's legislature in the past, and this time was no different. If Maxwell's words shamed the politicians into action, so much the better. The threat to resign, in contrast, presented serious problems for Washington. He could not encourage this kind of action on the part of his officers, who, unlike enlisted soldiers, could resign their commissions at any time. Their threat did not constitute mutiny. If successful, however, enlisted soldiers might infer that the threat of mutiny could bring material relief to their conditions. Second, Washington could not support the officers' methods. He quietly worked to defuse the situation without stifling the concern the officers demonstrated for their soldiers.

It might be argued that these officers acted more out of selfish motives than as representatives of their soldiers. After all, they expected the legislature to provide compensation to themselves as well as their enlisted men.[34] In addition, they believed themselves due a larger relative share of the settlement because of the greater responsibilities and sacrifices their service as officers required. Greed undoubtedly did play a part in the issue, but, in truth, it does not explain adequately their decision to take a stand. New Jersey's officers came from the state's upper and middle classes. As leaders of New Jersey society, they considered themselves gentlemen in the eighteenth-century meaning of the word. Service to the state was expected, most had other sources of income, and military pay did not constitute their primary support. Resignation would call their motives as well as their status as gentlemen into question. They could only lose from the bad publicity such an act would generate. The real benefactors of their decision to force the issue turned out to be their soldiers.

This attitude continued throughout the campaign. When Sullivan realized that a shortage of rations had become critical at the end of August, he requested rather than ordered the men to go on half-rations and promised compensation for the rations missed. Sullivan carefully crafted the request to elicit a positive response. Regardless of the wording, however, it was made in good faith. Those who did not wish to continue could return to Tioga.

Soldiers long after the war remembered the concern some of their officers had for their welfare. Private Nathan Davis recalled his regimental commander, Colonel Joseph Ciley, attempting to convince a young soldier named Richard Drout to drop from the march and return to Tioga when the army went to half-rations. Ciley walked the ranks to tell the men he would understand if circumstances prevented their continuing the march. When he reached Richard, a lad of only fifteen at the time, Ciley stopped and said, "Richard you must go back; you cannot endure the march." Drout replied he could withstand whatever the future held. Ciley persisted, citing Drout's youth as justification. Drout steadfastly remained in formation and claimed he could keep up with the other soldiers. "Besides," he said, "they will call me a coward, and I am not one." Ciley assured the young soldier that he would not think this of him and would flay any soldier who accused him of shirking. Drout wavered. "I enlisted to serve my country," the young man sobbed. "Do let me go on." Moved by Drout's response, Ciley relented and permitted him to continue the march.[35]

The performance of Sullivan's surgeons, hospital staff, and support soldiers at Tioga provided another example of the kind of concern Washington expected of his officers. Sullivan's medical staff set up a flying hospital at Tioga and general hospitals at Wyoming and Sunbury. The quality of the care provided in these facilities is difficult to determine and, given the state of medicine at the time, may have been as much a hazard as a benefit to the health of soldiers. The priority given to getting sick and wounded soldiers to some sort of treatment facility, rather than the quality of the care, stands out as significant. Sullivan suffered more than thirty casualties at Newtown on the afternoon of 29 August 1779. Of these the surgeons and their nurses found twenty-four soldiers in need of evacuation downriver. Returns from the general hospital at Sunbury record these men as being admitted on 4 September.[36] Despite one hundred and seventy miles of river between Newtown and the hospital at Sunbury, the surgical staff and the support garrison at Tioga accomplished the evacuation in six days.[37]

Ethical behavior rounded out Washington's concept of leadership. He expected high standards from his officers in their relationships with civilians and soldiers as well as with one another. He stressed the need for character and honor in his officers. Washington built the army's professionalism around high ethical standards, believing this foundation would bind the soldier to society.[38] Part of Washington's stress on ethics derived from the nature of the conflict the nation was fighting. The Declaration of Independence had made it clear that separation derived from a perceived violation of contract between governor and governed. The Continental Congress felt certain that justice rested on its side. The Continental army championed an aggrieved and righteous people. It would suffer and, if need be, die in the cause of the nation. The army's role carried undertones of chivalry and stoicism.[39] To make the concept function, officers had to maintain high ethical standards and strive to embed those standards into the army as a whole. The more the army's mission could be turned into a crusade, the more patriotic spirit could take the place of discipline in keeping the army to its task.

Driving the concept home was no easy task, particularly as the material conditions of the army degenerated. Soldiers seldom passed up the opportunity to liberate livestock from local farmers or steal wood from fences if they faced cold nights and hunger. Sullivan's army resembled the rest of the Continental forces in this regard. Sullivan could have overlooked minor transgressions in light of the less than timely support provided by the state of Pennsylvania; instead, he chose to make an issue of the problem. He reminded his men that "humanity dictates to every soldier that he should not add to their [local farmers] distresses, being already made miserable by a savage enemy."[40] When such warnings proved inadequate, Sullivan brought charges against soldiers caught pilfering. At Wyoming courts-martial tried and convicted thirteen soldiers for stealing hogs from the local farmers. With the army facing increasing problems with food, the punishments meted out usually proved light. John Thomas, for example, received the harshest sentence. The court awarded him fifty lashes and required that he make restitution to the owner. Others found guilty received sentences of twenty-five lashes. An army already suffering from too little food does not deal harshly with soldiers who steal an occasional hog or goose. But the key point Sullivan attempted to emphasize was that, regardless of circumstances, an army of the people could not be the people's oppressor.

Enemy civilians presented an ethical problem slighted by European theorists of war. The Swiss jurist Emmeric Vattel expressed the concept of eighteenth-century limited war most clearly, arguing that it concerned sovereigns only. Princes and their officers ought to wage it only in such a way as to minimize the harm done to their soldiers and to the civilian population.[41] Although this concept of limited war applied somewhat in the East, where Henry Clinton's army sparred with Washington's, it broke down on the frontier. Sullivan intended to bring the Iroquois to a decisive battle by destroying their towns and villages as well as the agricultural infrastructure that supported them. If decisive battle proved impossible, Washington hoped that the devastation would be severe enough to cause the Iroquois to rethink their decision to join the war. He understood that Sullivan's army would bring a winter famine to the Iroquois. The British would either have to feed their allies or let them starve. This was total war, and, in the emotionally charged environment resulting from the raids of 1778, it would be difficult to limit the violence exclusively to combatants.

The myths and distortions that grew out of the preceding year's battle at Wyoming hung over Sullivan's army and provided justification for the army's harsh mission. Nathan Davis revealed conflicting feelings about the coming campaign in his diary:

> Neither did it altogether escape our reflection what must be the inevitable consequences resulting from the destruction of all the sustenance of a multitude of natives. But when we reflected on the inhuman barbarities they had inflicted on our own people, the scalps that we had seen hanging around their wigwams, from the aged parent of grey hairs, down to the restless infant at breast, we could not but feel justified in the act, whilst we lamented the dreadful necessity that impelled us to it.[42]

Dr. Ebenezer Elmer, a surgeon in the New Jersey line, seconded Davis's thoughts. "I very heartily wish these rusticks [*sic*] may be reduced to reason, by the approach of this army, without their suffering the extremes of war," he recorded in his diary, "there is something so cruel, in destroying the habitations of any people (however mean they may be, being their all), that I might say the prospect hurts my feelings."[43] Other observers, such as Kirkland, laid the blame for Wyoming's devastation on George III.

> Havoc, devastation and waste salute our eyes wherever we walk over the fields of this once flourishing, now defoliated Country—& these objects create strange feelings in the breast—a just indignation & deep abhorrence of pretended british Clemency over so much boasted of now blended with savage barbarity. Upwards of one hundred & fifty widdows [*sic*] were here made upon this ground in the space of one hour & a half about a year from this time. Are these the fruits & effects of thy Clemency O George—thy tyrant of Britain & Scourge to Mankind! May he, to whom Vengence [*sic*] belongs pour forth his righteous Indignation in due time. . . . These once flourishing . . . but now melancholy fields, are now cultivated by the feble [*sic*] hand of disconsolate widdows [*sic*], & helpless orphans.[44]

Davis, Elmer, Kirkland, and others had visited the battlefield at Wyoming and saw human remains still unburied from the previous year's fight. In addition, the local inhabitants had not missed the chance to recount their version of the engagement complete with exaggerated stories of the massacre of prisoners that followed the defeat.[45] While the army was encamped at Wyoming, the Tory-Indian raids on Fort Freeland and Minisink provided additional grist for the atrocity mill. Kirkland noted in a letter to his wife that he had heard that neither women nor children were spared the hatchet in the attacks.[46]

Despite sentiment inflamed by such stories, Sullivan held to ethical high ground concerning the abuse of noncombatants. When Continental troops discovered an old Indian woman while engaged in burning Catherine's Town, a small Seneca settlement just south of Seneca Lake, Sullivan ordered them to build a bark cabin for her and provide bread, meat, and Indian corn sufficient to last six weeks.[47] Washington's orders to Sullivan mentioned taking women and children captive to use as a means to force an end to the raids; however, taking the old woman along would not further that goal. Given the hysteria following the previous year's raids in the lower valley, leaving her to die amid the ruins of her village would have been the easy way out for Sullivan. He chose, instead, to give her six weeks of food from the army's already tight supplies. Some enlisted men criticized Sullivan's gift of supplies in their diaries; most saw the old woman as an object of pity, not a trophy of war.[48]

The army returned by way of Catherine's Town several weeks later. The old woman still occupied the bark cabin. During the intervening weeks another much younger Indian woman had returned to the village and taken up residence with her. She had been shot dead sometime before the army reoccupied the village, probably the victim of a party of soldiers serving as messengers along Sullivan's line of communications. The court-martial records suggest that the murderer(s) escaped undetected. Nonetheless, many officers found they could not condone the incident. Lieutenant Colonel Hubley referred to the crime as "heinous" and expressed his disgust for the "breach of faith" by someone in the army. At worst a handful of soldiers committed the crime, yet Hubley feared their actions would taint the reputation of the entire army.[49] Sullivan ordered the young woman's burial then left a keg of salt pork, some biscuit, and a small amount of beef and flour for the old woman. Lieutenant William Barton noted that the gift represented no small sacrifice, since "no officer below the rank of a field officer had tasted any [salt pork] since leaving Tioga."[50]

Sullivan and his officers walked a fine line over the question of Indian relations. While at Wyoming, the army camped not far from the scene of John Butler's triumph of the year before. Soldiers walked the old battleground and listened to the grisly stories told by locals of the event.[51] Keeping this anger focused proved difficult. Several warriors who accompanied the expedition and rendered invaluable service as guides regularly faced verbal abuse from soldiers. Sullivan on more than one occasion instructed his officers not to tolerate this kind of behavior and reminded the army that

> nothing can be more ungenerous than to ridicule those who have come voluntarily to venture their lives in our aid; . . . All the warriors of the Oneida, Tuscarora and Stockbridge Indians are about

to join us. . . . The person, therefore, who after this notice gives the least discouragement to these people, must in malice to his country far exceed the most inveterate Tory, and must expect to be treated accordingly.[52]

Over the course of the campaign the animosity between soldiers and the Indians who accompanied them appears to have diminished, particularly after Hanyost Thaosagwat fell in combat while on Boyd's ill-fated patrol. Before the army departed Newtown on the way back to Wyoming, Sullivan and his officers celebrated the completion of the campaign with a feast honoring the Oneida, Tuscarora, and Stockbridge Indians.

Ethics within the army found its clearest statement in the disciplinary system. This legal structure governed relations between the individual and the army. Based on the British articles of war, the system Washington adopted provided a better balance between the rights of the individual and the army's need for order and discipline. The American system was generally less severe than that of the British. Both systems relied on whipping as the primary form of punishment. The British system placed no limit on the number of lashes; British courts-martial handed out sentences of five hundred and in some cases even two thousand lashes.[53] The Continental system placed constraints on the power of the courts, limiting lashes to thirty-nine. Later, at Washington's bidding, Congress raised the number to one hundred.[54] In some cases Continental courts-martial tried to increase the number of lashes beyond one hundred by using multiple charges. Washington disapproved of this tactic and ruled it illegal.[55] Other punishments common to the Continental army included running the gauntlet, imprisonment, and forfeiture of pay.

English common law, the basis of American civil law, provided far more guarantees for the individual than the military law practiced in the Continental army. Indictment by a grand jury did not exist and the accused represented himself before a jury of officers rather than his peers.[56] The court-martial of officers occurred with some regularity, although a board of inquiry normally investigated the charges before recommending the accused for trial. Safeguards existed to guard the rights of the accused. The administrative structure of the court system represented the first of these. Regimental or garrison courts-martial handled minor violations of the articles of war, while general courts-martial heard more serious offenses. This limited the judicial power of lower courts and insured that punishments fit the crime. The right of the accused to challenge a member of the court served as a second safeguard. If a soldier believed an officer sitting on his court-martial was prejudiced against him, he could challenge the officer's right to sit in judgment. The convening officer would then have to designate another member to sit in his place.[57] The fact that courts could only recommend punishment, not command its execution, provided the final safeguard. Though a general court could recommend the death penalty for certain offenses, only the convening authority, a general officer in command, could order its execution.

In Sullivan's army courts-martial convened frequently. Most records of regimental courts-martial have disappeared, but the surviving order books indicate that general courts-martial occurred at the rate of two or more a week while the army was in secure areas such as Easton, Wyoming, or Otsego. Sullivan continued to hold court during the campaign, though at a lessened rate during the march.

The judicial system maintained discipline in the army when more positive forms of motivation proved inadequate. With two exceptions punishments tended to be light and pardons frequent.[58] The courts touched officers as well as enlisted men. For soldiers the courts served largely as instruments of discipline. The majority of cases involving enlisted soldiers dealt with either accusations of desertion or theft of property. For officers the courts served as forums in which questions of competence could be heard before rumors and accusations destroyed careers and embittered feelings. Two field grade officers, Commissary Colonel John Street and Colonel Matthias Ogden, appeared before a court-martial, the former for unsatisfactory performance of the Commissary Department and the latter for disobeying orders at the Battle of Newtown.[59] The courts exonerated both men.

The courts also protected the rights of enlisted soldiers, although the punishments given to officers found guilty of abusing soldiers were exceedingly light. At worst abusive officers could be thrown out of the army, a sentence applied to the most egregious offenders. There were few instances of abuse in Sullivan's army, although two company grade officers did stand trial on such charges. In the first instance the court acquitted the accused. In the second the overwhelming evidence of abuse produced a guilty verdict; however, the penalty, public censure, proved less than Sullivan felt appropriate. Troubled by the light sentence, he sent a message to brigade and regimental commanders explaining his views on what constituted appropriate behavior for an officer:

> Tho the General will never countenance Soldiers in disrespectfull behavior to officers, and will entertain a poor opinion of any officer who suffers himself to be insulted without immediately chastising the soldiers who may attempt it, Yet he can never suffer officers to beat and abuse their soldiers wantonly. Blows should never be given except where they are necessary to the preservation of order and discipline and then unaccompanied with those marks of cruelty and malevolence which were apparent in the whole of Cpt. W. "Gans" Angels conduct.[60]

The court system served as the most overt structure in building an ethical and moral environment within the army. Sullivan also relied on his chaplains to accomplish the same thing but in a more subtle fashion. The religious life in Sullivan's army reflected that of the Continental army as a whole. Sunday services consisting of a sermon, prayers, and usually the administering of the Holy Communion were mandatory for officers and men alike. Only the immediacy of combat could cancel worship. On a daily basis chaplains reminded soldiers of God's expectations. This generally took the form of the daily prayer offered prior to the reading of the day's orders and roll call.[61]

Sullivan took his religion very seriously and actively encouraged his chaplains in the preaching of God's word. Kirkland, writing to his wife, Jerusha, noted that the commanding general frequently engaged him in conversation regarding theological matters. The authenticity of Scriptures, supremacy of God, and the nature and consequences of Deism were three topics of discussion in the evening hours under Sullivan's marquee tent. Regarding Deism, Kirkland wrote: "The General has undertaken to convince any Deist (of which there is no want in the Army) from principles of 'persuasion' that the Scriptures are of *Divine Original*—at least all the doctrinal & preceptive [*sic*] parts." To emphasize his point, Sullivan found the time to write a thirty-page tract arguing the existence of a Supreme Being and of the relationship of Jesus Christ to God and the world.[62] With a commanding general who took his religion very seriously, it should come as no surprise that chaplains played a key role in creating an ethical climate in the army.

The texts of most of the sermons delivered by Sullivan's chaplains no longer survive, but each chaplain assigned to the expedition recorded at least some of the Bible verses on which he based his sermons. Most of the messages, as expected, dealt with moral issues. All asked that soldiers keep their faith in God. But, in addition, the verses also suggest that the good soldier remain stoic in the face of adversity. Chaplains repeatedly reminded soldiers that they fought for a righteous cause blessed by God and should accept cheerfully all tribulations. The Reverend William Rogers reminded his listeners during a sermon delivered for a Fourth of July celebration that, "provided we fear God and are publicly as well as individually honest, what have we now to alarm us. . . . Our fathers trusted and the Lord did deliver them; they cried unto Him and were delivered; they trusted and the Lord did deliver them; they cried unto Him and were delivered; they trusted in Him and were not confounded."[63]

Helping soldiers deal with the hardships of army life became another persistent theme. Andrew Hunter chose Hebrews 12:13 as the text for one such lesson.[64] "Endure what you suffer as being a father's punishment, your suffering shows that God is treating you as his sons," Hunter admonished his soldiers. Israel Evans took a different approach in his sermons. At the completion of the campaign he painted the expedition's grisly job of destroying the Iroquois nation as God's will. In an early version of Manifest Destiny he spoke of seeing a day when the yeoman farmers of a new nation would till the lands of the Iroquois and certainly understood that many of the soldiers who listened to his words saw themselves as those yeoman farmers.[65]

Religion and the military justice system both served a role in maintaining the army's order. Their effectiveness rested, respectively, on fear of God and of the lash. Perhaps more important than religion or military justice, Sullivan made subtle use of ceremony in building unit esprit de corps and in maintaining its focus. Sullivan and Clinton staged several reviews of their regiments while in camp at Easton, Wyoming, and Otsego. On the return trip from the Iroquois homelands, Sullivan held reviews at Fort Reed and at Tioga. His intent was clear: he ordered the early displays to impress not only local onlookers but also the army of its own competency and ability. The later reviews accomplished the same thing while affording an opportunity for Sullivan to congratulate soldiers for their prowess.

At Fort Reed Sullivan brought his army in line and had them practice a *feu de joie*. The maneuver called for each soldier to fire his musket in succession, with only a fraction of a second between shots. Soldiers who had finished firing returned their muskets to order arms in the same sequential manner. The effect of a rolling musket fire and the precise movements of man and weapon made quite a sight when executed properly. It required coordination and teamwork on the part of individual soldiers because they had to be able to cover for their peers when a musket misfired. Unhappy with the first rehearsal, Sullivan had his soldiers repeat the drill. On the second attempt he mounted a horse and rode at full gallop down the line of soldiers as the muskets went off just behind him. The second attempt proved quite impressive, and the army burst into cheers after it was completed.[66] The ceremonies provided excellent positive reinforcement to the army. In this case Sullivan rewarded the army by giving an ox to each brigade to use in the day's feast and by returning the army to full rations.[67]

The army repeated the show at Tioga several days later. Davis recalled that his officers ordered the men to place a sprig of evergreen in their hats and whiten their hair with flour prior to departing Fort Reed.[68] Before marching onto the river flat at Tioga, Sullivan sent for his band and colors. The army's procession onto the old campgrounds at Tioga had all the appearance of a formal military parade. The band played and cannon salutes reverberated up and down the river. The whole affair may appear pretentious, but it served a purpose. Sullivan's army had not waged a regular military operation against professional soldiers. There had been only one opportunity to face an enemy in anything like normal eighteenth-century combat. It had been a calculated campaign against an entire nation, not simply its military forces. As a result, most soldiers knew that, because of their actions, the coming winter would bring hard times for the Iroquois with those most directly affected being women and children. The ceremonies attempted to bring some sense of civility to the operation, to somehow make it fit into an acceptable military framework by giving it the same trappings as other campaigns.[69]

Sullivan and his officers wanted to convince soldiers that civility was the most important trait separating them from their foes. The parades, toasts, and cheers that followed them contributed such an outlook. There was a dark side to military life, and this too had its ceremony. Sullivan used the funeral as another vehicle to perpetuate the idea of the army's moral superiority. The tempo of the campaign made it easier to attend properly to the dead. The officer corps made sure that this was done, as a way not only to pay respects to the deceased but also to maintain the concentration of the living. In April a party of Indians ambushed and killed two officers and four enlisted soldiers from the Eleventh Pennsylvania who had been scouting the trail from Easton to Wyoming. The soldiers who found their dead comrades buried the bodies where they lay, marking each officer's grave with a wooden board. The road that Sullivan's soldiers cut to Wyoming went past the grave site. Hand positioned his regimental band beside the graves then marched his brigade slowly by to the melodic sounds of "Roslin Castle." Rogers said that the makeshift cemetery and the music produced a sense of "universal gloom" in the soldiers.[70] It also sharpened their focus on the nature of their mission and of the threat presented by their foes. Later, at Tioga, Sullivan had Rogers perform a Masonic funeral service for the two fallen officers along with services for an enlisted man killed while on guard duty the preceding night. Sullivan had not known either officer, and the soldier was but a private, yet he believed the ceremony of sufficient importance to warrant not only his attendance but also that of his senior officers.

Once the army departed Tioga for the Iroquois homelands, funeral services became less elaborate but still part of the army's ceremonial routine. Funerals for the mangled bodies of Lieutenant Boyd and Private Parker only reinforced the contention that civility marked a key difference between the two sides.[71] Lieutenant Colonel Dearborn, upon viewing the dismembered bodies, wrote that "this was a most horrid spectacle to behold and from which we are taught the necessity of fighting those more than devils to the last moment rather than fall into their hands alive."[72]

The disposition of human remains did concern the officer corps, not only out of respect for the dead but also out of concern for the living. Soldiers wanted to believe that, if they died in combat, their comrades would not leave their remains to the mercy of an enemy capable of the kind of atrocities visited on Boyd and Parker. On the few occasions when combat brought fatalities, burial teams dug graves at irregular intervals then burned over the broken dirt of the graves to disguise them as the remains of campfires.

Washington's vision for an American style of leadership did eventually take hold in the Continental army. The process of change was not completed by 1779, nor would it ever yield an officer corps entirely built around service to the nation. Self-interest frequently stood behind some of the issues officers chose to champion. Only the year before the army's officers had begun to press their desire for half-pay for life pensions from the Continental Congress. They failed to demand any similar plan for their enlisted soldiers.[73] This deliberate oversight came not so much from unconcern for the future security of their soldiers as from their belief that they, more so than any other group in American society, had carried a disproportionate share of the burden for keeping the Revolution from being crushed by Britain's military might.[74] The officer corps had other related shortcomings as well. Officers still tied up considerable time in disputes over dates of rank, and boards of inquiry examined too many accusations of slander between officers. These problems continued throughout the war; nonetheless, Sullivan's expedition indicates that change was under way inside the officer corps. The real question is whether the evolving concept of leadership made any difference in the army's performance and cohesion.

At first glance the answer would appear to be no. Orderly books from Sullivan's and Clinton's units indicate that general courts-martial occurred with considerable frequency. Two charges predominated: desertion and theft. General courts-martial tried seventy-seven soldiers on ninety different charges. Forty-three percent dealt with desertion, and in every case the court found the accused guilty.[75] From August 1777 through June 1778, a period that included the trying times of Valley Forge, Washington's judicial system tied up only 18 percent of its time with soldiers charged with desertion.[76]

The problem with this comparison is that twenty-nine of the desertion charges came from one incident involving the German battalion assigned to Hand's brigade. Authorized 27 June 1776 by the Congress, this battalion consisted largely of Pennsylvania and Maryland Germans. Most of the men hailed from Philadelphia and surrounding counties. Recruited for three years, the regiment became part of the Pennsylvania line.[77] In June 1779 many of the soldiers assigned to this regiment were approaching the end of their three-year enlistments and indicated their plans to leave the army at the completion of their contract.[78] Sullivan, not having access to the enlistment records, made it clear that he would not permit them to go unless he received valid discharges. On 14 July thirty-three soldiers deserted, claiming that their contract had been fulfilled. Furious at their disobedience and willing to make an example of the offenders, Sullivan sent his cavalry troop to bring them back. Somewhere on the road between Wyoming and Easton the cavalry caught up with twenty-nine of the soldiers and returned them to the army at Wyoming. There a general court-martial found all guilty of desertion, sentencing five of the ring leaders to death and the rest to lesser punishments.[79] Sullivan probably conceded at least some merit to the argument of the condemned men, because he pardoned them all contingent upon receiving a pledge that they would serve until the end of the campaign.

Many issues prompted soldiers to desert the army. For the most part, however, they left when, in their opinion, the contract that bound them to the service had been violated. This could happen in response to inadequate rations, clothing, or shelter or because of delinquent or depreciated pay. Desertions came after an extended period in which the army's support structures failed to perform. In the case of the German battalion the soldiers who left had an even more valid complaint. Their time was up, and there was no question in their minds that they were owed a proper discharge.[80] It is important to keep in mind that the battalion had marshaled along with the rest of the army at Easton, a point only fifty miles from the unit's point of origin at Philadelphia. Soldiers who genuinely lacked a sense of self-discipline might have elected to quit the army a month early rather than accompany it to the Wyoming Valley. Getting home from Wyoming, after all, would require a trip alone along the wilderness road that crossed the Pocono Mountains. All of the soldiers who eventually deserted knew that the road home from Wyoming would be more dangerous than the way back from Easton. Yet they marched with the army to Wyoming. When their three years were up, they took matters into their own hands and deserted. A military tribunal no doubt would see the act as desertion, but the soldiers saw it as a legitimate option for a man serving in their type of revolutionary army.

Apart from the German battalion only 24 percent of the court's activity dealt with desertion, a number still high but certainly closer to the overall court-martial records of the period 1777–78. A comparison of the personnel returns for Sullivan's army suggests an even less serious problem with desertion. Returns do not exist for the months of August and September; however, Sullivan's monthly desertion rate for his fifteen regiments reporting in July 1779 was .5 percent. In October 1779, at the completion of the campaign and after the army's return to New Jersey, the rate dropped to .04 percent. The preceding year's returns for July and October, though not as complete as the 1779 figures, show desertion rates of .5 percent and 1.2 percent, respectively.[81]

Any review of desertion rates for the Continental army must be treated with a healthy degree of skepticism. Some unit returns consistently report desertions, while others seldom show any at all. It may be that some adjutants risked a court-martial offense by hiding their desertions as furloughs or "command/extra service details." A better measure of cohesion, morale, and combat readiness in the army might be the availability of soldiers for duty as a portion of the total regimental enrollments. Here, again, Sullivan's command seems to indicate that the army was improving. His infantry regiments showed an 87 percent availability for duty at the beginning of the campaign in July and 77 percent availability at its completion in October. The major factor accounting for the 10 percent decrease between July and October was a doubling in percentage of soldiers listed as sick (from 7.6 to 15 percent). Comparing these numbers to 1778 again, the same regiments show a 66 percent availability in July and a 65 percent availability in October. Sickness accounts for a large percentage of the nonavailable (16 percent in July and 21 percent in October). Also significant are the higher numbers of soldiers (12 percent in July and 18 percent in October) unavailable due to furlough or command/extra duty. Sullivan's army shows a 5.3 percent loss in July and 8.6 percent loss in October for these reasons.[82] In other words, even if adjutants were hiding desertions in the furlough or command/extra duty figures, no matter how one looks at the personnel returns, they indicate a lessening problem with desertion in 1779.

The scale of the thefts constituted a real problem, however, and probably show the degree to which Sullivan's logistics had broken down. In Washington's army during 1777–78 theft represented about 8 percent of the charges tried by the courts. For Sullivan's judges the rate hit 20 percent, most of which involved theft of food. Soldiers usually stole from local farmers, though there were several cases in which the theft occurred at the expense of other soldiers or the commissary. One incident in June involving a group of stragglers from the First New Jersey and the First New Hampshire regiments accounted for thirteen of the eighteen cases heard by the courts. Though prosecuted, the offenders received light punishments that could in no way serve as a deterrent to the crime. Sullivan found himself attempting to maintain the ethical standards Washington had set for the army while also trying to keep in mind the pernicious effect of his deplorable supply situation. He proved willing to try soldiers on even small breaches in military law but often pardoned a first offender.

The attempt to balance order with a realistic appreciation of the army's condition bore fruit. Only 4 percent of the cases heard by Sullivan's courts dealt with enlisted soldiers charged with challenging the authority of the officers and noncommissioned officers.[83] For Washington's courts during the period August 1777 to June 1778 the rate reached 15 percent.[84] Open insubordination was noticeably absent from Sullivan's small army, although minor infractions occurred throughout the campaign.

Two of the best examples of these involved swimming and the unauthorized discharge of firearms. In response to the urgings of his medical staff, who believed that swimming in the midday sun caused illness, Sullivan restricted swimming to the morning hours of Tuesday, Thursday, and Saturday.[85] Clinton took similar steps for his brigade at Lake Otsego.[86] Many soldiers chose to ignore the orders and took to the water anyway. Sullivan next authorized officers to administer twenty lashes to any soldier caught in the water against orders.[87] It is doubtful that the addition of a summary punishment dissuaded the soldiers from swimming. The problem probably says more about the motivation of the individual soldier than about the state of discipline in the army. A year earlier, at Valley Forge, Baron von Steuben had noted that, unlike European soldiers, the Continental soldier required clear orders explaining not only what was to be done but also why it was necessary. Soldiers held little regard for the opinion of Continental army surgeons, and the prohibition against swimming on a hot summer afternoon no doubt made little sense to soldiers whose own experience had convinced them that the practice did not cause disease.

The propensity of soldiers to discharge their muskets around camp had plagued Washington and his officers since the opening of the war. For Sullivan the deficiency proved costly. Captain Benjamin Kimball lost his life as a result of an accidental discharge of another soldier's musket.[88] The incident resulted in a court-martial, with the accused soldier being found innocent and the killing an accident. Although it is difficult to generalize from the ruling in this case, the frequency of accidental firings may have stemmed more from weapons technology rather than lax discipline. Muzzle-loading muskets and rifles are very difficult to unload short of firing them. Soldiers who loaded their muskets with a "running ball" (one using little or no wadding) might be able to shake the ball lose. A tightly packed ball required a gun worm to dig the ball from the base of the barrel. During the period that Sullivan's men operated in the wilderness, muskets and rifles remained loaded. The cleaning problem as well as the lack of any sophisticated safety device to keep flints from accidentally dropping on charged firing pans made accidental discharges a continuing hazard.

Other minor irritants also detracted from the army's sense of professionalism. Among the officer corps, petty jealousy and perceived slights took their toll on morale. Hand believed that neither Sullivan nor the other brigade commanders appreciated his talents. Hand had proposed while the army camped at Wyalusing that he steal a march on the enemy with his brigade of light infantry and strike the village of Chemung. He argued that he could depart camp under the cover of darkness, cross the Susquehanna, and strike out overland to the objective before the enemy knew he was gone. Most of the army's senior leadership believed that whatever opposition the army was yet to encounter would be directed and supplied from Chemung. Sullivan would not consent to the plan, but neither did he refuse it. Instead, he convened a council of the army's general officers and allowed Hand to present his concept. The council rejected the idea. Hand believed he had not received a fair hearing and that the council's decision simply reflected Sullivan's already known view of the proposal. In his journal he vented his bitterness over the matter: "This was the first time I found that my having command of the advanced corps had given jealousy or that it was possible that men engaged in their country's cause would oppose salutary measures because the honor of a brilliant action could not be immediately attributed to themselves, or to favorites who have perhaps no great desire to leave the beaten path."[89]

There were other problems as well. The advanced guard sent to meet Clinton's army on the way down the Susquehanna to Tioga consumed their eight days' rations in five days, a problem that did not bode well for an army facing a food shortage.[90] On another occasion Sullivan warned his soldiers not to imitate an Indian war cry while in camp, particularly with pickets patrolling the army's perimeter. Yet, viewed from the perspective of the army as a whole, few indicators suggested that Sullivan's army had anything other than minor problems with discipline.

The lack of major discipline problems within Sullivan's army does not prove that Washington had succeeded in inculcating the officer corps with his concept of leadership. The army's performance measured against the stresses of the campaign provides a better measure. Judged by this criterion, the commander-in-chief should have been pleased. Sullivan and his subordinates executed Washington's orders to the letter while overcoming significant difficulties in the process. They led the army forward not through a reliance on fear but, rather, on the development of a sense of unit cohesion and spirit which guided the actions of soldiers in the absence of their officers. This sense of cohesion and spirit was most strikingly present when Sullivan asked the soldiers to agree to accept half-rations for the duration of the campaign or until the commissary could improve the situation. Regimental commanders, at Sullivan's instruction, permitted those who did not feel they could to return to Tioga. This risky offer essentially granted veto power to the enlisted line on the question of continuing the operation. Not only did soldiers agree to stay; they did so by offering "huzzas" to the request.[91] The few soldiers who took Sullivan up on his offer to return to Tioga found themselves the brunt of ridicule from their peers. One Irish soldier in Clinton's brigade, who had earlier served in the British army, noted that he could never remember men cheering a request to accept half-rations.[92]

This enthusiasm continued throughout the campaign. The ceremonies at Fort Reed and Tioga revealed the effort soldiers made to execute drills with the same precision expected of a European regular, despite their ragged, threadbare, and often barefoot look. Yet, when Washington instructed Sullivan to hasten his march back to Easton, the army covered the 156 miles in eight days, an average of nearly 20 miles per day. When the army arrived at Easton on 15 October, inhabitants of the small village no doubt expected the taverns to be filled with soldiers eager to spend their available money on spirits. Lieutenant Erkuries Beatty wrote in his diary that tavern keepers had stocked their establishments "to the gills with liquor," expecting the soldiers to break ranks upon reaching town. With satisfaction Beatty noted that the soldiers marched past the temptations and to their campgrounds. The army no doubt did help innkeepers get rid of their liquor supply but only after orders had been given dismissing soldiers.

By 1779 the Continental army possessed a sense of cohesion and discipline derived from sound leadership. Although not a parade ground army (it would never be one), its men were soldiers in every sense of the word. The officers who led them marked the coming of age with pride. Ensign Daniel Gookin wrote in his journal that "to see with what patience the soldiers endured the fatigues of this march wading rivers, climbing mountains and a number of other things too tedious to mention, afford a pleasing prospect that in time we shall have soldiers equal to any in the world."[93]

Noted nineteenth-century military theorist Carl von Clausewitz referred to what had developed in Sullivan's army by 1779 as "military spirit." The product of sound leadership and a sense of unit cohesion built on shared experience, it was characterized by bravery, adaptability, stamina, and enthusiasm.[94] This attribute most separated the Continental army of the early years from the hardened veterans who laid siege to Cornwallis at Yorktown.

7

Civil-Military Relations

Sullivan's expedition primarily addressed the concerns of settlers in the western counties of Pennsylvania and New York. As a military undertaking, it provided a temporary halt to Britain's strategy of attacking the hinterland of the Middle Colonies but lacked an objective significant enough to affect seriously Britain's war-making capabilities. Designed to satisfy Congressional demands for action and rebuild popular support for the war in the area, Sullivan no doubt expected that state governments as well as the local populace would support his endeavor. He would be disappointed in this, for both states failed in varying degrees to provide the expected supplies and manpower. The failure in Pennsylvania eventually reached such proportions that Washington found it necessary to warn the state's executive council to "fix the problem before we perhaps lose an army."[1]

A Continental army essentially left on its own to conduct the campaign strongly suggests something was amiss between the military and the people and their civil governments. This was partly the army's own doing—the result of decisions made and deferred. Just as important, it also reflected on the government and the American people.

A poorly defined concept of civil-military relations, in which the army was expected to serve both the national government in the form of the Continental Congress and the states, lay at the root of the problem. Ostensibly, the army worked for the former, but its dependence on the latter for supplies and manpower made it loosely answerable to the states as well. Differences of opinion between the two levels of government and the army were to be worked out in a cooperative manner, with republican altruism mitigating when differences appeared irreconcilable. Whatever the intent, Sullivan's expedition revealed a different reality. A weak and inexperienced national government, state governments immobilized by political infighting, personality conflicts, and, at times, an indifferent populace combined to frustrate the efforts of all involved, bringing the undertaking closer to failure than any efforts mounted by the British or their Iroquois allies.

The American colonies found themselves in a unique position in their war against Great Britain. During a time when the aristocracy still dominated the government's of Europe, political authority in the colonies rested in an assembly representing a loose grouping of states, with each state demanding and receiving a considerable measure of sovereignty as the price of cooperation. The military arm responsible for implementing the policy of the state was itself divided, with the Continental army representing the national government, while each state retained its own militia.[2]

The political-military structure reflected popular American fear that powerful central governments invariably became corrupt and oppressive. The best guarantee for the continuation of liberty remained in a political arrangement in which the locus of power rested close to the people. Americans held tightly to this belief throughout the war, risking defeat rather than permit too much power to slip to the national government or the Continental army.

The army worked directly for the Continental Congress and relied on it for policy and administrative support. Had the members of Congress been of one mind, this situation might have yielded more favorable results. In reality the Continental Congress, even after independence, was a body frequently divided into conflicting groups of individuals, the effect of which was to slow the decision-making process. Furthermore, over time the composition of the Congress underwent considerable change.[3] The members who sweat through the debates that culminated with the Declaration of Independence represented the cream of America's political leadership. As the war progressed, however, the quality of the leadership began to decline when many of the original members left Congress to serve in the military or their state governments. Complicating the problem was the fact that the Congress stayed more or less in continuous session beginning in 1776. Delegates found themselves having to weigh the demands of their office with private concerns and family matters. The price Congress paid for all this came in the form of lower efficiency and loss of continuity.[4]

Early in the war differences of opinion existed within Congress over how best to direct the war effort. A few members went so far as to suggest moving the Congress to the major theater of the war to oversee the army's operations.[5] Members with a better understanding of the problems involved realized this concept was not workable and instead settled on the idea of creating a committee drawn from the Congress to administer the army. Created on 12 June 1776, the Board of War became the focal point for the war effort. Congress assigned it responsibility for maintaining an accurate count of officers and men on active duty and an inventory of the army's weapons and ammunition. The Congress also entrusted the board with responsibility for securing transportation for the army's use in moving men and supplies.[6]

The Board of War represented a reasonable solution to the problems inherent in a government trying to run a war without an executive branch. The concept did not work out as planned for a number of reasons. First, the original members, consisting of John Adams, Roger Sherman, Benjamin Harrison, James Wilson, and Edward Rutledge, universally lacked experience in military matters. Had they remained on the committee, this problem would have disappeared. None of them did, however, starting in motion a process of constant change in the committee's membership which hindered the development of institutional memory. The second flaw came in allowing the politicization of the committee. This occurred in November 1777 in an attempt to correct the committee's inexperience by adding a few military officers to the membership. Major General Horatio Gates took over leadership of the board with disastrous results. His involvement with the Conway Cabal undermined the board's standing with Washington. When the committee went beyond its traditional function as administrator for the army and attempted to implement its own military operations, the board became a genuine nuisance. Believing that Canada could be pulled into the American orbit at minimal cost, Gates had the board plan an invasion for the spring of 1778. The effort turned into a fiasco when the board failed to find the necessary soldiers and supplies to make the expedition possible.[7] With its influence clearly on the decline in 1779 due to its performance the preceding year, Sullivan found the board largely irrelevant in assisting with campaign preparations. Sullivan would have to depend on his ability to work with state governments in Pennsylvania and New York to satisfy these needs.

The governors of Pennsylvania and New York stood out among the most experienced war executives in the thirteen colonies, and both men intricately involved themselves with many of the preparatory aspects of the expedition. Reed had been governor of Pennsylvania only since December 1778, serving as a delegate to the Continental Congress since leaving the army in January 1778. He had been one of the brighter stars of the Continental army's officer corps, beginning the war as a lieutenant colonel in the Pennsylvania militia. Four days after Washington accepted command of the army, Reed was assigned to the general's staff, with a promotion to colonel soon to follow. The commander-in-chief eventually appointed him to the position of adjutant general. He served with distinction during the dark days of the Long Island campaign and helped Washington with the army's counterstrikes at Trenton and Princeton, for which he received a promotion to the rank of brigadier general. Reed served Washington diligently while on the general's staff, but the two had experienced some problems. While serving as adjutant general in November 1778, Reed wrote several letters to General Charles Lee critical of Washington's handling of military matters during the New York campaign.[8] Washington inadvertently discovered the correspondence then politely informed Reed that he knew the nature of the sentiments exchanged between Reed and Lee. The incident cooled what had been a close relationship between the two men, and Reed resigned from the army shortly thereafter.

George Clinton had also been no stranger to the smell of gunpowder prior to his election to governor of New York. Clinton had served in the military since the opening days of the war and had known the burden of an independent command. He held both militia and Continental commissions at the rank of brigadier general and had unsuccessfully defended Fort Montgomery and Fort Clinton against the British in 1777. Clinton suffered his share of criticism for the fall of the forts, although no one questioned his courage. Clinton retained his Continental commission throughout the war, ultimately rising to the rank of major general at war's end.

Both Reed and Clinton demonstrated an active interest in the welfare of their states' regiments, often spending weeks at a time visiting soldiers. They shared similar political views and had been forceful advocates of independence and republicanism. The Tory-Indian threat to their frontiers had produced considerable pressure on both men for a solution, and they applauded Washington's decision to detach part of the army to an Indian expedition. In the final accounting Clinton turned in a more forceful performance than did Reed, although neither governor completely met Washington's expectations. Reed certainly experienced more difficulty in working with the army than did Clinton, but personality differences alone do not explain the problem. The different political climates within the states provide a more complete glimpse into what went wrong.

Few of the thirteen colonies possessed a political environment less satisfactory for military operations than Pennsylvania or New York. In addition to a large section of their populations that opposed the war, those supporting independence showed little propensity to put aside differences in working for a common cause. This divisiveness meant that military commanders had to possess considerable finesse and ability in order to bring about the unity of effort so critical in military operations.

Pennsylvania represented the most cosmopolitan English settlement in North America and consisted of a patchwork of largely unassimilated minorities. Pacifist German sects such as the Amish and Mennonites, in addition to the Society of Friends (Quakers), opposed the use of war as a means to settle the differences between the colonies and England. The Quakers' opposition went far beyond simple nonparticipation in the fighting. They enjoined their members from participating in civil government, paying fines or taxes levied in lieu of military service, or engaging in any business pursuit likely to benefit from the war. All of these groups intended to maintain a strict neutrality but found their position under attack from supporters of the war, who saw no clear line between neutrality and loyalism.

Pennsylvania also possessed a sizable population of Loyalists, most of whom resided in the maritime regions along the Delaware River or in the settlements along the western frontier.[9] Until the British occupied Philadelphia in 1777, sympathy for England remained quietly hidden. The presence of a British army and their belief that the occupancy would be permanent brought some Tories out into the open. When Howe evacuated the city in June 1778, many of them found themselves having to leave as well, correctly fearing that many of their old neighbors might not be so tolerant of their now public loyalties.

New York's Loyalist elements easily matched that of Pennsylvania, with half the state's population opposing independence.[10] Land and the control of it politicized New Yorkers, energizing some of the most open support for the British cause to be found anywhere in the colonies.[11] Loyalists enlisted soldiers for the British service, blocked the selection of militia officers, and openly wished damnation on the Continental Congress.[12] Their centers of power eventually coalesced around British-occupied New York City, although strong support existed for George III in the Mohawk Valley and in some of the counties east of the Hudson River.

Despite the sizable numbers of Tories in both states, Sullivan did not find himself markedly delayed by their opposition. Some spied for Henry Clinton, while others fought among the ranks of Butler's Rangers and Johnson's Royal Greens. Washington had anticipated their contributions and accounted for them in his operational plans. Sullivan found the source of his biggest problems to be the political infighting among different factions supporting independence, with the problem most acute in Pennsylvania.

If Massachusetts carried the torch of rebellion boldly forward into the uncertainty of war, Pennsylvania followed along slowly and reluctantly, at times trying in desperation to extinguish the light in the hope of returning to a safer day. Pennsylvania represented one of the last proprietary colonies and had been the scene of considerable infighting among governing elites since Braddock's expedition during the French and Indian War. At the time of the Stamp Act, when other colonies focused almost exclusively on the trouble between themselves and the mother country, Benjamin Franklin, speaking on behalf of the Quaker-dominated provincial assembly, argued in London that the proprietorship ought to be abolished and replaced by a royal colony. Thomas Penn's supporters, drawn mainly from the Presbyterian churches in Philadelphia and enjoying the good graces of the governor's appointments, stood in opposition to the assembly's bid for dominance. Neither group represented the majority of the state's peoples. They held power because none of the numerous ethnic enclaves looked beyond their differences to make common cause with others outside the political structure.

England's deteriorating relationship with her colonies forced changes in the power relations between competing groups and politicized ethnic factions previously left out of the political process. Opposition to Parliament's policies developed along two paths. A conservative coalition made up of Quakers, older Anglicans, Germans from the nonfighting sects, and the commercial interests of Philadelphia favored a measured response to the problem and searched for a compromise solution.[13] These elements controlled the state's executive and legislative branches until 1776 and shaped the colony's response to the developing crisis.

Groups outside the government had little patience for the cautious approach. Deriving their membership from Presbyterians, young Anglicans, Germans, and the mechanical classes of Philadelphia, this group, often referred to by conservatives as "radicals," pushed for stronger countermeasures to British policy and took the lead in pushing the colony to accept independence. The radicals attempted to work their way into power through the normal structures of government but found themselves largely blocked by an experienced Quaker party and conservative proprietary interests. Unable to achieve their goals through the electoral process, the radicals used their control over many of the colony's committees of correspondence as an alternative road to power.

By 1775 the radicals had made some inroads into the provincial assembly. Their numbers proved inadequate to control the assembly but sufficient to paralyze it. Using absenteeism as a means of preventing the assembly from achieving a quorum, they set the stage for their own rise to power.[14] At the urging of John Adams and others in the Second Continental Congress, the radicals successfully pushed for a provincial convention to consider the question of independence. The radicals argued for the necessity of such a gathering on the grounds that the assembly could not be unbiased in a debate over its continued existence, let alone on the question of independence. After all, they argued, had it not been common practice for each session of the assembly to begin its business with a pledge of loyalty to the king?[15] When the conference finally came in June 1776, its first measure provided for a constitutional convention. The radicals had a clear agenda for the convention. Claiming to represent the interests of the poor masses over a rich entrenched elite, the radicals intended to write a constitution that would place power in the hands of the people.[16]

The resulting constitution institutionalized the radical view of government. Power rested squarely in the hands of a state assembly. To insure their control of the assembly, radicals lowered voting requirements and reconfigured representation to insure a more equitable balance between eastern and western counties. The constitution allowed for an executive branch but vested the powers in a council rather than a governor. Named the Supreme Executive Council, with its membership drawn from the assembly, the constitution used the pronoun *they* in subsequent references to symbolize the plural nature of the executive. The council consisted of one representative from each county and the City of Philadelphia, with maximum terms of three years.[17] One-third of the council's membership changed each year to minimize the chances for abusing the office and to maximize the number of people with experience in government. This policy had the unintended effect of institutionalizing a degree of inefficiency caused by the new member's lack of familiarity with the workings of government. With the approval of the assembly, members of the council could elect a president (sometimes referred to as governor) and vice president to be the presiding officers.[18] The constitution limited their powers, however, as decisions required a majority vote by a quorum of five members.

The constitution crafted by the radicals addressed the question of who would rule at home. The conservatives understood its aim and set about trying to insure that the government envisioned within its framework could not function. In 1777 they formed a group known as the Republican Society, whose purpose was to destroy the constitution. In times of peace this might have been acceptable behavior. During war it could have only undesirable effects.

By the time of the Sullivan expedition, Washington and many of his key subordinates believed that Pennsylvania's constitution of 1776 had institutionalized inefficiency in the state's government. Quartermaster William Hooper, a conservative and outspoken opponent of the document, referred to it as "a Beast without a head."[19] The pressures of war magnified the problem. As early as 1777, for example, the threat of a British invasion of Philadelphia created paralysis in the state government. The assembly had adjourned earlier, and the council lacked a quorum to conduct business. Washington feared that large quantities of army supplies stored in the city might be captured and pleaded that they be moved. He could not demand their removal, because the state rather than the Continental army controlled them. The Congress agreed with its commander-in-chief but could find no one in the state with the power to command the move. Facing imminent disaster, the Congress exceeded its authority, nearly ordering the council president and available members of the assembly in the city to take the required steps to move the supplies. Hoping to avoid angering Pennsylvanians for the appearance of heavy-handed direction, Congress asked that they cheerfully submit "to the exertion of an authority which is indispensably essential" for the good of the cause.[20] This near disaster should have been a catalyst for change, but, despite the clear inadequacies of the system, radicals had no intention of reforming the document and conservatives no willingness to set aside their attempts to subvert it. As a result, Sullivan found soon after assuming command of the expedition that he was dealing with a state government stricken by inertia.

In addition to the constitution, the radicals had fashioned the state's militia system to suit their needs. Although in many respects no worse than systems in other states, Pennsylvania's militia provided only peripheral assistance to Sullivan. During the colonial period Pennsylvania, like most colonies, had relied on British regulars for its defense needs. When provincial troops had been necessary, they usually consisted of volunteers enlisted to duty for a specified period. The militia units could provide some military training to civilians and often functioned as pools of able-bodied men from which to draw volunteer units. For the most part, however, by the late colonial period state militias lacked the small-unit training necessary for the demands of linear warfare.[21] With no militia laws on its books at the beginning of the war, Pennsylvania's militia system existed only in name.[22] A voluntary force of citizen-soldiers known as the "Associators" attempted to meet the state's requirements for internal defense.[23] The war brought widespread desertions among these volunteers and pointed up the need for a militia law, which the assembly passed in 1776. The law divided the state into districts, each of them responsible for providing a battalion of six hundred and forty men.[24] The assembly appointed county militia lieutenants to command the district battalions raised within the county and divided the militia into classes in order to spread the sacrifices associated with military duty equally across the militia-age male population.²⁵ To limit the hardships active service placed on families, the law specified that no units be kept involuntarily on duty longer than two months. In addition, it permitted a militia member to avoid service if he provided a suitable substitute.²⁶ Soldiers elected their own field and line officers, a practice not uncommon in other states at the start of the war.²⁷ Not surprisingly, the state's new law produced a militia preoccupied with local concerns rather than the welfare of the state.

Radicals controlling Pennsylvania's government and the militia enjoyed a reciprocal relationship. The Executive Council's power to appoint county lieutenants and sublieutenants gave the radicals influence over the militia and created a group of senior militia officers beholden to the radicals. Militia units, particularly those in the western regions of the state, proved to be among the radicals' most loyal supporters. To maintain this loyalty the radicals had to tread lightly on how and where the militia served as well as how frequently they performed duty.

The weakness of the militia system represented only part of the problem Sullivan eventually faced. Also complicating matters in Pennsylvania was a growing sense of frustration between the state government and the army. Pennsylvanians consistently believed that they provided a disproportionate amount of support to the Continental army and suspected they had been victims of unscrupulous commissary and quartermaster agents more than once. Hooper, the officer Greene assigned to build the critically important Easton depot, particularly angered the Executive Council. Hooper's political loyalties rested with the conservatives, and the state's radicals took his presence at Easton as a deliberate insult. In 1777 Hooper had refused to take Pennsylvania's loyalty oath, arguing that he worked for the Continental army, rather than the state. His stand against the oath led to problems with state officials, who eventually brought the matter before the Board of War. Thomas Mifflin, the army's quartermaster general, dismissed the charges against his subordinate as groundless and blamed the radicals controlling Pennsylvania's government for stirring up the trouble in the first place.²⁸ Hooper escaped dismissal but not the continuing ire of radicals, who pressed for his removal even as he began working to build a base of supplies for Sullivan's army at Easton.

Problems between council and the army extended beyond the quartermaster corps. During the winter of 1778–79 matters came to a head between the council and Benedict Arnold. Being the epitome of everything the council found reprehensible and dangerous in an army officer, Arnold impressed many observers as a haughty, self-important, and aristocratic individual. They believed he and men like him had designs on perpetuating themselves in power as a military elite after the war.[29] His circle of friends in Philadelphia included several Tory sympathizers, among them Peggy Shippen, the woman he eventually married. The public conflict between the council and Arnold had opened in the spring 1779. Speaking for the council, Reed accused Arnold of abusing his powers by using publicly hired wagons to move private cargo in which Arnold had an interest from a ship docked in New Jersey to Philadelphia. Reed demanded that Arnold be relieved of command pending an investigation. The council president intended that its officers would conduct the investigation. Instead, the Continental Congress appointed a special committee to investigate the charges for decision in a court-martial. This angered Reed, because it suggested that the Continental Congress represented a higher power within the borders of Pennsylvania than the council itself.[30] Fearing that the investigation might exonerate Arnold, Reed undertook to influence the findings. On 24 April he wrote to Washington to warn of the possible impact of a not-guilty verdict:

> Such is the dependence of the army upon the transportation of this state that should the court [martial] treat it as a light and trivial matter, we fear it will not be practicable to draw forth wagons in the future, be the emergency what it may, and it will have bad consequences.[31]

The radicals pressed their case against Arnold to the point of straining relations with Congress and the army. Congress ordered Washington to try Arnold on the charges, but the court-martial found him guilty of violating only one of the Articles of War. As to the use of public wagons for private purposes, the court termed it an indiscretion that did not violate the articles but should not be repeated.[32]

With the coming of spring in 1779, the Hooper and Arnold situations had created a strained relationship between the Executive Council and the army. Governor Reed and other radicals had become convinced that the army's officers might abuse their power. With the beginning of a new campaign season at hand and the focus of the new operations soon to shift westward to deal with the Indian threat, cooperation should have been the norm. The strained relations existing between the army and the state's government as well as the existence of a conservative opposition bent on destroying the state's new constitution made cooperation nearly impossible. Fortunately for Sullivan, this proved not to be the case in New York.

On the eve of the revolution New York possessed even less cohesion than that of Pennsylvania. In the years before the war the colony had been the scene of considerable disagreement among different social and economic groups which frequently turned into riots. By 1779, however, New York's state government demonstrated much greater ability to handle the demands of war than did Pennsylvania. The presence within the state of the largest British army on the North American continent provided the catalyst that produced a working government.[33] The threat forced cooperation among competing political factions, the critical element missing in Pennsylvania.

New York's political atmosphere loosely broke down into conservatives and radicals, with the former group consisting largely of wealthy merchants and a landed gentry. The latter drew its supporters from small traders, mechanics, and small farmers. Unlike in Pennsylvania, however, the conservatives did not attempt to block the move toward independence. They worked instead to control the momentum toward separation in order to maintain their political, economic, and social status after independence and intended to do so by controlling the provincial assembly, thereby denying radicals the means of changing the internal political structure.

Locked out of the government, the radicals turned to the revolutionary committees produced by the deteriorating situation between England and the colonies.[34] Their efforts eventually bore fruit as the committees managed to dominate the political landscape in many sections of New York. The old provincial government collapsed when the war came, and Howe's army drove Washington from New York City, leaving a void the committees filled. However successful the committee system proved to be in controlling local matters, it could not coordinate the needs of a state under siege.

At the end of 1776 New Yorkers found their southern counties and largest city under British control, a civil war raging on the frontier in Tryon

County, and the potential for further conflict in the eastern counties along the Hudson River, where anti-landlord sentiment had produced an unstable situation. Adding to this chaotic picture, small farmers in two counties east of Lake Champlain had declared their independence from New York and set to work forming an independent state they called Vermont.

Facing potential disaster, conservatives and radicals set their differences aside to write a new constitution. Their efforts provided the model for the men who wrote the federal Constitution in 1787. The new constitution divided power between a senate and an assembly, stipulating that elections for the assembly and one-third of the senate be held each year.[35] It apportioned representation by counties and broadened the electorate by easing voting requirements. Most important for the war effort, it gave the state a strong independent governor elected by the people rather than the legislature.[36]

George Clinton won the state's first election for governor. His victory married an experienced energetic leader with an office that granted freedom to act boldly. Clinton's public papers reveal that he understood both the state's security problems and the military assets under his control. Furthermore, he recognized the concept of unity of command better than many other wartime governors. When Washington informed him that he intended to launch an expedition against the Iroquois, Clinton stood ready to help. That his brother James would be second in command and a successful campaign might help extinguish Indian claims to the western areas of the state probably influenced his cooperation.

In addition to the factors already mentioned, it also must be conceded that Washington expected more of Pennsylvania than of New York. After all, the Wyoming Valley served as the operation's primary base of support. One reason for this was the belief that Pennsylvania could better provide the grain necessary to feed the army. In New York the preceding year's raids had taken a toll on grain production, even as demand for the commodity increased. Governor Clinton found himself under pressure to sell grain to nearby states such as Massachusetts and Rhode Island to meet shortages there.[37] He could barely meet the needs of his own state and the military forces stationed on its soil, let alone fulfill additional requirements.

The final factor working in New York's favor was the existence of a partial stockpile of food and other war materials gathered but not used for the ill-fated invasion of Canada, originally scheduled for 1778. Greene's officers found themselves able to put it to use feeding James Clinton's brigade.

In the spring of 1779 none of the Continental army's key leaders seemed to realize that neither state offered an acceptable starting point for the operation. With a strong governor, functional constitution, and, above all, a spirit of cooperation borne of necessity and opportunity, New York offered the right operational climate, but its shortage of grain largely negated the advantages. Pennsylvania possessed an abundance of grain, but the climate of paranoia, suspicion, and sometimes outright government hostility made it almost equally unacceptable. Neither Sullivan nor Washington appears to have understood the difficulties lurking in Pennsylvania.

The issue of how best to defend the frontier brought the controversy into the open. Congress created the Continental army to nationalize the war and because many high-ranking officers, Washington among them, believed that state militias could not stand up to British regiments in the field. Nathanael Greene disparagingly termed militiamen "people coming from home with all the tender feelings of domestic life" and "not sufficiently fortified with natural courage to stand the shocking scenes of war." "To march over dead men, to hear without concern the groans of the wounded," added Greene, "I say few men can stand such scenes unless steeled by habit or fortified by military pride."[38] Inability to master the intricacies of linear tactics did not mean, however, that the militias lacked purpose. Don Higginbotham noted that militias were to "enforce the 1774 Continental Association of Congress on non-importation, to compel people to take sides, to put down loyalist uprisings, to seize militia stores from royal governors, and to keep the slave population under control."[39] Soon after war broke out, defending the frontiers from Indian attacks also became one of their responsibilities.

The Tory and Indian raiding parties operating along the Pennsylvania and New York frontiers in 1778 did not arrive unexpectedly. Militia officers such as Pennsylvania's James Potter warned as early as 17 May 1778 that "the Indians are determined to clear the two Branches of the Susquehanna this moon."[40] Lacking the men necessary to defend the frontier, he feared for the results unless the state government offered assistance.[41]

In early summer 1778 both Clinton and Governor Thomas Wharton of

Pennsylvania intended to defend their frontiers with militias supplemented by a few regiments of Continental regulars. This plan broke down beneath the onslaught of Tory and Indian raiding parties that successfully depopulated the region in the summer and fall of 1778. Both men found themselves continually under pressure to do more to assist their western settlements. Petitions from besieged settlers as well as pleas for assistance from county militia lieutenants found their way to Kingston and Philadelphia.

In New York the raids intensified efforts to keep more militia on duty guarding the remnants of what had been a prosperous agricultural area. Wharton also adopted this approach but found his militia unready to meet the challenge. In Pennsylvania's badly stricken Northumberland County, Samuel Hunter, the county militia lieutenant, complained that half his men lacked weapons and the rest suffered for want of adequate powder and flints.[42] He also found food scarce and expensive, making it difficult to keep troops in the field for any extended time. To retain a militia presence on the frontier he ordered the people of the affected areas to catch and barrel fish for the use of militia units he hoped to station in the area. He suffered no illusions that this would be sufficient to meet long-term needs.[43]

With the raids on Wyoming and Cherry Valley it was soon apparent that the attempt at creating a working perimeter defense had failed. Clinton understood the problem. The sheer size of the area to be defended dwarfed the military capabilities of his militia. Writing to President John Jay of the Continental Congress, Clinton summarized his problems:

> Fatal Experience has more than sufficiently taught us the Impracticability of defending our extensive Frontiers by the Militia of the County and the small Proposition of regular Troops employed in that service against an Enemy acting upon a desultory Plan. There are so many Passes leading into the Different important Settlements to the Northward and Westward which equally claim attention, that when the present Force is distributed for their Defence it becomes too weak to resist the united strength of the Enemy employed against any particular Point.[44]

Only some other solution would secure the backcountry. Destroying their villages and fields had been the solution to fighting Indians since the first days of English settlement in North America. Militia officers in Pennsylvania suggested this early in the campaigning season. Hartley's small expedition against Tioga represented the response they favored; however, the undertaking only nibbled at the edges of the Iroquois lands. In New York Clinton also came to see offensive operations against the Indian settlements as the only long-term solution to the problem.[45] In a letter to Washington he suggested that conditions necessitated a major Indian expedition and promised to render every assistance to the commander-in-chief.[46] Clinton had in mind a large-scale operation consisting of both militia and Continentals. If the military situation in the East made this impossible, he was willing to accept smaller punitive raids such as Hartley had conducted along the Susquehanna to buy time.[47] He suggested and Washington approved one such punitive raid against the Iroquois village of Anaquaga on the Susquehanna, but such operations could not change the direction of the frontier war.

Washington made his decision in February 1779 to undertake an Indian campaign as the centerpiece of the army's activities in the early summer. For security he kept the decision secret among a small group of officers inside the army. Unaware that their wishes for a campaign would soon be granted, both governors looked upon the coming of spring with trepidation. In a letter to his state's delegates in the Continental Congress, Clinton warned that the people of western New York spoke of leaving their homes for relatives and friends to the east unless the Continental Congress took measures to insure their safety. He believed that calling out additional militia was a largely useless exercise and wanted to know if Congress meant to divert more of the Continental army to frontier defense or perhaps to "offensive measures against the savages."[48] If the Congress and army committed themselves to dealing with the problem, he promised his best effort to persuade the people to stay on their farms.[49] In truth he badly wanted them to remain. As early as January 1779, he understood that the preceding year's raids had created a grain shortage. In the short run prudent control over grain supplies might prevent the situation from growing worse. In the long run keeping the western farms in production offered the best solution. This could not be accomplished if further raids turned the remaining settlements into blackened ruins or if defending the frontier kept farmers on militia duty during the spring and summer. Pennsylvania suffered the same problem. The state's militia companies had spent considerable time patrolling the stricken areas during the preceding summer and fall. The approaching planting season seemed to promise more of the same, and this Reed hoped to avoid.

As the campaign took shape, Washington explained to both governors that the strategic situation facing the army at the beginning of the campaign season offered little solace. The dedication of nearly six thousand Continental regulars to a western Indian expedition far from the primary theater of the war demonstrated Washington's willingness to accept considerable risk. His forces guarding the strategically critical Hudson Valley might not be sufficient to secure West Point if Henry Clinton chose to press an attack from New York City. To compensate for the loss of Sullivan and his army, Washington ordered his subordinates in the Hudson Valley to establish a system of beacon signals on the high ground bordering the river to alert local militia forces and those in nearby Connecticut of a British attack.[50] Washington's efforts amounted to an economy of force operation in defense of the Hudson Valley. He believed that forces in the Hudson Highlands could hold the British until militia reinforcements arrived to tip the balance of power.[51] Patriot fortifications at West Point served as the primary defense. By 1779 they included a series of interlocking artillery positions and a massive iron chain that blocked navigation upriver. A series of landward defenses defended the chain and its batteries against ground attack. Washington understood that, once Sullivan's army disappeared into the mountains beyond Easton, he would not be able to count on them for assistance.

Washington also worried that Sullivan's army and Brodhead's small independent detachment on the Allegheny might not prove large enough to accomplish the mission should the British and their Indian allies marshal their forces against them. Particularly concerned that Sullivan might have to dedicate too many men to the task of maintaining his supply lines along the river, the commander-in-chief turned to Clinton and Reed for help.

Washington counted on the two governors for militia to supplement Sullivan's army. The commander-in-chief told Reed that he expected Sullivan to work closely with the militia officers in his area of operations but noted that help would be necessary to make the expedition a success. He asked Reed to provide six hundred militiamen, including four or five companies of rangers.[52] The men were to report for duty at Sunbury by 10 May and be on active duty for three months.[53]

Washington's request received a cool reception in Philadelphia. The arrival of spring had brought only additional misery to the frontiers. The raids resumed with no indication that Butler's or Hartley's efforts during the preceding year had any noticeable effect. Writing to Reed from Fort Augusta, Hunter emphasized the deplorable conditions in his county:

It is impossible to prevail on the inhabitants to make a stand, upon account of their Women and Children. . . . Our case is really deplorable and alarming, as we are surrounded by a cruel savage Enemy at this Present time, and Our Country on the Eve of Breaking up, as I am informed at the time I am writing this, by two or three Expresses that there is nothing to be seen but Disolation [sic], fire and smoke, as the inhabitants is collecting at particular places, the Enemy burns all their Houses they have evacuated.[54]

Reed had begun to raise five companies of rangers the preceding month. He hoped to enlist three of the companies from Hunter's badly devastated Northumberland County. Though the companies would serve the standard two-month period, Reed hoped to form a company of volunteers willing to serve for nine months from these companies.[55] If these units could be raised, their knowledge of the terrain and an obvious motivation to rid themselves of the continuing threat to their way of life would render them a valuable addition to the army. The Executive Council offered the possibility of a scalp bounty to spur enlistments. "We have it under consideration to offer a Reward for Indian scalps, but it involves in it some Considerations of a Political Nature affecting the general system of War with Great Britain," Reed wrote to Hunter. "However, if it will answer a Beneficient or Effectual purpose to you we shall not hesitate to do it."[56] Reed anticipated the need for rangers, but Washington's request for several hundred regular militia came as a surprise and sparked the first real controversy of the campaign between a state government and the army.

Reed wished to use as few militia units as possible during the summer. He understood the problems facing his frontier settlements but feared that any appreciable dependence on militia threatened the state's economy by keeping farmers from planting and tending their crops. Reed led Washington to believe that he would raise the soldiers requested and deliver them on time to the Continental army. Rather than have the state furnish soldiers to the Continental army, Reed hoped to provide the ranger companies and leave responsibility for the rest of the campaign to the army. Ideally, the governor desired to persuade Washington's subordinates to detail detachments of regulars to occupy several of the frontier posts normally garrisoned by militia. Reed's attempt to divert Continental soldiers to the backcountry began in March, when he informed Hunter, "A very Respectable force which has been stationed for some time at Scohary in the State of New York under Genl Hand is ordered to the frontiers of Northhampton [sic] and Northumberland and Will as far as any Stationary forces can do afford ample protection to those Counties."[57] Later he suggested that Hunter request assistance from Hand rather than ask the state to garrison the blockhouse at Muncy.[58] Washington had informed Reed on 27 February that he intended to conduct an Indian expedition during the summer; therefore, the governor undoubtedly understood Hand's mission and the importance of building the depot at Wyoming.[59] With only a regiment of soldiers at his disposal, Hand politely but firmly rejected the suggestion, noting that his orders directed him to focus on an objective "north of Wyoming." He regretted that this precluded his paying "much attention to Sunbury or the contiguous settlements."[60] The problem of frontier defense, Hand insisted, fell to Hunter's militia.

Reed refused to accept this answer. He asserted that he had been led (presumably by Washington, as the two men had met the previous week) to believe that Hand's mission included providing security for Sunbury and its environs. As a result, he had told the settlers of the Susquehanna Valley to stay on their land. He now regretted this decision, because he had sent the county's militia to Westmoreland County and left the valley at the mercy of the enemy.[61] Though his county lieutenants had begun raising additional companies, these were to be Sullivan's rangers and therefore not available for frontier defense.

Whether Washington actually promised the governor Continental regulars is unclear. The general's fixation on getting the expedition under way at the earliest possible time and his concern that manpower shortages among wagoners and boatmen might force Sullivan to divert soldiers to noncombat roles makes it unlikely. Any diversion of Hand's soldiers from transporting and stockpiling supplies could only increase the time necessary to prepare the depot and might render the site vulnerable to attack. The most likely cause for the misunderstanding is that Washington failed to explain the limits of Hand's mission. Reed probably assumed that Hand's security requirements for the depot extended to the frontier posts. Hand eventually did provide soldiers to Fort Augusta and Fort Jenkins, as both posts were along Sullivan's line of supply and could not be ignored. For a limited time, as more soldiers became available, Hand even permitted Hubley's men to garrison the blockhouse at Muncy. Regardless of how the misunderstanding occurred, Hand remained steadfast in his determination to avoid a permanent diversion of troops to the task of perimeter security.

Still wanting the army to assume as much of the burden as possible for the state's defense, Reed next attempted to change Washington's plans for the nonranger militia. Noting that he had mustered two hundred and fifty militia from the inner counties to protect the frontiers, Reed suggested that Washington use Brodhead's soldiers at Fort Pitt for this purpose while the new militia supported Sullivan.[62] The idea had merit. Brodhead's soldiers already patrolled the area, while the new militia companies faced several hundred miles of marching to reach the western counties. The suggestion, if accepted, would restrict the scope of the operation and ease the Tory-Indian problem of defending the homelands, but it would permit Reed to limit the militia call-up. As for the militia requested for Sullivan, Reed first informed the commander-in-chief that Pennsylvania's militia laws limited each soldier's period of active duty to two months at a time. Washington's wishes required calling out several classes of militia at staggered times to cover the period of the campaign. This complicated matters because units coming on duty would most likely be far removed from the action and out of touch with the tactical situation. Organizing and supplying their movement upriver also appeared difficult. In addition, Reed claimed that many of his militiamen lacked firearms because Continental army officers had confiscated their muskets to make up shortages in 1776 and 1777. Given these problems, the governor believed it impossible for the units to be ready by the requested date of 10 May; moreover, he questioned their value to Sullivan if available at a later date.[63] In an attempt to have the request for men reconsidered, he reminded Washington that calling additional units would put a strain on the people by making it difficult for the men to plant and tend their fields.[64] Reed went on to explain why the state should not attempt to meet Washington's request, accusing the general of favoring the interests of other states over Pennsylvania and arguing that the state should look after itself first.[65]

A series of charges and countercharges between the two men followed. Reed's accusation clearly bothered Washington, who responded that he favored no state over another. The Continental army's presence in his home state of Virginia, for example, fell short of that in Pennsylvania. On the issue of Hand's refusal to assist in frontier defense, Washington explained that he lacked the personnel to permit the diversion of regulars solely to this purpose. Hand's mission of building the depot at Wyoming simply held a higher priority. Pressing his views on this as well as Pennsylvania's sluggish response in raising militia units, Washington bluntly told Reed, "If the abilities and resources of the states cannot furnish a more competent force, assailable as we are on all sides, they will surely be more just than to expect from the army protection at every point."[66] He indirectly called into question the arms shortage in Pennsylvania's militias and explained that his own arsenals could not permit refit of Pennsylvania's militia. He understood and regretted the hardship militia calls caused farmers, but he had applied to Pennsylvania for six hundred men and now found himself locked in a contest over whether this constituted an unreasonable request. He explained to Reed that the governors of New York and New Jersey had received similar requests. In New York Clinton responded by authorizing a call for one thousand soldiers to meet various requirements generated by the campaign.[67] The comparison in the initial response between the two states reflected unfavorably on Pennsylvania.

Reed did not back down. He admitted pressures that made it difficult to "draw the eyes of the people from their own immediate danger to distant and general objects" and reminded his former boss that Pennsylvania had provided twelve regiments of infantry, a regiment of horse, the invalid corps, half the German battalion, and other support to the war effort. He went on to argue that Pennsylvania had contributed a greater number of soldiers to the Continental army than any other state.[68] Finally, with Pennsylvania's frontiers smoldering from the resumption of the Tory-Indian raids, he wanted to know why Washington chose to employ Pennsylvania's Continental regiments in New York and Virginia.[69]

Resolution of the conflict between the two men required Pennsylvania to continue its efforts to raise the militia with an understanding that, if ready in time, it would join the army as planned. Otherwise, Washington wanted them to secure Sullivan's line of supply on the Susquehanna or be assigned to serve on the frontier as circumstances dictated. As for the ranger companies, Reed agreed to provide them to Sullivan once they came up to strength.[70] With June rapidly approaching, this agreement should have cleared the way for better cooperation between the state of Pennsylvania and the army. Washington's and Reed's failure to include Sullivan in the agreement, however, soon generated new problems.

The relationship between Sullivan and Reed never had been good, and the governor clearly resented Washington's choice of the former New Hampshire lawyer to command the expedition. For his part Sullivan tended to be dogmatic and demonstrated little concern for the kinds of problems facing the states. Disagreement broke out between the two men soon after Sullivan arrived at Easton. Upon finding that Reed intended to send a sizable contingent of militia to the backcountry instead of fulfilling the commitment made to the expedition, Sullivan took the issue to Washington and the Board of War. Reed countered that Sullivan did not understand the disposition of Pennsylvania's militia; a change in their destination would anger the people of the state.[71] Sullivan, he reasoned, had confused these militia units with the five companies of rangers still being raised by county lieutenants. He reassured the board that, if Sullivan were patient, he could expect to receive the rangers once they were up to strength.

As May ended and material accumulated at Esthertown, Sullivan's quartermasters found themselves without sufficient soldiers to secure the supplies during their journey upriver. Sullivan reminded Reed that the ranger companies promised by the state originally had been committed to this task. If these units could not perform the mission, the general wanted to know if militia companies from Sunbury could fill in.[72] Reed responded by blaming the Continental army's quartermasters for the state's failure to deliver on its assurances. In an effort to recruit boatmen, Greene's quartermasters had searched the villages and hamlets of the lower Susquehanna. The army offered good pay for the job—$120 a month as well as one and a half rations a day and a suit of clothes.[73] Pennsylvania simply lacked the capacity to match this generous offer and thus raised few volunteer militia. In Sunbury, Hunter's efforts to enlist the promised ranger companies appeared to support Reed's contentions. In early June Hunter reported his ranger companies at only half-strength and not ready to move. When Reed instructed his lieutenant to use whatever resources he had to support Sullivan, Hunter responded that he had nothing to offer because of the requirements border defense placed on his militia. His men garrisoned both Fort Muncy and Fort Jenkins, leaving no one to spare for Sullivan.[74] In the end Hubley's regulars secured the line of supply from Sunbury to Wyoming and provided much of the muscle for moving supplies. As for security, in the interest of speed and against Hand's advice, Sullivan accepted Reed's opinion that the trip upriver from Esthertown to Sunbury required little vigilance.[75]

Washington intended that Sullivan attack the Iroquois homelands in June. By late May this appeared doubtful. Frustrated by the failure of his quartermaster and commissary officers, Sullivan also believed he lacked sufficient manpower to accomplish his mission. Reed had ordered his lieutenants to begin enrolling additional militia in March, but their efforts had largely failed. Few Pennsylvanians showed interest in volunteering, with the result that Sullivan still had not seen his first militia company march into camp by June. In fairness to Reed, the situation on his frontiers had worsened. In Westmoreland and Northumberland Counties frontier families increasingly abandoned their homes and congregated for protection around the stockades and larger forts in their areas. Most wanted to remain on their lands to plant and tend the crops. They expected protection but hoped to avoid having to provide it themselves in the form of militia companies. Continental regulars would be ideal for the mission. If this proved impractical, they saw militia from less-threatened areas of the state as an acceptable alternative. Eastern militiamen seldom shared this expanded concept of their responsibilities and resented attempts to station them beyond the bounds of their own county. Reed's efforts to strengthen the frontier regions by moving militia from less-threatened counties proceeded slowly or, in one case, not at all.

In Cumberland County, Lieutenant Colonel Alexander Brown, commanding the Fifth Battalion of Pennsylvania militia, received Reed's order to march his men westward to help defend Bedford and Westmoreland Counties. Brown refused, claiming that the inhabitants of Cumberland County needed their men for home defense. Reed responded to the insubordination with an exceptionally mild rebuke. Admitting that he understood why Brown had disobeyed, the governor explained that he had not issued the order without careful thought and added that the decision had been made in "concert" with Washington's desires. "It is much to be wished that a proper Confidence should always subsist between those who are to execute [orders] because in some Cases it being improper to disclose military Designs, they must fail of want of secrecy," Reed explained. "We would not send you to duty outside the county," he continued, "without the best of reasons and we would hope that you would understand and obey when such conditions arise."[76] In frustration Reed found himself explaining the obvious—that military officers ought to obey orders.[77]

Pennsylvania's militia commanders saw themselves first as defenders of their counties. The state's concerns were often secondary considerations. The reliance Pennsylvania's radicals had placed on the militia as a base of support rendered it difficult if not impossible for the state government to pressure militia commanders without paying a political price for the effort.

Most militia soldiers sought to avoid duty entirely. Even in areas victimized by raids, settlers who bravely remained on their land did so with the intention of working as farmers, not soldiers. Late in the summer the settlers of Penns Valley, Pennsylvania, an area badly hit by raids, petitioned the Executive Council for exemption from militia duty, citing troubles harvesting their crops. Militia service, they argued, did not pay enough to permit them to settle their debts.[78] The valley's settlers desired a military presence while they went about their chores but intended for someone else to provide it. The council denied the request and criticized the petition as "highly improper" and dangerous to "the Peace and comfort of their own Families."[79] From the level of the individual to that of the state, provincialism dominated all other concerns regarding the use of militia. Without a strong national government to force a broadening of the perspective, it should not have surprised Washington that Sullivan received little support from Reed or his subordinates.

July found Sullivan still without any significant militia augmentation and long out of patience with Pennsylvania.[80] Washington shared his subordinate's frustration. In an angry letter to Pennsylvania's Executive Council he stated that intelligence suggested that a large body of soldiers had reinforced Sullivan's enemies. He found himself unable to assist Sullivan because he had "stretched this string [the Continental army] as hard as it could possibly bear."[81] Without the promised militia, insisted Washington,

Sullivan had no choice but to employ his own men to guard the army's line of supply. If the British reinforced their Indian allies, Sullivan must face the possibility of defeat in detail. In a last attempt to spur the council to act, Washington implored the members to "fix the problem before we perhaps lose an army."[82]

Reed reassured Washington that he intended to deliver the promised ranger companies when his lieutenants had filled their ranks, but he suggested that it "is the universal Opinion [presumably of the council] that the Number of Men under General Sullivan is greater than can be fed when he proceeds a little farther on the Expedition."[83] Given the state of Sullivan's logistics in July, Reed was probably correct, but the contention neatly avoided Pennsylvania's role in creating the supply crisis. Reed repeated an earlier complaint that the enlistment of companies of boatmen had robbed the ranger's recruitment officers of their best source of soldiers.[84] The governor may have been setting the groundwork to excuse the failure of even the ranger companies to join Sullivan. Although the three companies Hunter reported at half-strength in May had not yet joined the army, the Executive Council granted a commission to Frederick Antes in July to recruit another ranger company in the same county.[85] Why provide money for the creation of another ranger company if the earlier companies remained understrength or if the formation of these units had depleted the area's pool of military-age men? It seems likely that the companies Hunter had raised already were employed on frontier duty and that he required additional units to supplement or replace them. The time necessary to raise a company renders it unlikely that the council intended Antes's company as a supplement for Sullivan.

Reed also resented Sullivan's tendency to complain directly to Washington rather than to the council when the state failed to meet its commitments. He wanted the practice stopped.[86] Now openly critical, Sullivan believed the council and its subordinates either incompetent or bent on deliberately sabotaging his efforts. Washington served as the logical point of appeal and no doubt enjoyed, despite earlier differences, a better working relationship with Reed than did Sullivan. Sullivan caught wind of Reed's contention that the manpower drain produced by recruiting boatmen had made militia recruitment nearly impossible, responding that he employed less than a hundred boatmen and only forty-two packhorsemen.[87] He did not think these numbers excessive and refused to believe they could have prevented recruitment of the ranger companies. Also taking issue with the idea that his army had grown too large, Sullivan claimed it consisted of only 2,312 rank and file, excluding Clinton or Brodhead's detachments. By the time he met all his requirements for boatmen, cattle drivers, and garrison soldiers, he estimated that he would have only 938 soldiers available for combat.[88] Washington later disputed these numbers, which do not mirror the returns available for the regiments that participated in the campaign.

There has been considerable disagreement about the number of soldiers present on Sullivan's expedition. Brodhead's men, though involved with the campaign, have never been counted among Sullivan's numbers. Albert Hazen Wright, after considerable research into the rosters as well as the journals of the expedition's participants, sets the number at approximately 6,000. Wright credits Sullivan with 3,500 men and Clinton with 2,107, excluding women, children, boatmen, wagoners, and packhorsemen.[89] This means Sullivan either lacked an accurate count of his army or deliberately undercounted his force to spur Reed into meeting his promises for militia support. Even if Sullivan had more soldiers available than he admitted, however, service and support requirements had taken a toll on his fighting strength.

As July ended, Sullivan appeared reconciled to the fact that he would receive no further support from Pennsylvania's governor. Reed seemed to understand that, while Sullivan operated upriver, the militia must look after the frontiers. The participation of Brodhead's soldiers at Fort Pitt promised to strip the frontiers of their last Continental army units. With luck the Iroquois would be too busy with Sullivan to mount new attacks—a hope that proved false. Facing their own problems with food shortages and realizing they lacked the power to confront Sullivan directly, Butler and Brant settled on a tactic of diversion as their best hope.

The strikes against settlements at Minisink and Fort Freeland provide the most notable examples of this strategy. Brant attacked Minisink on 20 July 1779 along with sixty Indians and twenty-seven Tory rangers. Failing to arrive in time for a dawn attack, the Mohawk chief reluctantly undertook to raid the settlement at noon. The endeavor achieved less than Brant had anticipated, and the following morning he began his withdrawal from the area with little to show for his efforts. One hundred and twenty militiamen from Goshen under the command of Colonel John Hathorn gave chase, finally catching Brant's men twenty-seven miles north of Minisink in the midst of fording the river. After a brief exchange the two sides took cover and kept up a sustained fire for nearly four hours before Brant managed to turn Hathorn's flank and rear.[90] In the melee that followed, Brant's warriors scalped forty of Hathorn's men, granting no quarter to the wounded.[91]

Along the Susquehanna Captain John MacDonald, a British regular temporarily assigned to Butler, commanding fifty rangers, a small detachment of British regulars, and about one hundred and twenty Seneca warriors led by Cornplanter, assaulted Fort Freeland on 28 July.[92] Warned in advance of MacDonald's approach, the garrison of thirty-three soldiers along with fifty women and children put up a determined resistance. During a lull in the fighting, MacDonald called a truce and offered the garrison the chance to surrender under terms. Inside the smoke-filled blockhouse, fear for the safety of the women and children and concern that help would not arrive before the powder gave out produced a favorable response. Acting as the garrison's commander, John Little agreed to surrender the fort, with the understanding that the men would be marched to Fort Niagara as prisoners of war and the women and children permitted safe passage back to Fort Augusta.[93] Unknown to Little, Captain Hawkins Boone had gathered a relief party of seventy to eighty men and marched to the sound of the guns. MacDonald later admitted to John Butler that Boone's small party nearly surprised him. "We had no intimation of their approach 'till they were very close upon us. The Scouts of Indians that were sent out having fell in with some Horses, which they pursued, neglecting the charge they were trusted with—The Indians upon the first appearance of the Rebels retired a little but soon recovered their surprise and came in upon their left Flank with great Fury while the Detachment of the 8th Regt. & Rangers attacked them in front, and put them immediately to the Route."[94] Boone, along with more than thirty of his men, died in the fighting, while the remainder of his detachment fled toward Fort Augusta.[95]

MacDonald attempted to convince Cornplanter of the need to press their advantage. Fort Augusta lay less than twenty miles downriver and offered an inviting prize situated along Sullivan's line of supply. "I did every thing in my power to prevail upon the Indians to pursue their success, but they were too glutted with Plunder, Prisoners, & Scalps, that my utmost efforts could not persuade them from Retreating," lamented the British captain.[96] Elements of his raiding party got to within eight miles of Fort Augusta and found the area deserted. After destroying five blockhouse forts and torching a thirty-mile strip of what MacDonald described as a "close and settled country," he ordered his men to withdraw from the valley, believing he had passed up a rare opportunity to strike a more significant blow against Sullivan.[97]

Brant's raid on Minisink concerned Sullivan little. MacDonald's attack at Freeland produced more of a stir, though not with Sullivan. The loss of the blockhouse as well as the successful defeat of the relief party renewed a sense of panic on the west branch of the Susquehanna similar to that of the previous year. Remaining settlers departed the area immediately. William Maclay, a Sunbury resident and member of the Continental Congress, described the town as nearly defenseless for lack of manpower and appealed to Reed for help. Maclay's dislike for Sullivan emerged clearly in his loud and persistent appeals for assistance. Maclay's large stone house overlooking the river nearly a mile from the protective wall of Fort Augusta served as one of Sullivan's magazines and would be an obvious target in the event of a Tory-Iroquois raid. The combination of distance and the small number of soldiers in garrison at Fort Augusta complicated the problem of defending the house without additional reinforcements.[98] Maclay believed that Sullivan's army offered the only possible source of reinforcements capable of defending the frontiers and intended to force the diversion of part of it to this duty. He repeated Hunter's contention that the village and surrounding area could not defend itself, as most of the military age men had enlisted in the boat service. He lectured Reed that a failure to reinforce the garrison at Fort Augusta threatened the success of the expedition. "In short nothing seems wanting on their part But a proper degree of Spirit (and upon some occasions they have manifested enough of it) for to make one bold push for Sunbury, and destroy the Magazine which is now collecting there for the Support of the Army," he warned.[99] Maclay overstated the danger to the expedition. By late July Sullivan had already moved most of his powder upriver. Whatever powder did exist in Sunbury represented only an operational reserve available in the event the army expended its carry-along supply in a major battle.

Northumberland County residents and their militia lieutenants renewed pleas for assistance to Reed as well as Sullivan after the fall of Fort Freeland. The governor reluctantly convinced the Executive Council to authorize a call-up of militia forces from Lancaster and Cumberland Counties and attempted again to convince Sullivan to return some soldiers to Fort Augusta. Under orders from Washington to avoid weakening the army, Sullivan sent polite but firm rebuffs to requests for support to Colonels Hunter and John Cook. "I feel for you, and could wish to assist you, but the good of the service will not admit it," Sullivan wrote to Hunter. "The Object of this Expedition is of such a nature, and its Consequences so Extensive that to turn the course of this Army would be unwise, unsafe and impolitic."[100] Cook received an even more curt reply. "Nothing Could afford me more pleasure than to Relieve the Distress'd, or to have it in my Power to add to the Safety of your Settlement," stated Sullivan, "but should I Comply with the Requisition made by you it would Effectually answer the Intention of the Enemy, and Destroy the Grand Objective of this Expedition. . . . For your present Safety I must refer you to the Council of your State for assistance. Certainly it will be granted without much inconvenience as the State has neglected to furnish the Troops promis'd for this Expedition."[101]

Reed bridled at Sullivan's intransigence. Not surprisingly, the governor went to the Board of War to get Sullivan's decision overturned. Reed had found support for his opinions from a source inside the army at Wyoming and intended to use it in the appeal. Unknown to Sullivan, Hubley had written Reed several times concerning the expedition. Hubley's earlier letters had been sympathetic to Sullivan, steadfastly defending his superior from charges that the delays plaguing the army came as a result of Sullivan's failings. With the fall of Fort Freeland, however, Hubley began questioning his superior's decisions. Hubley informed Reed that Sullivan could have spared five hundred soldiers for duty on the Susquehanna's west branch to "scour the country."[102]

Was Sullivan capable of sending the men? The answer depends on the ratio of the army's field strength to the size of the enemy force thought to oppose it. The need to garrison the line of communications from Wyoming forward meant that, as the army progressed, its capabilities diminished. Washington had warned Sullivan to expect an enemy force numbering about two thousand. In modern combat the minimum desired ratio for a successful attack is three to one in favor of the attacker. Although no such doctrinal guidance existed at the time of the Revolution, the ever cautious Sullivan could not have been happy with the relative balance between the two sides, especially given that his adversaries possessed more extensive knowledge of the terrain. Satisfying Reed's request, particularly if Sullivan accepted Washington's figures on the enemy's strength, would threaten the expedition's chances for success.

Under a modern command structure Hubley's actions regarding the letter constituted disloyalty. Within the Continental army the practice of officers writing directly to their governors and bypassing their superiors did not stand out as unusual. The lack of a clear chain of command and the importance Continental army officers placed in the support of their states for administration rendered it prudent for regimental commanders like Hubley to keep their governors informed and to offer an opinion when asked. Such correspondence also made it easy to second-guess the decisions of military commanders. In this case Reed used Hubley's opinion to support his appeal of Sullivan's decision.[103] Rather than take the plea to Washington, Sullivan's immediate superior, Reed carried it directly to the Board of War. It arrived well after Sullivan had departed Wyoming, making it difficult if not impossible to overturn the decision. The fact that Reed found it necessary to carry the request directly to the Board of War, nonetheless, indicates the tension existing between the army and the state of Pennsylvania.

Sullivan marched northward with his small army largely intact and free from the distraction of providing frontier security. Still, Sullivan could not have been happy. Though he had sidestepped the attempts of Reed and his subordinates to divert part of the army, Sullivan found that Reed had eluded him as well. Neither the ranger companies nor the militia support materialized. Only Brodhead's small army operating from Fort Pitt benefited from a significant militia presence. Sullivan proceeded northward, hoping that James Clinton and his men found New York's government better able to assist the operation.

Logistics turned out to be less a problem for James Clinton because of the supplies accumulated the previous year for an attack into Canada. These would carry James Clinton's small army through the summer at Lake Otsego and eventually served as a valuable, though inadequate, supplement for

Sullivan once the two armies joined at Tioga. Greene's quartermaster and commissary agents still found themselves required to use impressment warrants to move supplies to Otsego. Unlike in Pennsylvania, no running battle occurred over the need for these warrants. George Clinton generally signed impressment warrants without delay. In the interest of his state he did sometimes caution Greene's officers to avoid inconveniencing the civilian community with unreasonable requests. He explained to these officers the need to safeguard the public's faith in its military by not employing agents who had been involved in past impressment controversies.[104] Thanks to a cooperative effort between the state and the army's supply officers, James Clinton's brigade was fully supplied and ready to move from Lake Otsego well in advance of the main army at Wyoming. Only in the area of personnel did New York's government fail Washington.

As had been the case in Pennsylvania, Washington asked George Clinton to supplement his brother James with soldiers from the militia. The commander-in-chief particularly desired that Clinton provide several companies of rangers.[105] Clinton responded by attempting to raise one thousand volunteers. He planned to use half the men to fill out the New York regiments of Continentals assigned to the expedition; the rest he intended to station on the frontiers. Clinton's correspondence to Washington and Sullivan lacks the kind of excuses Reed offered in response to requests for assistance, although conditions on New York's frontiers mirrored those of Pennsylvania. Clinton's one lapse came in June, when the situation in Vermont prompted him to write Washington. He cautioned Washington that the dispute might render it impossible for him to be of much assistance in preparing for the expedition against the Iroquois. To make a point, Clinton asked Washington for the return or replacement of six brass cannon New York had loaned to the Continental army in 1776 and threatened to use flour accumulated for his brother James to supply his own expedition against the rebelling counties of Vermont.[106] The governor probably intended the letter more as a bluff than as a real threat. His subsequent correspondence indicates no moves to reposition New York militia to deal with the problem in Vermont.

Clinton had ordered Colonel Albert Pawling, one of his militia lieutenants, to begin gathering the soldiers promised to Washington and to move them to the Susquehanna River in time to join with James Clinton's expedition as it moved westward to Tioga. While Pawling collected his force, Brant struck the colonial settlements at Minisink. No doubt under local pressure to react, Pawling wrote the governor for instructions.[107] Here Clinton showed the mettle that separated him from Reed. He told his lieutenant that sending soldiers to Minisink would waste manpower, as Brant and his warriors probably had departed the area. He gave Pawling the latitude to extend his patrols westward toward the stricken settlements but made it clear that Pawling's job remained that of supporting the expedition, not patrolling the frontiers.[108]

Clinton had not lost his concern for conditions in the backcountry. He realized that the situation had deteriorated over the summer and believed that a speedy beginning to the expedition offered the best remedy. Getting the expedition started would serve to draw Brant's and Butler's forces back to the Iroquois homelands and thereby afford respite to the frontiers. By July the governor had become clearly disappointed with Sullivan for not getting under way. Unaware of the conditions under which Sullivan labored in Pennsylvania, Clinton appears to have assumed that Sullivan himself deserved the lion's share of blame for the delay. In a letter to a friend the governor complained that "the unaccountable Delay of General Sullivan at Wyoming" had produced considerable suffering in his western settlements.[109] Yet, unlike Reed, Clinton largely kept his dissatisfaction to himself rather than allow it to complicate further the tenuous relationship existing between the states and the army.

Clinton did not have to wait long for the news he wanted to hear. Both Washington and Sullivan informed the governor during the first week of August that the army at Wyoming had begun its move upriver and asked that Pawling commence his march toward a junction with James Clinton.[110] The governor informed his brother that he could expect Pawling to join him on 17 August at the Indian village of Onoquaga on the Susquehanna River.[111]

The governor sent specific instructions to Pawling concerning the movement. He spent considerable time reviewing procedures that were becoming common in the Continental army, including guidance on how to make a secure camp in hostile terrain and cautions concerning effecting a rendezvous with another friendly force. Pawling commanded only three hundred soldiers, two-thirds of these being recruits for the Continental regiments and the rest militia. Clinton intended that Pawling's militia go home after the two forces joined. They were to take Clinton's packhorses with them, presumably for return to the main body of the Continental army.

James Clinton's army arrived at Onoquaga on the afternoon of 14 August and remained in the village until the appointed day for the rendezvous. Clinton sent a detachment of light infantry consisting mostly of soldiers from the Fourth Pennsylvania to find Pawling and escort him into the camp. The patrol found no sign of the expected reinforcements and returned empty-handed. On the morning of 17 August Clinton ordered one of his artillery crews to fire a shot as a last attempt to signal Pawling that the army was bivouacked nearby and to hurry his march. The sound reverberated among the surrounding hills and valleys. Clinton and his men listened intently for some return signal, but none came. Not long afterward the army set out for Tioga. Pawling arrived at Onoquaga after Clinton had departed. Problems with provisions as well as rainy weather that had swollen the streams had conspired to make it impossible for him to arrive in time to be of any assistance.[112] Rather than attempt to catch Clinton, Pawling chose instead to retrace his steps to the Delaware Valley.

In one sense Pawling's failure to find Clinton aided Sullivan. Had the rendezvous gone according to schedule, Clinton would have lost his packhorses. As the campaign unfolded in the following weeks, these horses proved critical for the movement of the army. As for manpower, Clinton found himself devoid of support from the state of New York, a condition with which Sullivan could sympathize.

Neither state met Washington's expectations. Both states placed large numbers of militia units into frontier service but failed to reinforce Sullivan's army at Wyoming or Lake Otsego. In New York the leadership made a concerted effort to get the soldiers promised to Clinton, but difficult terrain, inadequate coordination, and bad luck doomed the effort. In Pennsylvania the reasons behind the failure went much deeper. Without shared priorities for the expedition and no clear hierarchy between the army and the state, Pennsylvania's leaders pursued their own ends at the expense of the expedition. For the most part, Pennsylvania's leaders believed themselves responsible first to their constituents and lacked either the insight or political courage necessary to subordinate state issues to national ones. They saw their state militia as primarily a home defense force and took issue with both Washington and Sullivan when it became clear that the army envisioned another use for these soldiers.

The army showed itself in many ways no better in dealing with Pennsylvania. Sullivan never troubled himself to understand the state's internal political struggles and demonstrated little sympathy for anything less than acquiescence to the demands they made on the state's leaders and people. Having faced nearly two years of an unremitting guerrilla war against their homes and crops, farmers in the interior expected the Continental army to do the work of putting an end to the problem. Sullivan's demands for food and additional men suggested that more sacrifices were to follow. Most believed that they had done their part and that the army's requests exceeded what was necessary or right to give.

In a broad sense Sullivan's expedition turned up problems in the relationship among the government, its people, and the military which would plague the nation for decades. Assumptions concerning a virtuous citizenry willing to suffer the hardships of soldiering had been proven largely false. By midwar the average civilian showed scant inclination to enlist for altruistic reasons. Many considered duty in the militia the most that reasonably could be asked of them. The militias by this time were poorly trained and inadequate to most military tasks other than that of controlling the Loyalist population. The problem of frontier defense proved especially troublesome, and in the case of Pennsylvania most persons expected the Continental army to help secure the settlements from attack. Most civilians happily would have given the mission entirely to the army. This did not reflect Washington's view. His attempt to have militiamen perform this duty produced resistance from within the militias and their state governments. The latter considered militias to be their home defense force and generally demanded a voice as the price of cooperation. Any large-scale operation requiring state support thus depended on cooperation and compromise. This worked at cross-purposes to Washington and the Continental army. The greater number of people involved in decisions consistently threatened operational security. More important, lacking a central government capable of coercion when time and circumstances made compromise difficult, the army often found itself woefully undermanned, badly fed, and inadequately clothed. It could have been a recipe for disaster.

8

Conclusions

Most accounts of the Sullivan expedition have centered on whether the venture could be considered a success and the degree to which it contributed to the formation of post–Revolutionary War America. This study has taken a different approach, focusing instead on how the Continental army operated in the field at midwar. The two questions are not unrelated. A well-motivated, trained, and led fighting force certainly has a better chance of gaining success on the battlefield and having an impact in any war. In the case of Sullivan's expedition, disagreement over the significance of the campaign has overshadowed what the operation has to say about the Continental army. It is necessary therefore to lay to rest the first question before dealing with the second.

The historical debate over the importance of the expedition really began at the centennial celebration staged in honor of the event on 29 August 1879. General William T. Sherman, a man who certainly knew war and was no stranger to fighting Indians, had agreed to address the crowd of fifty thousand assembled to remember Sullivan and his army. From the vantage point of the hilltop where the crowd had gathered, the valley stretched out below appeared the picture of tranquility, a place of small farms with the nearby town of Elmira hinting at a more industrialized future for the region. This to Sherman's eye marked progress, and he blessed it, crediting

Sullivan for making it possible. Perhaps answering his own critics as much as Sullivan's, Sherman acknowledged that the kind of war Sullivan brought to the valley was harsh but the ends justified the means:

I know it is very common, and too common a practice, to accuse General Sullivan of having destroyed peach trees and corn fields, and all that nonsense. He had to do it, and he did do it. . . . Whenever men raise up their hands to oppose this great advancing tide of civilization, they must be swept aside, peacefully if possible, forcibly if we must.[1]

In Sherman's mind Sullivan had provided the model for the army's role in advancing the interests of the nation. He had commanded the army's first Indian campaign with a mission similar to that of the post–Civil War army in the West—that is, to punish the Indian for his savagery and sweep him from the path of white civilization. Sherman's argument that Sullivan had broken the Iroquois and opened western New York and Pennsylvania to white expansion became the basic contention of the expedition's earliest historians, Craft and Norton. This line of argument, however, simply does not bear up under close examination.

During the winter and early spring of 1780, Sullivan's efforts did bring comparative peace to the frontiers. The destruction of the Iroquois villages and crops in conjunction with one of the harshest winters on record took its toll. It did not, however, break the Iroquois will to resist. The loss of staging areas near frontier settlements may have been the primary reason for their temporary absence from the fight. One chief, writing to Sir Guy Johnson, noted "that the Difficulty of sending out Parties against them [the Americans] from hence [Fort Niagara] is very great, especially as so many of our Villages where we congregate ourselves and get supplied are destroyed."[2] Nonetheless, he reassured Johnson, "we do not look upon ourselves as defeated for we have never fought."[3] One of the Cayuga chiefs at Niagara had voiced similar sentiments, vowing to British officers that, come spring, they would take revenge on the whites "and if it is the will of the Great Spirit leave our Bones with those of the Rest of our Brethren rather than evacuate our Country or give our Enemy Room to say we fled from them."[4]

The Iroquois kept their promises. In the spring of 1780 nine hundred warriors led by Brant, Cornplanter, and Butler rekindled the war against the frontiers of the Middle Colonies. The campaign opened as early as February, with an attempt to blockade Fort Stanwyx. The following month an Iroquois and Tory force overwhelmed a militia garrison at Shenesborough. In succession they attacked Riemendsnyder's Bush, Harpersfield, Cherry Valley, Johnstown, Little Falls, Schoharie, and German Flats, destroying 1,000 homes, 1,000 barns, and 600,000 bushels of grain.[5] They also repaid the Oneida and Tuscarora for the assistance they had provided Sullivan, putting their villages to the torch. Not even Kirkland's old church at Kanowalohale escaped the onslaught. In Pennsylvania the situation proved little better. By April 1780 Reed had already begun to consider the possibility of mounting another raid, at state expense, into the Iroquois homelands. In the Susquehanna Valley, Maclay proposed that the hard-hit valley be abandoned if something could not soon be done.[6] The raids continued throughout 1780 into 1781. By 1782 the situation had grown so bad that Reed started in motion preparations for a raid on the Genesee towns, appointing Potter to command the endeavor.[7] Before Potter could gather his forces and begin the march up the Susquehanna, Washington requested that Reed abandon the plan. With the war finally coming to a close, Washington had pressed for and received promises from Guy Carleton that the British would use their influence to bring the incursions to a finish.[8]

Carleton kept his word. When peace came to the frontiers, the Iroquois found themselves weakened but unbroken. So long as the British continued to support them with supplies, they did not believe it unreasonable that the damage done by the war could not be repaired. The Treaty of Paris that officially ended the war, however, did not leave them with the protection they expected. While failing to mention the disposition of Indians, the treaty's provisions granted all lands south of Canada and east of the Mississippi River to the United States, including the lands reserved for the Iroquois in the Treaty of Fort Stanwix. Having always believed that they were a separate and independent nation, Iroquois leaders met the news that the British had ceded their lands with disbelief. Brant strongly reminded Haldimand of the commitments the British had made to the Iroquois. Haldimand proved sympathetic but powerless to change decisions already put to paper. What followed was a series of persistent American efforts, pushed by Governor Clinton, and aimed at moving the Iroquois from their lands.[9] Sullivan's raid undoubtedly helped weaken the Iroquois, making them vulnerable to American pressures, but provisions of the Treaty of Paris limiting British support for the tribes proved the deciding factor in the demise of the Six Nations.

Sullivan's raid, then, neither brought peace to the frontier nor measurably assisted in the final outcome of the war. On a practical level the expedition turned out to be a well-executed failure. The blame for this rests not with Sullivan but, rather, with Washington. Sullivan's mission had been to destroy the Iroquois homelands, and this he had done. Washington, on the other hand, failed to give his enemy his due. Like most whites of his day, he did not hold Indians in high regard. Not surprisingly, he had little understanding of the history of the Six Nations. Sullivan's raid was not the first time a European army had penetrated deep into Iroquoia. The French had done it several times during the seventeenth century. In 1666 Marquis Prouville de Tracy led an army of a thousand soldiers against the Mohawks with orders to "exterminate" the Five Nations.[10] He burned their villages and destroyed their crops but could not force them to stand and fight his numerically superior army. Another French army under Jacques-René de Brisay de Denonville attacked the Senecas in 1687, again finding only villages and fields against which to vent its power, as the Seneca sought safety with the Cayuga. Over the next two years New France paid in blood for Denonville's invasion, as Iroquois raiding parties took their revenge on French settlements along the St. Lawrence.[11] Nine years later the Oneida and the Onondaga fled before French arms. These attacks against the Iroquois certainly took their toll and occasionally forced the Confederation into making concessions to the French, but they never threatened its destruction. What they did accomplish was to push the Confederation closer to the British. Sullivan's raid had exactly the same effect. What he and his soldiers accomplished was largely to remove Iroquois options. If the Americans won, none of the pro-British Iroquois could have any doubt that the loss of more tribal land would soon follow. If the British won, the Iroquois had good reason to believe they would keep their lands. Spokesmen for the Crown had promised them that George III would not forget their sacrifices.

To be successful, Washington needed to take Fort Niagara and cut the British supply line to the Iroquois. Although Washington hoped that the fates would deliver Niagara into Sullivan's hands, he never equipped his subordinate with the weapons necessary to take the fortress, nor did he specify it as the primary objective of the campaign. The campaign did not

CONCLUSIONS

produce the results desired because Washington assigned Sullivan an operational objective too limited in scope to bring about the desired strategic objective. As a result, the final outcome of the campaign largely depended on how many Iroquois perished in the snows blanketing the woods and fields around Fort Niagara in the winter of 1779–80. When the British managed to find the supplies to sustain their allies, Sullivan's scorched-earth offensive served as a catalyst to increase Iroquois commitment to the British cause.

The expedition's failure should not diminish the progress the army had made over the four years since Boston. Washington's planning, particularly in areas of operations and intelligence, stands out as thorough and imaginative. His use of multiple routes to concentrate his forces against the Iroquois homelands confused and hindered the reaction of his foes. The elaborate diversion provided by Hazen's Canadians along the Connecticut reinforced British uncertainty.

Tactically, Sullivan's army turned in a solid but not perfect performance. The constant fixation on security successfully blocked every Tory and Indian attempt to disrupt the march. Security consciousness meant more than simply a challenge and password system and the stationing of flankers. The army's ability to move rapidly, such as its thirty-minute crossing of the Susquehanna River, often denied the enemy time to make use of their superior knowledge of the terrain. Sullivan's reliance on aimed fire to cover the movement of the maneuver element during the Battle of Newtown also stands out as an appropriate adaptation to the demands of frontier warfare. At the junior-officer level the army exhibited some problems. At Chemung, for example, Sullivan found some musket-equipped units firing at will rather than responding to the direction of their officers.

Washington had given considerable thought to what he expected of officers. Competency, bravery, loyalty, and a willingness to suffer the discomfort of soldiering along with one's men stand out as the characteristics he most wanted to inculcate in the Continental army's officer corps. Building a solid officer corps was in no way complete in 1779, nor would it be when the final gun sounded at Yorktown. Sullivan's officers still spent needless energy arguing over dates of rank and other matters of honor. Nonetheless, Sullivan's campaign suggests that some officers had begun to learn that soldiers follow an officer into battle out of respect more than fear. These were the officers who read books on military subjects by the light of campfires, waded rivers with their soldiers, and wrote letters to their legislatures when their men wore rags and marched on empty stomachs.

That Washington's logisticians failed to feed and clothe Sullivan's army adequately across the summer of 1779 stands out as a most glaring weakness of the Continental army. A number of factors combined to produce the poor showing. Inadequate time to plan for the operation, low water levels in the rivers during the summer, inflated currency, and, most important, a dysfunctional relationship between the army and the civil governments combined to force Sullivan to improvise. This he did well, relying on the discipline of his soldiers to make foraging the Iroquois lands a suitable alternative.

Sullivan's inability to gain cooperation from Pennsylvania's government severely hurt the campaign and provides a good example of the problems inherent in the civil-military relations of revolutionary America. War is first and foremost a political act requiring a nation to coordinate its resources and manpower to accomplish the task before it. Throughout the colonial period provincial governments had participated in England's wars only as secondary players. British leaders formulated political and military objectives then raised the armies and navies to achieve them. In 1776 the Americans found themselves on their own and to a considerable degree fell short in linking together the state, its military, and the people. Neither the Continental Congress nor the state governments ever managed to put aside completely the political infighting that in peacetime is part of the democratic landscape but in war sets the stage for potential disaster.

The internal struggle, when linked to the perception that the war came about because of Britain's tyrannical treatment of the colonies, combined to produce state constitutions that institutionalized weak government as the best protector of liberty. Wars drive even the most democratic of governments toward curtailing liberty as the price of military effectiveness. This was a lesson that Americans largely refused to acknowledge. Pennsylvanians appeared particularly reluctant to assist Sullivan and expected their state government to mitigate, if not block, his demands for support. Sullivan's army achieved its operational objectives despite the governments and the people it served, not because of them.

Conclusions

Taken as a whole, Sullivan's army turned in a credible performance in its operations against the Iroquois. Detractors may argue that the destruction of the Iroquois homelands did not represent enough of a military achievement to render any verdict on the army. Projecting military power inland in the colonial period was not easy, given the logistical requirements involved. Furthermore, Sullivan's opponents, although outnumbered, did have the manpower to delay the advance until supply shortages and the lateness of the season brought the expedition to a halt. That they failed was largely the doing of Sullivan and his men. It should not be forgotten that Sullivan's expedition occurred under wartime conditions, with the colonies facing multiple threats. Following the war the United States government tried twice to duplicate Sullivan's accomplishments. Both Josiah Harmar's and Arthur St. Clair's expeditions in 1790 and 1791 met with disaster, victims of poorly trained soldiers, inadequate logistics, and an enemy willing to take advantage of the weaknesses. It would not be until 1794 at the Battle of Fallen Timbers that Anthony Wayne, the other hero of 1779, would lead the army's second successful Indian expedition. He followed the same basics as Sullivan, relying on a solid plan of attack, good leadership, and trained soldiers.

To say the Continental army had finally come of age in 1779 probably overstates the case. All things being equal, the army was not in 1779, nor would it be in 1781, the equal of its British counterparts. In war, however, all things are never equal. The American victory at Saratoga had brought France into the war, widening the conflict and complicating Britain's military situation. As a result, the cost of the conflict rose even more steeply, while new military demands strained the empire's resources. In addition, the British army's inability to penetrate into the rich farming areas of the interior left the army dependent on a line of supply stretching back to England. These problems, in conjunction with the Continental army's growing prowess, meant that by midwar the scales had tipped back to relative equilibrium. For Britain victory required smashing Washington's army in a battle of annihilation. The showing produced by Sullivan's men in the summer of 1779 indicated that this had become no small task.

Notes

Chapter 1: Introduction

1. Gates to Sullivan, 16 March 1779, in *The Letters and Papers of Major-General John Sullivan, Continental Army*, ed. Otis G. Hammond (Concord, N.H.: New Hampshire Historical Society, 1931), 2:534.

2. Washington to Gates, 6 March 1779, in *The Writings of George Washington from the Original Manuscript Sources, 1745–1799*, ed. John C. Fitzpatrick (Washington, D.C.: U.S. Government Printing Office, 1936), 14:198–201. A month later in a letter to John Jay, Washington confessed that his first choice for the command had been Philip Schuyler, but the New Yorker's health made his continued service in the army uncertain. See Washington to Jay, 14 April 1779, in ibid., 384.

3. Gates to Washington, 16 March 1779, in *The Writings of George Washington*, ed. Jared Sparks (Boston: Little, Brown, 1858), 6:189.

4. Sullivan to Gates, 17 March 1779, in Hammond, *Sullivan Papers*, 2:535.

5. Sullivan to Gates, 23 March 1779, in ibid., 542.

6. Lt. Col. Adam Hubley, 30 September 1779, in *Journals of the Military Expedition of Major General John Sullivan against the Six Nations of the Indians in 1779*, ed. Frederick Cook (Freeport, N.Y.: Books for Libraries Press, 1972), 166.

7. Sullivan to Jay, 30 September 1779, in Hammond, *Sullivan Papers*, 3:134.

8. Militia representation among the expedition's number was nearly nonexistent. Only two companies of militia accompanied Sullivan, with most of these men coming from the Wyoming Valley. See William S. Stryker, *General Maxwell's Brigade of the New Jersey Line in the Expedition against the Indians in the Year 1779* (Trenton, N.J.: W. S. Sharp, 1885), 7.

9. Sullivan reported losing only forty-one men from all causes, and no proof exists to suggest that his opponents suffered much more than this. See Sullivan to Jay, 30 September 1779, in Hammond, *Sullivan Papers*, 3:134.

10. George Bancroft, *History of the United States from the Discovery of the North American Continent* (Boston: Little, Brown, 1875), 10:230–32.

11. Benson J. Lossing, *Pictorial Field Book of the Revolution* (New York: Harper and Brothers, 1860), 1:277.

12. A. Tiffany Norton, *History of Sullivan's Campaign against the Iroquois; Being a Full Account of that Epoch of the Revolution* (Lima, N.Y.: By the author, 1879), v.

13. David Craft, *The Centennial Celebration of General Sullivan's Campaign against the Iroquois in 1779* (Waterloo, N.Y.: Waterloo Public Library and Historical Society, 1879), 90.

14. Alexander C. Flick, "New Sources on the Sullivan-Clinton Campaign in 1779," *New York State Historical Association Quarterly Journal* 10 (October 1929): 316.

15. Howard Swiggett, *War out of Niagara: Walter Butler and the Tory Rangers* (Port Washington, N.Y.: Ira J. Friedman, 1933), 185.

16. Christopher Ward, *The War of the Revolution* (New York: Macmillan, 1952), 2:645.

17. Morris Bishop, "The End of the Iroquois," *American Heritage* 20 (October 1969): 28.

18. Donald R. McAdams, "The Sullivan Expedition: Success or Failure?" *New York Historical Society Quarterly* 54 (January 1970): 80.

19. Barbara Graymont, *The Iroquois in the American Revolution* (Syracuse, N.Y.: Syracuse University Press, 1972), 222.

20. Ibid., 192.

21. Don Higginbotham, *The War of American Independence: Military Attitudes, Policy, and Practice, 1763–1789* (Boston: Northeastern University Press, 1983), 329.

22. Robert Middlekauff, *The Glorious Cause: The American Revolution, 1763–1789* (New York: Oxford University Press, 1982).

23. Bradford Perkins, "The Peace of Paris: Patterns and Legacies," in *Peace and the Peacemakers: The Treaty of 1783*, ed. Ronald Hoffman (Charlottesville: University of Virginia Press, 1986), 209.

24. The French intended to limit the United States to the land east of the Appalachians, effectively granting the Ohio lands to the British. See Thomas Perkins Abernethy, *Western Lands and the American Revolution* (New York: Russell and Russell, 1959), 286.

25. The Continental Congress authorized money for a campaign against the Iroquois in New York and the British at Detroit as early as 11 June 1778 but found themselves having to postpone the undertaking until the following year for lack of supplies. See Alexander C. Flick, "New Sources on the Sullivan-Clinton Campaign in 1779," *New York State Historical Association Quarterly Journal* 10 (July 1929): 211.

Chapter 2: The Frontier in Flames

1. In military terms the backcountry provided the army with strategic depth.

2. Britain divided the colonies into two geographic districts, with the Mason-Dixon line serving as the boundary for the purpose of regulating Indian relations. Tribal claims often skirted this English imposed boundary, forcing the superintendents to work together on Indian problems. The leadership in Whitehall was divided on the question of how many soldiers to provide for frontier posts. With the value of the fur trade on the decline, then secretary of war William Wildman Viscount Barrington argued in 1763 that the American interior ought to be left as an Indian "desert." Small numbers of soldiers could not defend the settlements nor pacify the tribes. Barrington's views did not prevail, but Britain's commitment to the western posts did wane over the decade that preceded the outbreak of the American Revolution. See John Shy, *Toward Lexington: The Role of the British Army in the Coming of the American Revolution* (Princeton, N.J.: Princeton University Press, 1965), 237.

3. Francis Jennings, *The Ambiguous Empire: The Covenant Chain Confederation of Indian Tribes with English Colonies from Its Beginning to the Lancaster Treaty of 1744* (New York: W. W. Norton, 1984), 14.

4. At the Peace of Utrecht in 1713 ending Queen Anne's War, clause 15 of the treaty stated clearly Britain's view of the Iroquois Confederation's place in the empire: "The Subjects of France inhabiting Canada shall hereafter give no Hindrance or Molestation to the Five Nations or Cantons of Indians subject to the Dominion of Great Britain nor to the other natives of America who are Friends to the same." See Peace of Utrecht, clause 15, as stated in Ian K. Steele, *Warpaths: Invasions of North America* (New York: Oxford University Press, 1994), 159.

5. Peter Cooper Mancall, *Environment and Economy: The Upper Susquehanna Valley in the Age of the American Revolution* (Ph.D. diss., Harvard University, 1986), 114.

6. Johnson exceeded his instructions for two reasons. First, the board's instructions only partially recognized existing settlements. Johnson's work to extend the line westward may have been designed to prevent an Indian war by paying the Iroquois for a fait accompli. Second, there is evidence to suggest that Johnson and his chief lieutenant, George Crogan, may also have been attempting to placate several groups of land speculators who were interested in opening the new lands. See Ray A. Billington, "The Fort Stanwix Treaty of 1768," *New York Historical Association* 25 (April 1944): 184–85; and Albert T. Volwiler, *George Croghan and the Westward Movement, 1741–1782* (Cleveland: Arthur H. Clark Company, 1926), 222.

7. Deed of Cession by the Six Nations and Others to the British Colonies, Fort Stanwix Treaty, 5 November 1768, in *Indian Affairs Papers: American Revolution,* ed. Maryly Barton Penrose (Franklin Park, N.J.: Liberty Bell Associates, 1981), 2.

8. This proved to be one of the least clear provisions of the agreement, as the term *Tiadaghton Creek* had been applied to two different streams on the upper river, Pine Creek and Loyalsock Creek. See Mancall, *Environment and Economy,* 116.

9. Anthony F. C. Wallace, *The Death and Rebirth of the Seneca* (New York: Alfred A. Knopf, 1970), 122–23.

10. Friedenshütten was built with the permission of the Cayuga. The village grew to include twenty-nine log houses and thirteen bark huts. As with all Moravian efforts, the centerpiece of the town was the chapel, a beautifully built structure of hewn logs. Gardens, orchards, and pasture rounded out the setting. Although there were exceptions, most of the townspeople came from the various Delaware clans. The Iroquois deeded away all the villages east of the Susquehanna in the Treaty of Fort Stanwix. See C. A. Weslager, *The Delaware Indians: A History* (New Brunswick, N.J.: Rutgers University Press, 1972), 283–84.

11. Mancall, *Environment and Economy,* 128.

12. Missionary Philip Vickers Fithian, 6 July 1775, Journals of Fort Augusta in the American Revolution, Northumberland County Historical Society, Sunbury, Pa.

13. Charles Sellers makes the point that the transition from subsistence production to market production had already begun prior to the Revolution in many frontier regions. The Susquehanna Valley particularly fell into this category, with some farms selling as much as 30 percent of its produce to eastern or southern markets. See Charles Sellers, *The Market Revolution: Jacksonian America, 1815–1846* (Oxford: Oxford University Press, 1991), 15–16.

14. Founded in 1772, Pennsylvania's government made Sunbury the county seat of Northumberland County, intending a prosperous future for the town. Town planners designed the village to be a small version of Philadelphia. It was to have eighty-foot-wide main streets and sixty-foot-wide side streets, with lanes and alleys twenty feet across. Building specifications for town dwellers stipulated that homes were to be at least twenty-foot-square with a brick or stone chimney. If building specifications were not met within three years, the owner's title to the land could be voided. Mancall, *Environment and Economy,* 161–62.

15. Jack M. Sosin, *The Revolutionary Frontier, 1763–1783* (New York: Holt, Rinehart, and Winston, 1967), 172.

16. Weslager, *Delaware Indians,* 297.

17. There remains considerable debate about when the Confederation was ac-

tually founded. Most scholars accept that the League was founded between a.d. 1400 and 1600. Some traditional Iroquois sources, however, place the date as early as a.d. 1000. See Daniel K. Richter, *The Ordeal of the Longhouse: The Peoples of the Iroquois League in the Era of European Colonization* (Chapel Hill: University of North Carolina Press, 1992), 300.

18. Most of the Tuscarora tribe came north during the conflict into the spring of 1714. The inclusion of the Tuscaroras added fifteen hundred to two thousand people to the Confederation. It would not be until the 1720s that the Confederation recognized the Tuscaroras as the sixth member of the Confederation. Ibid., 238–39.

19. Both Pennsylvania's colonial government and the various groups of displaced persons who lived in the area recognized Shikellamy as the League's representative. David Richter argues, however, that the League was split politically, making it unclear whether the Confederacy's council viewed the Oneida headman as its spokesman. Iroquois claims to the Susquehanna Valley were also dubious. Pennsylvania land agents such as James Logan found that the way around the refusal of the Shawnee, Delaware, and Conestoga tribes to sell their lands east of the Susquehanna was simply to deny that these tribes owned the lands in the first place. With Iroquois acquiescence in 1731, Logan and Pennsylvania's governor, John Penn, simply argued that the Iroquois had conquered the peoples of the Susquehanna Valley in the seventeenth century. The decision to open parts of the valley to white settlement rested with the Iroquois alone. The Iroquois understood the value of playing along with this charade. Not only could they derive the benefit that came from using the Susquehanna Valley as a buffer state to block access to Iroquoia; they also stood to gain materially through the systematic sale of the area. Only the Shawnee, Delaware, and Conestoga stood to lose from the deal. A series of less than forthright treaties followed, culminating in the "Walking Purchase" of 1737, which effectively removed most of the Delaware from eastern Pennsylvania. See Richter, *Ordeal of the Longhouse,* 274–75; and Barry C. Kent, *Susquehanna's Indians* (Harrisburg: Pennsylvania Historical and Museum Commission, 1989), 100–101.

20. Journal of Frederick Post, 19 January 1759, Division of Archives and Manuscripts, Pennsylvania Historical and Museum Commission, as cited in Paul A. Wallace, *Indians of Pennsylvania* (Harrisburg: Pennsylvania Historical and Museum Commission, 1981), 109–11.

21. Jennings, *Ambiguous Iroquois Empire,* 288.

22. German Flats Treaty with the Six Nations, 15 August 1775, in Penrose, *Indian Affairs Papers,* 6–9.

23. Ibid., 22.

24. German Flats Treaty with the Six Nations, 31 August 1779, in ibid., 28.

25. Wallace, *Death and Rebirth of the Seneca,* 127–28, 130.

26. Germain's belief that the majority of the countryside favored an end to the war on British terms appears as a continuing theme in his writings. See Germain to Henry Clinton, 23 January 1779, in Sir Frederick Haldimand: Unpublished Papers and Correspondence, 1758–84, reel 16.

27. Piers Mackesy, "British Strategy in the War of American Independence," *Yale Review* 52 (June 1963): 548.

28. Unlike western tribes, the Mohicans of Stockbridge, Massachusetts, lived surrounded by their European neighbors. In their daily lives they felt the pressure being exerted by advocates of separation from England. Unlike western tribes who the English could woo by promising to defend their tribal homelands in the event of a British victory, the king's record of support for Stockbridge land claims had been long on rhetoric and short on action. Finally, the Mohicans had in years past been dominated by the Mohawks. The Six Nations' early decision to remain neutral freed the Mohicans to follow a diplomatic policy of their own choosing. The Mohicans' commitment to the American cause remained steadfast throughout the war. At a meeting called by the Continental Congress' commissioners to treat with representatives from the Confederacy and the Mohicans at Albany in August 1775, Solomon, a Mohican warrior, informed his listeners: "Brothers, appointed by the Twelve United Colonies: We thank you for taking care of us and supplying us with provisions since we have been at Albany. Depend upon it, we are true to you, and mean to join you. Wherever you go, we will be by your sides. Our bones shall lie with yours. We are determined never to be at peace with the red coats, while they are at variance with you. . . . If we are conquered, our lands go with yours; but if we are victorious, we hope you will help us to recover our just rights." Victory would in the end come to the American cause, but the Mohicans' appeal for justice regarding their land claims never did. Patrick Frazier, *The Mohicans of Stockbridge* (Lincoln: University of Nebraska Press, 1992), 196–97, 199, 204.

29. Ibid., 206.

30. Shy, *Toward Lexington,* 31.

31. Gage became particularly adamant about the need to raise both Canadians and Indians once Ticonderoga fell into American hands. Gage to Dartmouth, 12 January 1775, in *The Correspondence of General Thomas Gage with the Secretaries of State, 1763–1775,* ed. Clarence Edwin Carter (New Haven, Conn.: Yale University Press, 1931), 1:404; Bancroft transcripts, England and America, January–August 1775, 296, New York Public Library (NYPL), as quoted in Graymont, *The Iroquois in the American Revolution,* 80; and Frazier, *Mohicans of Stockbridge,* 207.

32. Frazier, *Mohicans of Stockbridge,* 207.

33. Isabel Thompson Kelsay, *Joseph Brant, 1743–1807, Man of Two Worlds* (Syracuse, N.Y.: Syracuse University Press, 1984), 156.

34. Piers Mackesy, *The War for America, 1775–1783* (Cambridge, Mass.: Harvard University Press, 1964), 58.

35. Ibid., 59.

36. Reference here is to St. Dominique, Jamaica, and the Leeward Islands, where both Britain and France maintained numerous profitable sugar plantations. Mackesy notes that many influential men in Britain believed that the British economy depended on the profitability of their holdings in the West Indies. Lose these islands, and the British economy would collapse. Furthermore, they believed that the French had been able to rebuild their navy largely because of the monies generated by French sugar plantations located here. Seize control of the French sugar islands, and France would be forced out of the war, leaving the thirteen colonies once again alone and vulnerable. Ibid., 182–84.

37. Eric Robson, *The American Revolution in Its Political and Military Aspects, 1763–1783* (New York: W. W. Norton, 1966), 120.

38. Mackesy, "British Strategy," 550.

39. This idea dates back to Britain's earlier orientation on New England. See Mackesy, *War for America*, 59.

40. Claus to Haldimand, 30 August 1779, in Claus Papers, 2:131–33, National Archives of Canada, as quoted in Graymont, *Iroquois in the American Revolution*, 159.

41. Whitehall would come to depend primarily on two Tory regiments as well as the Iroquois to fight the war in the interior of Middle Colonies. William Johnson's son, John Johnson, raised the first of these regiments in the summer of 1777. Designated the Royal Greens, this regiment consisted primarily of men who had been tenants or neighbors of the Johnsons in the Mohawk Valley. Many of them came from Scotch-Catholic ancestry. See Tom Martin, "Royal Greens," in *The American Revolution 1775–1783*, ed. Richard L. Blanco (New York: Garland Publishing, 1993), 2:1440. John Butler organized the second regiment in the summer and fall of 1777. Named Butler's Rangers in honor of its founder, the rangers consisted of a diverse band of poor landless whites, fugitives from the law, some Senecas, and at least one Continental army deserter. Unlike the Royal Greens, the rangers rapidly earned a reputation for cruelty for their tactics along the frontiers. See Tom Martin, "Butler's Rangers," in ibid., 1:226; and Tom Martin, "Joseph Brant," in ibid., 162.

42. Graymont, *Iroquois in the American Revolution*, 97–98.

43. Ibid., 99.

44. Robert Fruit, September 1776, in Journals of Fort Augusta, vol. 15.

45. Wallace, *Death and Rebirth of the Seneca*, 131.

46. Samuel Kirkland accompanied the expedition in order to assist Sullivan with problems of Indian diplomacy. Kirkland had served as a missionary to the Iroquois for many years prior to the war, ministering first to the Senecas and later to the Oneidas and Tuscaroras. He had successfully Christianized many Indians, particularly among the Oneidas and the Tuscaroras. His influence alone accounts largely for the Oneida's decision to participate actively on the American side. See Graymont, *Iroquois in the American Revolution*, 329.

47. Wallace, *Death and Rebirth of the Seneca*, 132–33.

48. James E. Seaver, *The Life of Mary Jemison: The White Woman of the Genesee* (Jersey Shore, Pa.: Zebrowski Historical Services and Publishing Company, 1991), 116–17.

49. Other estimates of Indian casualties range from a high of about 150 to a low of 62. See Craig L. Symonds, *A Battlefield Atlas of the American Revolution* (Annapolis, Md.: Nautical and Aviation Publishing Company of America, 1986), 43; Francis Whiting Halsey, *The Old New York Frontier* (New York: Charles Scribner's Sons, 1901), 192; and Graymont, *Iroquois in the American Revolution*, 138.

50. Ibid., 149.

51. The commission was empowered to enter into negotiations with the Continental Congress "as if it were a legal body." Among the list of concessions they could offer was: no standing army in the colonies in times of peace without the assemblies' consent; the colonies could maintain their own military forces; Congress would continue in being if the Americans insisted, provided its powers did not conflict with that of Parliament's. See Mackesy, *War for America*, 188.

52. Casualty figures for this engagement vary. John Butler claimed that his rangers and Indians took 227 scalps. Adam Crysler of Butler's Rangers stated that the militia suffered 450 dead, leading one to expect that the militia probably numbered over 500 before the start of the battle. This number is too high. Zebulon Butler, the Continental army officer in command of the militia, stated that 301 of his men lost their lives. Other sources suggest that the militia numbered somewhere between 300 to 400 at the start of the battle and place the death toll at 160. Regardless of whose figures one accepts, put in perspective, this means the engagement ranks as one of the most costly frontier battles in the nation's history. See John Butler to Mason Bolton, 8 July 1778, in Sir Frederick Haldimand: Unpublished Papers and Correspondence 1758–84 (London: World Microfilms Publications Ltd., 1977), reel 42; Swiggett, *War out of Niagara*, 133; Charles Miner, *History of Wyoming, in a Series of Letters from Charles Miner, to His Son William Penn Miner, Esq.* (Philadelphia: J. Crissy, 1845), 228; Oscar J. Harvey, *A History of Wilkes-Barre* (Wilkes-Barre, Pa.: Raeder Press, 1909), 2:1006; and Graymont, *Iroquois in the American Revolution*, 171.

53. William C. Kashatus, "The Wyoming Massacre: The Surpassing Horror of the American Revolution, July 3, 1778," *Valley Forge Journal* 4 (December 1988): 117.

54. Ibid.

55. Butler to Bolton, 8 July 1778, in Sir Frederick Haldimand: Unpublished Papers, reel 42.

56. Robert Covenhoven's Account of the Great Runaway, n.d., Journals of Fort Augusta, vol.21.

57. Lt. Col. Thomas Hartley to the Continental Congress, 20 September 1778, in Papers of the Continental Congress, National Archives, Washington, D.C., reel 96.

58. The Sheshequin, Towanda, and Great Warriors paths were the three major trails that led north toward Tioga from the forks of the Susquehanna at Sunbury. The Shehequin departed the Susquehanna Valley at the Indian village of Ostonwakin (present-day Montoursville) and ran along Lycoming Creek to its source. After a small ascent it descended into Sugar Creek valley, terminating at Sheshequin. The Towanda led from Muncy across the Allegheny mountains to Towanda, a village fifteen miles downriver from Toga. The Great Warriors path, although the longest of the three, had the advantage of being the easiest to use. There were no high mountains to cross, and most of the trail ran along the north branch of the Susquehanna. See Wallace, *Indian Paths of Pennsylvania*, 5.

59. John B. B. Trussell Jr., *The Pennsylvania Line: Regimental Organization and Operations, 1776–1783* (Harrisburg: Pennsylvania Historical and Museum Commission, 1977), 144–45.

60. Halsey, *Old New York Frontier*, 228.

61. Draper MSS 4F55; and Trussell, *Pennsylvania Line*, 71.

62. William Butler to George Clinton, 12 October 1779, in George Clinton, *Public Papers of George Clinton, First Governor of New York* (Albany: State of New York, 1900), 4:223–28.

63. Butler to Haldimand, 17 November 1778, in Sir Frederick Haldimand: Unpublished Papers, reel 42.

64. Graymont, *Iroquois in the American Revolution*, 190.

65. Germain to Haldimand, 16 April 1779, in Sir Frederick Haldimand: Unpublished Papers, reel 16.

66. Germain to Haldimand, 3 March 1779, in ibid.

67. Arriving in January 1776, Brant had gone to London to discuss the Iroquois' position on the war and hopefully to overturn Carleton's orders concerning the employment of Indians in the fighting. While there, Brant sat for a portrait that became the source of the prints Germain later decided to distribute among the

Iroquois villages. Germain to Sir Henry Clinton, 23 January 1779, in Great Britain War Office Correspondence, Sir Henry Clinton's Correspondence with the War Office, General Washington, and Other Officers, Manuscripts Division, Library of Congress, Washington, D.C.; and Germain to Clinton, 3 Mar 1779, in Sir Frederick Haldimand: Unpublished Papers, reel 16.

68. Germain to Haldimand, 16 April 1779, in ibid.

69. McAdams, "Sullivan Expedition," 63–65.

70. Arthur F. Lykke Jr., "Toward an Understanding of Military Strategy," *The Strategic Environment: Selected Readings* (Fort Leavenworth, Kans.: U.S. Army Command and General Staff College, 1991), 38.

CHAPTER 3: STRATEGY AND OPERATIONS

1. Russell F. Weigley, *A History of the United States Army* (New York: Macmillan Company, 1967), 65. The term *Fabian strategy* comes from the strategy adopted by Quintus Fabius Maximus to meet the superior battlefield prowess of Hannibal during the Second Punic War. Following Hannibal's victories over Roman armies at Trebia (218 b.c.) and at Lake Trasimene (217 b.c.), the new Roman commander, Fabius, adopted a strategy built around fighting delaying actions designed to wear down and exhaust the Carthaginian army, with the hope that it would be ultimately forced to leave Italy. The Romans intended to avoid decisive engagements at all costs unless they found the odds overwhelmingly in their favor. Such a strategy proved a two-edged sword. Though it did wear down Hannibal, it also stretched the patience of the Roman public, eventually bringing Fabius's relief. See Elmer C. May and Gerald P. Stadler, *Ancient and Medieval Warfare* (Wayne, N.J.: Avery Publishing Group, 1984), 57.

2. Dave Richard Palmer, *The Way of the Fox: American Strategy in the War for America, 1775–1783* (Westport, Conn.: Greenwood Press, 1975), 201–2.

3. Russell F. Weigley, "American Strategy: A Call for a Critical Strategic History," in *Reconsiderations on the Revolutionary War*, ed. Don Higginbotham (Westport, Conn.: Greenwood Press, 1978), 40.

4. Washington considered the interior his only safe source of supplies. Because of the British navy, he refrained from building depots within a day's march of the coast. This was particularly true in Connecticut. Intent on guaranteeing himself a source of supply should his army be pushed inland, Washington had Greene build a series of grain depots in the interior: 200,000 bushels at Head of Elk; 200,000 on the Schuylkill; 200,000 total in depots between Lancaster and Wright's Ferry; and 100,000 between the Delaware and the Hudson. Greene located all of the depots above the fall line of nearby rivers and therefore beyond the reach of the British navy. John W. Wright, "Some Notes on the Continental Army," *William*

and Mary Quarterly 12 (July 1931): 187.

5. Thomas G. Frothingham, *Washington: Commander in Chief* (Boston: Houghton Mifflin, 1930), 107.

6. Howard Swiggett, *War out of Niagara: Walter Butler and the Tory Rangers* (Port Washington, N.Y.: Ira J. Friedman, 1933), 185.

7. James Thomas Flexner, *Washington: The Indispensable Man* (New York: NAL/Penguin, 1984), 182.

8. Higginbotham, *War of American Independence*, 328.

9. Frederick the Great warned his generals: "There is an ancient rule of war that cannot be repeated often enough: hold your forces together, make no detachments, and, when you want to fight the enemy, reassemble all your forces and seize every advantage to make sure of your success." See Frederick the Great, "Instructions of Frederick the Great for His Generals, 1747," in *Roots of Strategy*, ed. Thomas R. Phillips (Harrisburg, Pa.: Stackpole Books, 1985), 343–44.

10. Martin L. Van Creveld, *Command in War* (Cambridge, Mass.: Harvard University Press, 1985), 24.

11. On the return march Sullivan did insure the widest possible destruction to the Iroquois homelands by detaching several regiments from the main force and having them burn bypassed villages. One of these detachments proceeded back to Fort Stanwix, while the others rejoined the main army at Fort Reed.

12. Brian Leigh Dunnigan, *Siege—1759: The Campaign against Niagara* (Youngstown, N.Y.: Old Fort Niagara Association, 1986), 9.

13. Fort Niagara's basic design remained true to that of its original French military engineers. A good description of the fort's appearance in 1779 appears in a ration invoice for a rum purchase made for the garrison in the spring of 1779. See Expenditure of Rum at Niagara, 11 May 1779, in Sir Frederick Haldimand: Unpublished Papers, reel 41.

14. Sebastien Le Prestre de Vauban served as Louis XIV's chief engineer. Vauban synthesized much of the new discoveries in mathematics and engineering coming out of the Enlightenment into an advanced science of siege craft. He produced only one published treatise on siege craft, but his views dominated the military thinking of his age. See Henry Guerlac, "Vauban: The Impact of Science on War," in *Makers of Modern Strategy: From Machiavelli to the Nuclear Age*, ed. Peter Paret (Princeton, N.J.: Princeton University Press, 1986), 72–73.

15. Dunnigan, *Siege—1759*, 108–9.

16. Howard H. Peckham, *The Colonial Wars: 1679–1762* (Chicago: University of Chicago Press, 1964), 182. Also see Lawrence Henry Gipson, *The Great War for the Empire: The Victorious Years, 1758–1760* (New York: Alfred A. Knopf, 1949), 7:348–55.

17. Christopher Duffy, *The Fortress in the Age of Vauban and Frederick the Great, 1660–1789* (London: Routledge and Kegan Paul, 1985), 274.
18. Middlekauff, *Glorious Cause*, 309.
19. Haldimand to Germain, 25 July 1778, in Sir Frederick Haldimand: Unpublished Papers, reel 16; Bolton to Haldimand, 1 June 1779, and Bolton to Haldimand, 6 July 1779, in ibid., reel 42.
20. Bolton to Haldimand, 24 May 1779, in ibid.
21. Disposition of Troops in the Back Country as of 21 October 1779, in ibid.
22. Washington to McIntosh, 15 February 1779, in Fitzpatrick, *Writings of Washington*, 14:116.
23. Washington to Brodhead, 22 March 1779, in ibid.
24. Washington to Sullivan, 3 May 1779, in Papers of the Continental Congress, reel 183.
25. Washington to Sullivan, 31 May 1779, in Hammond, *Sullivan Papers*, 3:50–52.
26. Ibid., 49.
27. Ibid.
28. Ibid., 53.
29. Schuyler to Washington, 1 March 1779, in Papers of the Continental Congress, reel 183.
30. Schuyler told Washington that, under optimum conditions, the expedition would be faced by 700 Seneca; 200 Cayuga; 120 Onondaga; 80 Mohawk, Oneida, and Tuscarora; 300 Ottawa and Chippewa; 250 Delaware, Mingo, and Nanticoke; 200 Tories; and 150 British regulars. See Schuyler to Washington, in ibid.
31. Deane to Schuyler, 1 April 1779, in ibid., reel 189.
32. Washington to Schuyler, 11 February 1779, in Fitzpatrick, *Writings of Washington*, 14:94.
33. Schuyler to Washington, 4 February 1779, in Papers of the Continental Congress, reel 183.
34. Sullivan's ability to take hostages depended on how his army approached the Seneca and Cayuga villages in the Finger Lakes. A single axis attack would not provide much opportunity to take hostages. With a superior knowledge of the terrain, the Seneca and Cayuga could always find a way to stay beyond the reach of Sullivan's army. Only a dual-axis advance, with one of the elements attacking west from Fort Stanwix, offered any hope of taking significant numbers of hostages.
35. Schuyler to Washington, 1 March 1779, in ibid.
36. Hand's methods for collecting information proved very similar to

Washington's. He used a questionnaire and surveyed only men who he was sure knew the upper reaches of the river. In Zebulon Butler's questionnaire he asked the following kinds of questions: How much in the way of provisions and forage would be necessary? What is the distance to Chemung? Are the river and creeks frozen? and Are snow shoes necessary? Hand's work did not stop with Washington's assumption of the intelligence collection effort. Well after Hand moved his regiments to Wyoming, he continued to solicit information from officers such as Thomas Hartley, who had led the preceding year's raid against Toga. See Hand to Z. Butler, 17 December 1778, in Papers of Zebulon Butler, Wyoming Valley Historical Society, Wilkes-Barre, Pa.

37. Washington to Reed, 27 February 1779, in *Pennsylvania Archives*, ser. 1, 7:210.

38. Returns on Washington's Questionnaires, n.d., in Papers of the Continental Congress, reel 183.

39. Carl Van Doren, *The Secret History of the American Revolution* (Clifton, N.J.: Augustus M. Kelley Publisher, 1973), 219.

40. Ibid.

41. Lt. John Jenkins, 6 April 1779, in Cook, *Journals of the Military Expedition*, 169; Indian Expedition Questionnaire, in Papers of the Continental Congress, reel 183; and Fitzpatrick, *Writings of Washington*, 14:314–18.

42. Washington to Maxwell, 7 March 1779, in Fitzpatrick, *Writings on Washington*, 14:207.

43. Washington to Philip Van Cortlandt, 13 April 1779, in *Correspondence of the Van Cortlandt Family of Cortlandt Manor, 1748–1800*, ed. Jacob Judd (Tarrytown, N.Y.: Sleepy Hollow Restorations, 1977), 2:300–301.

44. Washington to Schuyler, 21 March 1779, in Fitzpatrick, *Writings of Washington*, 14:397.

45. Ibid.

46. Ibid.

47. Ibid.

48. Washington to George Clinton, 17 April 1779, in ibid., 397.

49. Tactical security can come on one hand from taking the time to examine carefully the route of march or on the other from simply relying on speed. Fast-moving units provide their own security by traveling faster than the enemy's ability to react.

50. Washington to Schuyler, 19 April 1779, in Papers of the Continental Congress, reel 183.

51. Washington to Sullivan, 15 April 1779, in Hammond, *Sullivan Papers*, 3:2–3.

52. Washington to Brodhead, 21 April 1779, in Fitzpatrick, *Writings of*

Washington, 14:421; and Washington to Reed, 27 April 1779, in *Pennsylvania Archives,* ser. 1, 7:351–55.

53. Washington to Sullivan, 29 July 1779, in Hammond, *Sullivan Papers,* 3:88.

54. Brodhead to Sullivan, 6 August 1779, in ibid., 93.

55. Washington was under pressure from both Gates and Hazen to attack Canada by way of the Connecticut. Permitting Hazen to go ahead with the plan quieted both of its proponents while serving Washington's purposes regarding Sullivan. See Allan S. Everest, *Moses Hazen and the Canadian Refugees in the American Revolution* (Syracuse, N.Y.: Syracuse University Press, 1976), 68–69.

56. McAdams, "Sullivan Expedition," 66.

57. Washington to Weare, in Fitzpatrick, *Writings of Washington,* 14:290.

58. Wright, "Some Notes on the Continental Army," 12:187.

59. Haldimand to Robinson, 28 July 1779, in Sir Frederick Haldimand: Unpublished Papers, reel 16.

60. Entry, 9 May 1779, Thomas Hughes, *A Journal by Thos. Hughes for His Amusement, & Designed Only for His Perusal by the Time He Attains the Age of 50 If He Lives So Long* (Cambridge: Cambridge University Press, 1947), 65.

61. Samuel Gustine to Zebulon Butler, 23 April 1779, in Papers of Zebulon Butler; and Christopher Sowers to Henry Clinton, March 1779, in Papers of Henry Clinton, Clements Library, University of Michigan, Ann Arbor, 54:37.

62. Intelligence extract, 1 February 1779, in Great Britain War Office Correspondence.

63. Pennsylvania Packet, 3 April 1779, in Papers of Henry Clinton, 55:38.

64. Cortland Skinner to Henry Clinton, 11 May 1779, in ibid., 57:50.

65. Bowler Metcalf to Henry Clinton, 1 May 1779, in ibid., 8.

66. Butler to Bolton, 3 July 1779, in Great Britain War Office Correspondence; and Alexander C. Flick, "New Sources on the Sullivan-Clinton Campaign in 1779," *New York State Historical Association Quarterly Journal* 10 (July 1929): 266–67.

67. Benedict Arnold to Henry Clinton, 18 June 1779, in Papers of Henry Clinton, 59:1, Arnold to Clinton, 11 July 1779, in ibid.

68. Roger Kaplan, "The Hidden War: British Intelligence Operations during the American Revolution," *William and Mary Quarterly* 47 (January 1990): 126.

69. Clinton to Haldimand, 2 April 1779, in Great Britain War Office Correspondence.

70. "Extracts of Intelligence Received at Quebec," 20 May 1779, in ibid.

71. Sir George Beckwith to Unknown, 14 June 1779, in Papers of Henry Clinton, 61:1.

72. Arnold to Henry Clinton, 18 June 1779, in ibid., 59:1.

73. Arnold to Henry Clinton, 11 July 1779, in ibid. The inaccuracies in Arnold's correspondence raise the question of whether they were deliberate. With Washington's high regard for Arnold, it appears strange that Arnold would not know Sullivan's objective. Arnold's desire to prove himself to the British, however, renders it unlikely that the misinformation was deliberate. Properly concerned for security, Washington more likely deliberately limited information concerning the expedition to officers possessing a need to know. Evidence exists to support this contention. Henry Clinton had already expressed interest in the plans to the fortifications at West Point. When pressed, Arnold had to admit that only Washington and the engineers had access to the plans. See Joseph Stansbury to John Andre, August or September 1779, in ibid., 67:7.

74. Haldimand believed the enemy could threaten his command in five different areas. From west to east, they were: (1) Detroit, (2) Niagara, (3) Montreal, by way of Lake Champlain, (4) Quebec, by way of the Connecticut River, and (5) Quebec, by way of a French naval invasion up the St. Lawrence River. In the case of the latter, see Haldimand to Germain, 18 June 1779, in *Documents of the American Revolution, 1779–1780,* ed. K. G. Davis (Dublin: Irish Academic Press, 1977), 16:121.

75. Germain to Gage, 12 April 1776, in Papers of Thomas Gage, vol. 30, Clements Library, University of Michigan, Ann Arbor.

76. Haldimand to Henry Clinton, 10 November 1778, in Davis, *Documents of the American Revolution,* 14:73.

77. Clinton to Haldimand, 21 May 1779, in ibid., 104.

78. Clinton to Unknown Recipient, 15 May 1779, in Papers of Henry Clinton, 58:13.

79. Haldimand to Clinton, 26–31 May 1779, in Davis, *Documents of the American Revolution,* 16:108.

80. Clinton to Haldimand, 28 July 1770, in Great Britain War Office Correspondence.

81. Clinton did tell Haldimand in September that he had intended to assist in the defense of Canada by attacking Sullivan's depot at Easton. The plan could not be executed, Clinton claimed, because Whitehall had not delivered on promises to send reinforcements to New York. See Clinton to Haldimand, 9 September 1779, in ibid.

82. From the early days of the war Washington maintained spies in Canada. With the approach of Sullivan's raid the commander-in-chief took steps to increase his spy network in Canada. See Washington to Bagley, 5 May 1779, in Fitzpatrick,

Writings of Washington, 14:503; Schuyler to Deane, 15 April 1779, in Diplomatic Extracts of the Continental Congress, National Archives, Washington, D.C., 3:438–41; and Schuyler to the Board of War, 15 April 1779, in Papers of the Continental Congress, reel 189.

83. Schuyler to Sullivan, 21 June 1779, in Hammond, *Sullivan Papers,* 3:64.

84. Butler to Bolton, 3 July 1779, in Flick, "New Sources," 266–67.

85. Haldimand to Bolton, 23 July 1779, in Papers of the Sullivan Indian Campaign, State Archives of New York, Albany.

86. Haldimand to Butler, August 1779, in ibid.

87. Ibid.

88. McDonald to Butler, 24 July 1779, in Sir Frederick Haldimand: Unpublished Papers, reel 42.

89. Flick, "New Sources," 290.

90. Haldimand to the Six Nations, May 1780, in Daniel Claus Papers, Manuscripts Division, Public Archives of Canada, Ottawa, MG 19, ser. F1, 25:176–79.

91. Washington to Sullivan, 15 April 1779, in Hammond, *Sullivan Papers,* 3:4.

92. Weigley, *History of the United States Army,* 268. Custer's defeat at the Little Big Horn was the most notable instance in which this violation of military principle brought disastrous results. For a discussion of Lt. Gen. Philip H. Sheridan's plan for the campaign in the Powder and Yellowstone River Basin, which culminated in Custer's defeat, see Robert M. Utley, "Last Stand," *Quarterly Journal of Military History* 1 (Autumn 1988): 114–17.

Chapter 4: Tactics

1. John Shy, *Toward Lexington: The Role of the British Army in the Coming of the American Revolution* (Princeton, N.J.: Princeton University Press, 1965), 93.

2. Beckles Willson, ed., *The Life and Letters of James Wolfe* (London: W. Heinemann, 1909), 131.

3. Shy, *Toward Lexington,* 100.

4. Some historians have made much of the fact that Sullivan failed to take Fort Niagara. As discussed in chapter 2, Fort Niagara was never more than a target of opportunity. The fort fell to the British in the French and Indian War only after an extensive siege conducted according to Vauban's doctrine for such operations. It included the use of artillery up to eighteen pounds. Sullivan carried no such artillery with him. His largest guns were only six-pound pieces. A six-pound brass cannon excluding carriage weighed nearly five hundred pounds. Anything larger would have been too difficult to move in roadless terrain. Several of Sullivan's offic-

ers, including James Clinton, had fought in the siege of Niagara in 1759. Their presence makes it highly unlikely that Sullivan would have departed intent on laying siege to the fort while lacking the necessary artillery. See Joseph Brant Papers, State Historical Society of Wisconsin, Draper Manuscript Collection (1727–1891), 7F2; and Brian Leigh Dunnigan, *Siege—1759: The Campaign against Niagara* (Youngstown, N.Y.: Old Fort Niagara Association, 1986), 52–53.

5. Most of the scouts who eventually accompanied the army came with Clinton's brigade from Lake Otsego. Sullivan probably had a few with him at Wyoming. How much these warriors knew about the route Sullivan elected to take beyond Toga remains unclear. Undoubtedly, some of the Oneida and Tuscarora warriors had traveled along the trail system that linked the southern door Cayuga and Seneca villages. As for the Stockbridge, a sizable number of Stockbridge Mohicans had elected to settle with the Oneida under Kirkland's watchful eye. It is not unlikely that these men also had at least a rudimentary knowledge of the area. Washington had taken an active role in their recruitment. While at West Point, he directed William Goodrich, a member of the Stockbridge Mohicans, to recruit scouts for Sullivan and authorized him to pay them a private's pay, "unless you find it necessary to distinguish the chief of each tribe by some little pecuniary or other encouragement." See Peter Gansevoort to Caty Gansevoort, 5 July 1779, in Gansevort-Lansing Papers, box 21/1/61; and Patrick Frazier, *The Mohicans of Stockbridge* (Lincoln: University of Nebraska Press, 1992), 227.

6. Good nurses were hard to find and harder still to keep. Washington's chief physician, Dr. James Craik, lamented: "I wish some method could be fallen upon to employ women that can be depended on. The General [Washington] says we may enlist them for at least the same money as are paid soldiers, for he can no longer bear having an army on paper and not have them in the field." The Continental army did make an effort to pay the nurses well. A matron received fifty cents per day plus one food ration, a rate of pay twice that of an army sergeant. Nurses received the same ration and twenty-four cents per day in wages. Linda Grant DePauw, "Women in Combat: The Revolutionary War Experience," *Armed Forces and Society* 7 (Winter 1980): 214.

7. Ibid., 212.

8. Joseph Brant Papers, 7F2.

9. Geoffrey Parker, comments on "The Japanese Army as a Bureaucracy" (paper presented at the History of War as Part of General History Symposium at the Institute for Advanced Studies, Princeton, N.J., 13 March 1993).

10. Russell F. Weigley, "American Strategy: A Call for a Critical Strategic History," in *Reconsiderations on the Revolutionary War,* ed. Don Higginbotham

(Westport, Conn.: Greenwood Press, 1978), 66.

11. Maurice of Nassau had used a battalion formation of about 500 soldiers as his primary tactical unit. Gustavus employed squadrons consisting of 408 soldiers (216 pikemen in the center with 96 arquebusiers on each of the wings). See Albert Sidney Britt and Jerome A. O'Connell, *The Dawn of Modern Warfare* (Wayne, N.J.: Avery Publishing Group, 1984), 47; and Archer Jones, *The Art of War in the Western World* (New York: Oxford University Press, 1987), 222.

12. Jones, *Art of War in the Western World*, 289–90.

13. There had been previous attempts to produced a drill manual applicable to the American soldiers. Timothy Pickering wrote *An Easy Plan of Discipline for a Militia* in 1775 in anticipation that England and its colonies would not peacefully settle their differences. Using the British model for drill as a base, Pickering simplified the instructions. A year later Lewis Nicola argued in *A Treatise of Military Exercise* that the American soldier could not be reasonably expected to compete on a par with British regulars; therefore, simplifying the drill instructions did not represent an answer for the army's tactical needs. Rather than attempt to match the British in volume of fire, Nicola recommended instead that the Americans rely on the rifle for aimed fire and a looser concept of tactics, bearing a closer approximation to guerrilla warfare. Concerned that his emphasis on aimed fire might appear too radical for more conservative thinkers, he wrote: "Using rifles in war is certainly savage and cruel, but the Americans may allege in their defense the law of absolute necessity, which supersedes all other obligations; for they, undisciplined and unused to arms, are compelled to make use of every advantage Providence has put in their power, in order to effectually resist regular and well disciplined troops." See Timothy Pickering Jr., *An Easy Plan of Discipline for a Militia* (Salem, Mass.: Samuel and Ebenezer Hall, 1775); and Lewis Nicola, *A Treatise of Military Exercise Calculated for the Use of the American* (Philadelphia: Styner and Cist Printers, 1776), 2. Neither of the two attempts proved totally satisfactory. In the case of the latter, Washington found very early that he did have to find a way to build an army capable of standing up to the British in the open field.

14. For the purposes of this discussion, I am defining *tactics* as "the planning, training, and control of the ordered arrangements (formations) used by military organizations when engagement between opposing forces is imminent or under way." See John I. Alger, *Definitions and Doctrine of the Military Art, Past and Present* (Wayne, N.J.: Avery Publishing Group, 1985), 7. In the eighteenth century *drill* and *tactics* constituted nearly interchangeable terms. The drill formations of the parade field mirrored the movements units had to perform under fire.

15. Frederick William Baron von Steuben, *Baron von Steuben's Revolutionary War Drill Manual: A Facsimile Reprint of the 1794 Edition* (New York: Dover Publications, 1985), 118.

16. Ibid., ii.

17. Fire power in an eighteenth-century army was based on two key factors: numbers and the rate of fire. Constant mind-numbing drill as well as the introduction of an iron ramrod made it possible for Frederick's infantry to deliver a rate of fire often double that of less proficient armies. See Britt and O'Connell, *Dawn of Modern Warfare*, 105; Russell F. Weigley, *The Age of Battles: The Quest for Decisive Warfare from Breitenfeld to Waterloo* (Bloomington: Indiana University Press, 1991), 170; and Hew Strachan, *European Armies and the Conduct of War* (London: Unwin Hyman, 1983), 16.

18. Jay Luvaas, ed., *Frederick the Great on the Art of War* (New York: Free Press, 1966), 144.

19. Richard A. Preston, Alex Roland, and Sydney F. Wise, *Men in Arms: A History of Warfare and Its Interrelationships with Western Society* (Fort Worth, Tex.: Holt, Rinehart and Winston, 1991), 123.

20. J. F. C. Fuller, *British Light Infantry in the Eighteenth Century* (London: Hutchinson and Company, 1925), 67.

21. Washington liked the light infantry concept and directed that each regiment create one company of light infantry from among its ranks, consisting of agile young men who were good shots. During a campaign they could be formed into a light infantry corps. See Wright, "Some Notes on the Continental Army," 12:192–93; and Strachan, *European Armies and the Conduct of War*, 28.

22. Fuller, *British Light Infantry*, 65.

23. Neither the Prussian drill manual nor its British counterpart included a command to aim. See Britt and O'Connell, *Dawn of Modern Warfare*, 103.

24. Steuben, *Revolutionary War Drill Manual*, 28–29.

25. Steuben, in his zeal to professionalize the American army, moved the army toward standardized weapons by eliminating any other infantry weapon but the bayonet-equipped smoothbore musket. By 1779 this process was nearly complete, although several companies of Morgan's famed rifle corps continued to exist. Washington assigned these to Sullivan. In November 1779 the rifle corps received orders to turn in their rifles to be boxed and stored over the winter. In the spring the quartermasters would reissue the rifles on an "as-needed" basis. See Neil R. York, "Pennsylvania Rifle: Revolutionary Weapon in a Conventional War," *Pennsylvania Magazine of History and Biography* 103 (July 1979): 314–15. Also see John K. Mahon, "Anglo-American Methods of Indian Warfare, 1676–1794," *Mississippi Valley Historical Review* (September 1958): 265; and Wright, "Some Notes on the Continental Army," 12:197.

26. The differences in diameter between the muzzle of a smoothbore musket and its ball frequently was as great as 6/100ths of an inch. This decreased the effect of fouling, but it also permitted the escape of burning gases around the ball rendering the weapon inaccurate. In a rifle the ball size nearly mirrored that of the barrel. See York, "Pennsylvania Rifle," 305.

27. Robert Wright, "Greene's Southern Campaign" (paper presented for Special Warfare Command at Ft. Bragg, N.C., 13 December 1994).

28. There is little written on this troop, although the men appear to have been assigned to Hubley's regiment at the start of the operation. They were probably a troop of dragoons, and their only notable mission involved bringing back the deserters from the German battalion that had left Wyoming for Easton. Before the army left Wyoming, Sullivan dismounted them and made use of their horses for other duties. Hubley to Hand, 17 June 1779, in Emmett Collection, Manuscripts Division, New York Public Library, New York.

29. John Morgan Dederer, *War in America to 1775: Before Yankee Doodle* (New York: New York University Press, 1990), 62.

30. Ibid., 109.

31. Peter E. Russell, "Redcoats in the Wilderness: British Officers and Irregular Warfare in Europe and America, 1740 to 1760," *William and Mary Quarterly* 35 (October 1978): 641, 645.

32. Joseph P. Tustin, ed., *Diary of the American War: A Hessian Journal* (New Haven, Conn.: Yale University Press, 1979), 108.

33. *Doctrine* is "the accepted body of ideas concerning war." The term first entered common usage in the nineteenth century. See Alger, *Definitions and Doctrine*, 7.

34. George Washington, "The Braddock Campaign," *American History Illustrated* 5 (November 1970): 17.

35. See Vegetius, " Military Institutions of the Romans," in *Roots of Strategy*, ed. Thomas R. Phillips (Harrisburg, Pa.: Stackpole Books, 1985), 132–34; and Maurice de Saxe, *The Reveries on the Art of War* (Harrisburg, Pa.: Military Service Publishing Company, 1944), 261.

36. Washington, "Braddock Campaign," 16.

37. Ibid.

38. Ibid., 19; and Russell, "Redcoats in the Wilderness," 642–44.

39. Washington to Sullivan, 3 May 1779, in Papers of the Continental Congress, reel 183.

40. Vegetius, "Military Institutions of the Romans," 132.

41. Ibid., 125.

42. Saxe, *Reveries*, 298.

43. When the army left Wyoming, Proctor's artillery went by boat rather than overland, as originally specified in the movement orders. Difficult terrain and the detrimental effect it would have on the army's speed probably explains the decision.

44. The Continental army's procedures for crossing defiles required elements of the advanced guard to halt the army then clear and secure the obstacle. Once this was accomplished, the army resumed its march, with the security guard falling in at the rear and then presumably working its way back to the front. John W. Wright, "Some Notes on the Continental Army," *The William and Mary Quarterly* 11 (April 1931): 85.

45. Assigning light artillery to line units was not unusual. Artillery is most effective when fired in battery, but the terrain made such concentrations difficult and command nearly impossible. Sullivan's answer was to attach some of his individual guns (usually the light three-pound pieces) to individual brigade commanders to employ as they saw fit while he kept the rest of Proctor's regiment in reserve and under his own control. See American Revolution Orderly Book (unit unspecified), 23 August 1779, in Military Records Collection, Wyoming Valley Historical Society, Wilkes-Barre, Pa.

46. Lt. Col. Henry Dearborn, 31 July 1779, in Cook, *Journals of the Military Expedition*, 68.

47. Rev. William Rogers, 25 July 1779, in ibid., 253.

48. For a Continental army platoon this meant an eight-man front. This represented an attempt to copy Prussian march methods. See Nathan Davis, "Nathan Davis' History," *Historical Magazine* 3 (April 1868): 199; Order Book of Lt. Col. Francis Barber, entry 4 August 1779, in *Notes from the Collections of Toga Point Museum and Its Centennial Celebration of 1879*, ed. Louise Welles Murray (Athens, Pa.: Toga Point Historical Society, 1929), 59; and Henry Lloyd, *History of the Late War in Germany between the King of Prussia and the Empress of Germany and Her Allies* (London: S. Hooper, 1781), 2:130.

49. William Barton, 10 August 1779, in Cook, *Journals of the Military Expedition*, 6.

50. Sullivan's river crossing follows almost exactly the procedures put forth by Maurice de Saxe and by Frederick the Great. See Saxe, *Reveries*; Phillips, *Roots of Strategy*, 96; and Frederick, "Instructions," 364.

51. Lt. Col. Adam Hubley, 11 August 1779, in Cook, *Journals of the Military Expedition*, 151.

52. Dr. Ebenezer Elmer, 11 August 1779, in ibid., 85.

53. Sullivan reconfigured his brigade organizations once Clinton joined him at Toga. The reorganization generally attempted to incorporate all state regiments

into the same brigade. Hand's brigade consisted of predominantly Pennsylvania units. New England regiments came under Enoch Poor's command. Clinton gained all the New York regiments, and Maxwell received the New Jersey troops. See Albert Hazen Wright, *New York Historical Source Studies: The Sullivan Expedition of 1779, Regimental Rosters of Men,* ser. no. 34 (Albany: New York State Historical Society, 1965), 1–4.

54. Thomas Grant, 11 August 1779, in ibid., 139.

55. Sullivan to Shreve, 24 August 1779, in *The Letters and Papers of Major-General John Sullivan, Continental Army,* ed. Otis G. Hammond (Concord: New Hampshire Historical Society, 1931), 3:103.

56. American Revolutionary Orderly Book (unit unspecified), 23 August 1779, Military Records Collection, Wyoming Valley Historical Society, Wilkes-Barre, Pa.

57. Haldimand was very concerned about Fort Sullivan and ordered Bolton to have it reduced. Bolton delegated the task to Sir John Johnson. Johnson told Bolton that he was preparing a force to destroy the post. In addition to a sizable force of Tories and natives, Johnson reported that he would take two six-pound brass cannons and requested that Bolton forward one or two coehorns to assist in the siege. Sullivan and his men destroyed the post before departing Tioga, but this was still unknown to Johnson. See Haldimand to Bolton, 16 September 1779, and Johnson to Bolton, 29 September 1779, in Papers of the Sullivan Indian Campaign.

58. Lt. William McKendry, 28 August 1779, in ibid., 203.

59. The drum signals permitted commanders to widen or narrow the unit fronts as needed depending on the terrain and the enemy situation. See Orderly Book of Spenser's Fifth New York, 4 August 1779, in Orderly Books of the Revolution, Manuscript Division, New York Public Library, New York, reel 9; and Order Book of Lt. Col. Francis Barber, 4 August 1779, in Murray, *Notes from the Collections of Toga Point Museum,* 59.

60. Ibid., 43.

61. Peter Gansevoort to Caty Gansevoort, 10 August 1779, in Gansevoort-Lansing Papers, Box 21/1/68.

62. Martin L. Van Creveld, *The Transformation of War* (New York: Free Press, 1991), 101–5.

63. Lt. John Jenkins, 11 August, in Cook, *Journals of the Military Expedition,* 170.

64. One issue raised by the composition of Cummings's patrol is its lack of Indian scouts. Most of the Indians who joined Sullivan came with Clinton. See Christine Sternberg Patrick, "The Life and Times of Samuel Kirkland, 1741–1808: Missionary to the Oneida Indians, American Patriot, and Founder of Hamilton

College" (Ph.D. diss., State University of New York at Buffalo, 1993), 331; and Herbert John Lennox, "Samuel Kirkland's Mission to the Iroquois" (Ph.D. diss., University of Chicago, 1932), 132–33.

65. Sullivan to Washington, 15 August 1779, in Hammond, *Sullivan Papers,* 3:98.

66. Ibid.

67. Lt. Col. Henry Dearborn, 12 August 1779, in ibid., 70.

68. Journal of Nathan Webb, 13 August 1779, in Joseph Brant Papers, 7F4.

69. Lt. Col. Henry Dearborn, 12 August 1779, in Hammond, *Sullivan Papers* 3:70.

70. Sullivan described his artillery as "one howitzer" in a letter he wrote to the president of the Continental Congress then told Washington it was a coehorn mortar. The latter is more likely because the army's howitzers were simply too heavy to transport forty miles across broken country at night. A small coehorn weighed not much more than two hundred pounds and could be carried by hand. See Sullivan to the president of the Continental Congress, 15 August 1779, in Hammond, *Sullivan Papers,* 3:96; and Sullivan to Washington, 15 August 1779, in ibid., 99.

71. The numbers vary depending on whose account one accepts. Sullivan lists seven killed and thirteen wounded in his letters. Ibid., 97.

72. Ibid., 100.

73. Order Book of Francis Barber, 13 August 1779, in Murray, *Notes from the Collections of Toga Point Museum,* 67.

74. Maj. Jeremiah Fogg, 26 August 1779, in Cook, *Journals of the Military Expedition,* 94.

75. Ibid.

76. Lt. William Barton, 28 August 1779, in ibid., 7.

77. Butler to Bolton, 21 July 1779, in Alexander C. Flick, "New Sources on the Sullivan-Clinton Campaign in 1779," *New York State Historical Association Quarterly Journal* 10 (July 1929): 270.

78. Butler to Bolton, 3 June 1779, in ibid., 220.

79. Butler to Bolton, 18 June 1779, in ibid., 265.

80. Butler to Bolton, 24 June 1779, in Papers of the Sullivan Indian Campaign.

81. Haldimand to Henry Clinton, 29 August 1779, in ibid.

82. Germain to Henry Clinton, 20 September 1779, in Sackville Germain Papers, Clements Library, University of Michigan, Ann Arbor, vol. 10.

83. Haldimand to Henry Clinton, 29 August 1779, in Papers of the Sullivan Indian Campaign.

84. McDonald to Butler, 5 August 1779, in ibid.

85. Butler to Bolton, 3 June 1779, in ibid.

86. Iroquois leaders generally held these sentiments in check until after the Battle of Newtown. Following the defeat, they did not hesitate to voice their disappointment with their perception that the British had abandoned them. "The Six Nations have been long threatened by the Rebels and they have for these three years past been running a Race against Numbers of British antagonists," wrote Chief David in a letter to Haldimand. "They are now almost out of breath." See David (a Mohawk) to Haldimand, 13 September 1779, in *Iroquois Indians: A Documentary History of the Diplomacy of the Six Nations and Their League*, ed. Francis Jennings (Woodbridge, Ct., 1985), reel 34.

87. Butler to Bolton, 10 August 1779, in Papers of the Sullivan Indian Campaign.

88. Bolton to Haldimand, 16 August 1779, in ibid.

89. Butler to Bolton, 31 August 1779, in Sir Frederick Haldimand: Unpublished Papers, reel 42; and Flick, "New Sources," 282–84.

90. Kelsay points out that Indian traditions held that the chiefs from the most directly threatened villages had the final say in these matters. See Kelsay, *Joseph Brant*, 259; and the Journal of R. Cartwright, 26 August 1779, in Joseph Brant Papers, Draper MSS 6F48.32.

91. Native American tribes east of the Mississippi River preferred to employ a half-moon formation in which decisions occurred as a result of the two wings of the formation falling on the enemy's flanks and rear. Surprise and maneuverability were key to success. The attackers had to close quickly and capitalize on the chaos and fear such tactics created in their opponent's ranks. The French and Indian forces who stopped Braddock's army just short of its objective, Fort Duquesne, employed the formation. Good security was the most important means to avoid being caught in such an ambuscade. Once caught, the key was to maneuver so as to drive the Indians out of the formation and prevent the wings from collapsing inward. See Leroy V. Eid, "'A Kind of Running Fight': Indian Battlefield Tactics in the Late Eighteenth Century," *Western Pennsylvania Historical Magazine* 71 (2 April 1988): 148,155, 160–66.

92. Journal of R. Cartwright, 26 August 1779, in Joseph Brant Papers, Draper MSS 6F48.32; and Butler to Mason, 31 August 1779, in Sir Frederick Haldimand: Unpublished Papers, reel 42.

93. Ibid.

94. Kelsay, *Joseph Brant*, 260.

95. Lt. Erkuries Beatty, 28 August 1779, in Cook, *Journals of the Military Expedition*, 26.

96. Maj. Jeremiah Fogg, in ibid., 94.

97. Dr. Jabez Campfield, in ibid., 55.

98. Ernest Cruikshank, *Butler's Rangers: The Revolutionary Period* (Niagara Falls, Ont.: Renown Printing Company, 1988), 71.

99. Kelsay, *Joseph Brant,* 261.

100. Lt. John Jenkins, 29 August 1779, in Cook, *Journals of the Military Expedition,* 173.

101. This adaptation may have had its roots in the Hartley expedition of the preceding year. In his report to Congress following his raid on Toga, Hartley made a point of noting that musketeers, with their inaccurate smoothbores, labored under considerable disadvantages in woodland combat. He suggested that the use of rifle armed light infantry offered a better means of dealing with the demands of warfare in broken terrain. See Thomas Hartley to the Continental Congress, 8 October 1779, in Papers of the Continental Congress, reel 96.

102. Samuel McNeill, 29 August 1779, in *Pennsylvania Archives,* ser. 2, 15:756.

103. Sullivan to Washington, 30 August 1779, in Hammond, *Sullivan Papers,* 3:109.

104. Sgt. Maj. George Grant, 29 August 1779, in Cook, *Journals of the Military Expedition,* 110.

105. Sgt. Moses Fellows, in ibid., 88.

106. Lt. Col. Dearborn, in ibid., 72; and Joseph Brant Papers, Draper MSS 6F45.

107. Davis, "Nathan Davis' History," 200.

108. Butler to Bolton, 31 August 1779, in Sir Frederick Haldimand: Unpublished Papers, reel 42.

109. Butler was not alone in the dim view he took of Indian performance. Although noting that the thirty Indians who accompanied McDonald gave good service, R. Cartwright, one of the rangers, noted in his journal, "The behaviors of the Indians on this occasion has fully convinced me, that thou they may exert themselves against defenseless people or an enemy taken at surprise with great fury, they will soon give way when taken at equal terms in the field." See Journal of R. Cartwright, 29 August 1779, in Joseph Brant Papers, Draper MSS 6F47; and Howard Swiggett, *War out of Niagara: Walter Butler and the Tory Rangers* (Port Washington, N.Y.: Ira J. Friedman, 1933), 198.

110. Samuel McNeill, 29 August 1779, *Pennsylvania Archives,* ser. 2, 12:756; and Butler to Bolton, 31 August 1779, in Sir Frederick Haldimand: Unpublished Papers, reel 42.

111. Casualty figures vary considerably depending on source. Sullivan lists three dead and thirty-nine wounded. Most other American sources place Sullivan's losses at somewhere between thirty and forty. See Sullivan to Washington, 30 August

1779, in Hammond, *Sullivan Papers*, 3:111; and Albert Hazen Wright, *New York Historical Source Studies: The Sullivan Expedition of 1779, The Losses*, ser. no. 34 (Albany: New York State Historical Society, 1965), 24–25.

112. Swiggett, *War out of Niagara*, 198.

113. Sullivan to Washington, 30 August 1779, in Hammond, *Sullivan Papers*, 3:110.

114. Daniel K. Richter, "War and Culture: The Iroquois Experience," *William and Mary Quarterly* 40 (October 1983): 533.

115. Ibid., 537.

116. Ibid., 535–36.

117. Butler to Bolton, 31 August 1779, in Sir Frederick Haldimand: Unpublished Papers, reel 42.

118. During the Battle of Saratoga, Morgan had required the assistance of Dearborn's line infantry regiment to protect them against a British attack. See Don Higginbotham, *Daniel Morgan: Revolutionary Rifleman* (Chapel Hill: University of North Carolina Press, 1961), 77; and Preston, Roland, and Wise, *Men in Arms*, 153.

119. Maj. Jeremiah Fogg, 1 September 1779, in Cook, *Journals of the Military Expedition*, 96.

120. Sullivan to Jay, 30 September 1779, in Hammond, *Sullivan Papers*, 3:129.

121. R. W. G. Vail, ed., *The Revolutionary War Diary of Lt. Obadiah Gore* (New York: New York Public Library Publications, 1929), 28.

122. Wright, *Sullivan Expedition of 1779*, 26.

123. Murphy had made his reputation at Freeman's Farm during the Saratoga campaign. Fearing General Simon Fraser might be successful in rallying British and Hessian forces, Morgan had called on Murphy, a native of the Susquehanna Valley, to kill the British officer. Murphy climbed a tree, took aim, and fired. Accounts relate that the first round cut the crupper on Fraser's horse, the second creased the horse's mane, and the third hit Fraser, mortally wounding him. See Higginbotham, *Daniel Morgan*, 73–74.

124. Sullivan to Jay, 30 September 1779, in Hammond, *Sullivan Papers*, 3:130.

125. Boyd did not stand up well under interrogation. Butler reported that Boyd disclosed Sullivan's troop and artillery strength, the order of battle, the campaign's objective, and the army's supply situation. With Boyd's information Butler realized that Sullivan did not have the capability of threatening Niagara. Butler's letter did not indicate that Boyd's information was yielded under duress, yet it is unlikely that he could have been ignorant of the fate that awaited the two men once they had provided the information he desired. See Butler to Bolton, 14 September 1779, in Sullivan Indian Campaign, box 1 F 3.

126. Ibid.; and Patrick, "Life and Times of Samuel Kirkland," 335.

127. Alger, *Definitions and Doctrine*, 5.

128. Stephen Griffin Journal, 12 September 1779, in Manuscript Division, New York State Library, Albany.

129. Preston, Roland, and Wise, *Men in Arms*, 153.

130. McDonald to Bolton, 24 July 1779, in Sir Frederick Haldimand: Unpublished Papers, reel 42.

131. Butler to Bolton, 26 August 1779, in Papers of the Sullivan Indian Campaign.

132. Butler to Bolton, 31 August 1779, in Sir Frederick Haldimand: Unpublished Papers, reel 42.

Chapter 5: Logistics

1. L. Andre, ed., *Le Testament politique du Cardinal Richelieu* (Paris: 1947), 480; quoted in Martin L. Van Creveld, *Supplying War: Logistics from Wallenstein to Patton* (Cambridge: Cambridge University Press, 1986), 17.

2. Washington to Wadsworth, 14 February 1779, in *The Writings of George Washington from the Original Manuscript Sources, 1745–1799*, ed. John C. Fitzpatrick (Washington, D.C.: U.S. Government Printing Office, 1936), 14:113.

3. John R. Elting, *Swords around a Throne: Napoleon's Grande Armée* (New York: Free Press, 1988), 554.

4. Van Creveld, *Supplying War*, 27.

5. Supply problems are only one of a number of factors that could propel an army to its culminating point. Personnel losses due to combat or disease also impact on the issue. *FM 100–5 Operations* (Washington, D.C.: Department of the Army, 1986), 181–82.

6. Washington to Schuyler, 21 March 1779, in Papers of the Continental Congress, reel 183.

7. Greene to Washington, 17 March 1779, in *The Papers of General Nathanael Greene*, ed. Richard K. Showman (Chapel Hill: University of North Carolina Press, 1986), 3:346–47.

8. Ibid., 325.

9. Durham boats first appeared on the Delaware River about 1750. They were approximately sixty feet long, eight feet wide, and two feet deep. They possessed a keelboat shape similar to an Indian bark canoe and carried a crew of five. Though the craft carried a two-sail mast, it was more likely that the crew would propel it using setting poles.

10. Greene to Washington, 23 April 1779, in Fitzpatrick, *Writings of Washington*, 14:438.

11. The word *dollar* here refers to the Spanish milled dollar, which the Congress chose to use as the standard measure of specie. See Thomas Robert Veleker, "Pennsylvania's Performance under the Old Money Requisition System during the American Revolution" (master's thesis, Kansas State University, 1976), 9–11.

12. Erna Risch, *Supplying Washington's Army* (Washington, D.C.: Center of Military History, United States Army, 1981), 18.

13. Ibid.

14. Greene to Washington, 5 January 1779, in Showman, *Papers of General Nathanael Greene*, 3:144–45.

15. Lewis to Greene, in ibid., 241.

16. Greene to Lewis, 10 February 1779, in ibid., 226.

17. The Continental army was no different from its European counterparts. Most eighteenth-century armies relied on private contractors for wagons. Few were happy with the results. It was not until the nineteenth century, when armies made the decision to develop and maintain their own service and support branches, that the problem improved.

18. There was a move afoot to create a wagon corps organic to the Continental army, but it was not in place by the spring of 1779.

19. Greene to Hay, 26 February 1779, in Showman, *Papers of General Nathanael Greene*, 3:309.

20. E. Wayne Carp, *To Starve the Army at Pleasure: Continental Army Administration and American Political Culture, 1775–1783* (Chapel Hill: University of North Carolina Press, 1984), 80–81.

21. Benedict Arnold had been accused of this during his stay in Philadelphia and in fact had used public wagons to transport his private property. He had, however, paid for the use of the wagons. The Executive Council had also charged Hooper with this during the army's stay at Valley Forge. Hooper denied the charges, and the Board of War dismissed them without bothering to hear the Executive Council's case against Hooper. The situation created considerable ill will inside the Executive Council, with the result that their dislike for Hooper got in the way of taking care of Sullivan. Risch, *Supplying Washington's Army*, 431–32.

22. Sullivan to Reed, 11 May 1779, in *The Letters and Papers of Major-General John Sullivan, Continental Army*, ed. Otis G. Hammond (Concord: New Hampshire Historical Society, 1931), 3:19.

23. Forrest to Sullivan, 20 May 1779, in ibid., 27; and Pettit to Reed, 20 May 1779, *Pennsylvania Archives*, ser. 1, 7:420.

24. Reed to the Board of War, in ibid., 424–25. Reed was no supporter of Sullivan. He believed him the wrong man for the job and made his views known to Greene. Greene did his best to convince Reed that Washington's decision to place

Sullivan in command came after considerable deliberation, but it does not appear that Reed was convinced. Additionally, neither Reed nor the rest of the council were happy over the fact that Sullivan wanted the warrants delivered to Hooper. Greene to Washington, 26 April 1779, in Showman, *Papers of General Nathanael Greene*, 3:430.

25. Pennsylvania Council to Sullivan, 21 May 1779, in Hammond, *Sullivan Papers*, 3:28.

26. Ibid., 29.

27. Ibid.

28. Sullivan to Reed, 26 May 1779, in ibid., 41–42.

29. Sullivan to Washington, 26 May 1779, in ibid., 42.

30. General Henry Clinton's intelligence apparatus did use the contracting system as a source of intelligence. British spies in Philadelphia reported that the Continental army was planning some sort of operation on the frontier based on the number of pack saddles being produced under army contract in Philadelphia. See Intelligence Extract, 1 February 1779, in Great Britain War Office Correspondence.

31. Hooper to Hart, 27 April 1779, in Revolutionary War Records (Records Group 93), National Archives, Washington, D.C., reel 122.

32. Risch, *Supplying Washington's Army*, 78.

33. Hooper to Greene, 5 May 1779, in Showman, *Papers of General Nathanael Greene*, 3:450.

34. Order Book of Lt. Col. Francis Barber, in *Notes from the Collections of Toga Point Museum and Its Centennial Celebration of 1879*, ed. Louise Welles Murray (Athens, Pa.: Toga Point Historical Society, 1929), 2.

35. Orderly Book of the Fifth New Jersey, 27 July 1779, in Orderly Books of the Revolution.

36. Lt. Charles Nukerck, 18 September 1779, in *Journals of the Military Expedition of Major General John Sullivan against the Six Nations of the Indians in 1779*, ed. Frederick Cook (Freeport, N.Y.: Books for Libraries Press, 1972), 218.

37. Washington to Malcolm, 17 April 1779, in Fitzpatrick, *Writings of Washington*, 14:402–3.

38. Sullivan to Washington, 12 May 1779, in Hammond, *Sullivan Papers*, 3:20.

39. Route reconnaissance in eighteenth-century armies fell under the auspices of the quartermaster. Washington did ask Greene to query Charles Stewart, one of Greene's subordinates, about the condition of the trail between Easton and Wyoming. The information Stewart provided indicated that the path would be usable after some improvement. No other record exists to suggest that Washington asked

anyone else about the path. Washington appears to have assumed that the existing path would require some work but that it would be usable in a short time. Greene to Stewart, 17 April 1779, in Showman, *Papers of General Nathanael Greene*, 3:415; also Sullivan to Washington, 8 May 1779, in Hammond, *Sullivan Papers*, 3:14–15.

40. Sullivan to Washington, 31 May 1779, in Hammond, *Sullivan Papers*, 3:14–15.

41. Nathan Davis, "Nathan Davis' History," *Historical Magazine* 3 (April 1868): 198.

42. Philip Van Cortlandt to Pierre Van Cortlandt, 20 June 1779, in *Correspondence of the Van Cortlandt Family of Cortlandt Manor, 1748–1800*, ed. Jacob Judd (Tarrytown, N.Y.: Sleepy Hollow Restorations, 1977), 326.

43. Rev. William Rogers, 20 June 1779, in Cook, *Journals of the Military Expedition*, 247.

44. Greene to Col. John Davis, 26 February 1779, in Showman, *Papers of General Nathanael Greene*, 3:308.

45. Washington to Jeremiah Wadsworth, 20 April 1779, in Papers of the Continental Congress, reel 183.

46. Washington had directed that the boats be capable of carrying three to four tons, but Greene's fears about the carrying capacity of the river in summer forced a revision, downward to two tons. The records that survive indicate that Sullivan did receive a substantial number of boats larger than two tons, though no record of exact numbers has survived. Greene estimated that he would need 140 boats to adequately support Sullivan. Showman, *Papers of General Nathanael Greene*, 3:325.

47. Greene to Jay, 19 September 1779, in ibid., 395–97.

48. Blaine to Sullivan, 24 May 1779, in Hammond, *Sullivan Papers*, 3:39.

49. Claiborne to Greene, 6 May 1779, in Showman, *Papers of General Nathanael Greene*, 3:458–59.

50. Washington's commissary officers had assured him that there would be no shortage of food on the lower Susquehanna. In April, Royal Flint, the assistant commissary of purchases, boasted, "I make no doubt that several armies may be comfortably subsisted through the campaign." See Flint to Washington, 30 April 1779, in Papers of the Continental Congress, reel 183. Had all of the food Blaine claimed present been usable, Sullivan should have had on hand seventy-seven days' worth of meat, given that the Board of War's standard for individual meat rations was 1.25 pounds of beef, 1 pounds of pork, or 1.25 pounds of fish per day. Risch, *Supplying Washington's Army*, 190.

51. Washington to Measam, 20 April 1779, in Fitzpatrick, *Writings of Washington*, 14:419.

52. Washington to Wadsworth, 14 February 1779, in ibid., 113.
53. Washington to the Board of War, 20 March 1779, in ibid., 265.
54. Risch, *Supplying Washington's Army,* 87.
55. Washington to McIntosh, 5 February 1779, in Papers of the Sullivan Indian Campaign.
56. Brodhead to Washington, 16 September 1779, in Cook, *Journals of the Military Expedition,* 307.
57. Ibid., 308.
58. James Clinton to Washington, 28 May 1779, in Papers of the Sullivan Indian Campaign.
59. Sullivan to Washington, 12 June 1779, in Hammond, *Sullivan Papers,* 3:60.
60. Steele to Stewart, in "Supplies for General Sullivan: The Correspondence of Colonel Charles Stewart, May–September 1779," ed. Marion Brophy and Wendell Tripp, *New York History* 60 (July 1979): 274.
61. Ibid.
62. Though not blaming Washington outright, the Board of War did explain to Sullivan in July that the commissary problems stemmed from a shortage of men and materials. Specifically addressing the barrel problem, the Board admitted that, with an inadequate supply of properly dried wood, the quartermasters had used green wood in the barrels, a solution that everyone involved recognized as inadequate for a summer campaign. Board of War to Sullivan, 21 July 1779, in Hammond, *Sullivan Papers,* 3:79.
63. Hubley to Sullivan, 2 July 1779, in ibid., 70.
64. Order Book of Lt. Col. Francis Barber, 26 June 1779, in Murray, *Notes from the Collections of Toga Point Museum,* 22.
65. Ens. Daniel Gookin, 21 July 1779, in Cook, *Journals of the Military Expedition,* 104.
66. Blaine to Sullivan, 24 May 1779, in Hammond, *Sullivan Papers,* 3:39.
67. Sullivan to Jay, 21 July 1779, in ibid., 82.
68. Wadsworth to Harrison, 3 July 1779, in Papers of the Continental Congress, reel 183.
69. The commissary department computed rations based on the assumption that each soldier should receive 1.25 pounds of beef per day and that a live cow could yield 130 pounds of usable meat, once butchered. This meant that Sullivan's additional 270 cattle could, under ideal conditions, yield 28,080 rations, or about seven days of meat for an army of four thousand men. Diary of Ebenezer Elmer, 19 July 1779, in Cook, *Journals of the Military Expedition,* 83.
70. Maj. John Burrows recorded in his diary that only one in twelve of his soldiers possessed blankets. See Maj. John Burrowes, 25 August 1779, in ibid., 43.

71. Washington to Sullivan, 5 July 1779, in Hammond, *Sullivan Papers,* 3:71.
72. Sullivan to Washington, 10 July 1779, in ibid., 75.
73. Greene was particularly concerned that Sullivan's accusations were damaging his own reputation as well as that of his subordinates. Writing to Wadsworth, Greene noted that he had received dispatches from the army on the Susquehanna and that, as usual, Sullivan found himself "surrounded with difficulties and perplexed with mazes." Greene went on to say that, if Sullivan accomplished his mission, he would forgive him (the accusations he had made against the quartermasters and commissaries), but, if he returned "without doing any thing, with his Mouthful of complaints, I shall take the liberty to abuse him, in a genteel way." Greene to Wadsworth, 19 August 1779, in Showman, *Papers of General Nathanael Greene,* 3:330.
74. Blaine to Washington, June 1779, in Papers of the Continental Congress, reel 183.
75. Washington to Sullivan, 29 July 1779, in Hammond, *Sullivan Papers,* 3:87.
76. Sullivan to Shreve, 24 August 1779, in ibid., 102.
77. Rev. William Rogers, in Cook, *Journals of the Military Expedition,* 265.
78. The Iroquois fields could have provided Sullivan's soldiers with most of the dietary needs, including protein, had the science of nutrition been more advanced in the eighteenth century.
79. Maj. John Burrows, 25 August 1779, in ibid., 43.
80. The need for a depot at Toga had been part of the original plan for the operation. Washington's intelligence varied in quality, but it was the general consensus of those he polled that Toga was the logical place for the army's last major depot.
81. Sullivan's Address to the Army, 30 August 1779, in Hammond, *Sullivan Papers,* 3:112.
82. The first return indicates 425 cattle, plus 4 barrels of salt beef, 2 barrels of salt pork, and 2 barrels of salt fish. Using the standard ration set for the army, this is 46,240 rations, or 8.4 days of rations for an army of fifty-five hundred men. The second return lists 254 cattle, 1 barrel of salt beef, 534 pounds of pork, and 197 pounds of salt fish. This is 27,349 rations, or 4.9 days of rations. Revolutionary War Records (Records Group 93), reel 122.
83. Davis, "Nathan Davis' History," 203.
84. Maj. Jeremiah Fogg, in Cook, *Journals of the Military Expedition,* 98.
85. Ibid.
86. Ibid., 98.
87. Fort Reed was little more than a blockhouse located near present-day Elmira, N.Y.

88. Estimates vary as to the number of deaths suffered by Sullivan's army. Sullivan himself reported he lost fewer than forty men, with almost all the deaths occurring as a result of combat, not disease.

89. Van Creveld, *Supplying War,* 27.

CHAPTER 6: LEADERSHIP

1. George Washington to Lund Washington, 20 August 1775, in *The Writings of George Washington from the Original Manuscript Sources, 1745–1799,* ed. John C. Fitzpatrick (Washington, D.C.: U.S. Government Printing Office, 1936), 3:433.

2. General Orders, 1 August 1775, in ibid., 383.

3. General Orders, 2 August 1775, in ibid.

4. General Orders, 10 August 1775, in ibid., 412.

5. Washington to Lund Washington, 20 August 1775, in ibid., 433.

6. Leadership was apparently seen largely as a personal characteristic, more the product of birth than a developed trait. James Wolfe provided the most applicable advice on the subject in *Instructions to Young Officers.* He cautioned officers to take care of their soldiers before themselves and to become familiar with their names. Besides these commonsense pieces of advice, he left the subject alone. A latter tract published in America early in the war, Lewis Nicola's *Treatise of Military Exercise Calculated for the Use of the Americans* Lewis (Philadelphia: Styner and Cist Printers, 1776), cautioned officers that they should procure the goodwill of their soldiers by "doing strict justice to the men in all their rights" and by keeping them to their duty without unnecessary harshness or cruelty. Nicola said that soldiers were kept to their duty largely by fear of punishment but admitted "that soldiers have sometimes principles and a way of thinking superior to the common run of mankind." See General James Wolfe, *Instructions to Young Officers* (London: Printed for J. Millan, 1768); and Nicola, *Treatise of Military Exercise,* 89–90.

7. Allen Bowman, *The Morale of the American Revolutionary Army* (Washington, D.C.: American Council on Public Affairs, 1943), 34–35.

8. James Kirby Martin and Mark Edward Lender, *A Respectable Army: The Military Origins of the Republic, 1763–1789* (Arlington Heights, Ill.: Harlan Davidson, 1982), 161–63.

9. Soldiers did kill one officer and mortally wound two others during the Pennsylvania line's mutiny. See Mark Edward Lender, "The Enlisted Line: The Continental Soldiers of New Jersey" (Ph.D. diss., Rutgers University, 1975), 234–35.

10. The American army was probably not the equal of its British opponent at the end of the war, but it was beginning to approach parity and may have actually surpassed its opponents in some areas, such as the proficiency of artillery units. A

British victory would have required additional expenditures of manpower, money, and time—resources that Whitehall no longer possessed the will to use.

11. Two other issues threatened the positions of colonial elites. First, the British government viewed power as emanating from England outward to the colonies. Elites in America ruled because Britain let them. Second, a growing, dispersed, and diverse population had started to render ineffective the old "face-to-face" methods elites had once depended on to rule. See John Shy, *A People Numerous and Armed: Reflections on the Military Struggle for American Independence* (Ann Arbor: University of Michigan Press, 1990), 123–24.

12. Gordon S. Wood, *The Radicalism of the American Revolution* (New York: Alfred A. Knopf, 1992), 189.

13. Ibid.

14. Charles Royster, *A Revolutionary People at War: The Continental Army and American Character, 1775–1783* (New York: W. W. Norton, 1979), 49–50.

15. Voluntary enlistments did not constitute the sole source of manpower for the Continental line. Some states used drafts from the militia to fill the ranks. The use of substitutes was also common.

16. Ibid., 373–74.

17. Lender, "Enlisted Line," 149.

18. In the case of the Pennsylvania Line the mutiny revolved around issues involving back pay and the question of their terms of enlistment. The enlistment contracts were vague. Soldiers believed they had signed on for the duration of the war or three years, whichever occurred first. The state as well as the army's leadership subscribed to the idea that they had signed on for the duration of the war. When the mutiny broke out, the soldiers killed one officer, seriously wounded two others, and roughed up several others. The officers had been engaged in trying to quell the riot and did not represent the focal point of the men's anger. The mutineers intended to march on Philadelphia to force the Congress and the Assembly to meet their demands. The state eventually worked out a compromise that largely yielded to the soldier's demands. See Paul David Nelson, *Anthony Wayne, Soldier of the Early Republic* (Bloomington: Indiana University Press, 1985), 118–20; and Carl Van Doren, *Mutiny in January: The Story of a Crisis in the Continental Army* (New York: Viking Press, 1943), 44–46.

19. Charles H. Lesser, ed., *The Sinews of Independence: Monthly Strength Reports of the Continental Army* (Chicago: University of Chicago Press, 1976), 252.

20. Officers and men alike left Newburgh believing they would be ignored. Many had not been paid in months. Describing the scene to his brother-in-law Charles Bruce, Lt. Benjamin Gilbert wrote in disgust: "Those brave men who were for the war and who have been fighting from four to eight years in defense of their

Country and for the preservation of its liberty, are now discharged the service, and are retiring from the field of Glory with Joy in their countenances, but poverty in their pockets.... I am at some times almost tempted to wish I had not lived to see the day when those brave heroes, the deliverers of my Country, should be drove from the field of Glory without one farthing of reward for their services, Where is the Justice, where is the propriety of the Army's bearing the whole burden of the war." See John Shy, ed., *Winding Down: The Revolutionary War Letters of Lieutenant Benjamin Gilbert of Massachusetts, 1780–1783* (Ann Arbor: University of Michigan Press, 1989), 107.

21. Wright, "Some Notes on the Continental Army," 11:44.

22. Samuel Tallmadge, 3 August 1779, in *Orderly Books of The Fourth New York Regiment, 1778–1780, the Second New York Regiment, 1780–1783 with Diaries of Samuel Tallmadge, 1780–1782 and John Barr, 1779–1782*, ed. Almon W. Lauber (Albany, N.Y.: Division of Archives and History, 1932), 68.

23. David A. Armstrong, "Order: Steuben's Contribution to the Patriot Cause," *Military Review* 56 (June 1976): 58.

24. Joseph P. Tustin, ed., *Diary of the American War: A Hessian Journal* (New Haven, Conn.: Yale University Press, 1979), 108.

25. Shy, *Toward Lexington*, 393.

26. Washington to Sullivan, 17 April 1779, in Revolutionary War Records, Roll 4. See also Fitzpatrick, *Writings of Washington*, 14:400.

27. Lt. Charles Nukerck, 18 September 1779, in *Journals of the Military Expedition of Major General John Sullivan against the Six Nations of the Indians in 1779*, ed. Frederick Cook (Freeport, N.Y.: Books for Libraries Press, 1972), 218.

28. Sgt. Maj. George Grant, 11 August 1779, in ibid., 109.

29. Thomas Grant, 11 August 1779, in ibid., 139. This would not be the only time Hand's actions drew the attention of soldiers. Samuel McNeill noted that Hand, sword in hand, would have personally led an attack on the enemy's position at Newtown had not Sullivan sent orders to prevent it. See Samuel McNeill, *Pennsylvania Archives*, ser. 2, 14:755.

30. Sullivan's Orderly Book, 14 August 1779, in Papers of the Sullivan Indian Campaign.

31. Lender, "Enlisted Line," 221.

32. Ibid., 220.

33. Ibid., 223.

34. New Jersey's legislature eventually did vote two hundred dollars to each officer and forty dollars to each enlisted man. Officers felt this justified. Unlike the enlisted men who served for a set period of time, officers served for the duration of the war or until they resigned. They did not receive bounties or bonuses yet had to function in a system having a lower disparity between officer pay and enlisted pay

than was the case in the British army. Furthermore, they were expected to pay out of their own pockets for uniforms and other accoutrements associated with their rank. See Stirling to Washington, 10 May 1779 in *Correspondence of the American Revolution Being Letters of Eminent Men to George Washington,* ed. Jared Sparks (Boston, Mass.: Little, Brown, 1853), 2:298; and Bowman, *Morale of the American Revolutionary Army,* 24.

35. Nathan Davis, "Nathan Davis' History," *Historical Magazine* 3 (April 1868): 200.

36. John W. Jordan, ed., "Continental Hospital Returns, 1777–1780," *Pennsylvania Magazine* 23 (1898): 212.

37. The Susquehanna flows from Toga to Sunbury through an area of rolling hills. The current seldom exceeds three miles per hour during normal water levels and, in some of the river's broad stretches, fails to reach this speed. Moving bateaux thirty miles a day, even with the current, required considerable effort.

38. Ibid., 18.

39. We know that Washington had been introduced to Seneca's *Morals* and Addison's play *Cato.* Dederer argues that Washington readily adopted stoicism, choosing to live the philosophy. His guidance to officers is filled with the notion that sacrifice is part of their responsibilities. See Dederer, *War in America to 1775,* 67.

40. Entry in Regimental Order Book, 12 June 1779, in American Revolution Orderly Book. Also Order Book of Lt. Col. Francis Barber, 11 July 1779, in Murray, *Notes from the Collections of Toga Point Museum,* 32.

41. Martin L. Van Creveld, *Supplying War: Logistics from Wallenstein to Patton* (Cambridge: Cambridge University Press, 1986), 37.

42. Davis, "Nathan Davis' History," 203.

43. Jabez Campfield, 11 August 1779, in Cook, *Journals of the Military Expedition,* 54.

44. Samuel Kirkland to Jerusha Kirkland, 5 July 1995, in Papers of Samuel Kirkland, Hamilton College, Hamilton, N.Y., 78a.

45. The Esther (Catherine) Montour story mentioned previously provided the most frequently mentioned incidence of alleged Indian barbarity. One soldier supposedly escaped Esther's knife and made his way to the river. It is his account of the massacre that made the rounds of Sullivan's army, though there is now some question about whether the story may have been fiction. It is true that many of the militia soldiers killed on the field were scalped by the raiding party, and some of them may well have been scalped by members of Butler's Rangers rather than the Iroquois warriors who accompanied Butler. For an idea of operating conditions inside Butler's Rangers, see Tustin, *Diary of the American War,* 166–67.

46. The allegations were not true in either case, but this did not prevent them from being accepted as fact. Samuel Kirkland to Jerusha Kirkland, 30 July 1779, in Papers of Samuel Kirkland, 78b.
47. Samuel McNeill, 1 September 1779, in *Pennsylvania Archives,* ser. 2, 14:757.
48. Ibid.
49. Lt. Col. Adam Hubley, 23 September 1779, in ibid., 40.
50. Lt. William Barton, 23 September 1779, in ibid., 12.
51. Rev. William Rogers, 8 July 1779, in ibid., 252.
52. Order Book of Spenser's Fifth New Jersey, Orderly Books of the Revolution, 24 June 1779; and Frazier, *Mohicans of Stockbridge,* 228.
53. Maurer Maurer, "Military Justice under General Washington," *Military Affairs* 28 (Spring 1964): 11.
54. Ibid., 12.
55. Ibid.
56. Ibid., 10.
57. Ibid.
58. Sullivan approved the execution of three soldiers from the Eleventh Pennsylvania who had been convicted of the murder of an innkeeper at Easton. Clinton executed one of three deserters sentenced to death in trial proceedings at Otsego. He pardoned the other two. Only five men of the seventy-seven brought before the courts received sentences of one hundred lashes, the maximum physical punishment permitted short of death at the time; one of these had his sentence pardoned. The most common sentence was that of twenty-five lashes. See "Order Book of the German Regiment," in *Pennsylvania Archives,* ser. 6, 14:24–65; and "Order Book of Hand's Brigade from Wyoming to Toga," in ibid., 69–121.
59. Sullivan had ordered Ogden to flank the ambuscade at Toga from the left. Ogden's route ran along the river, making it far less difficult than Poor's. Nonetheless, Ogden failed to get his regiment into position prior to the enemy's abandoning the works.
60. Orderly Book of Spenser's Fifth New Jersey, 11 August 1779, in Orderly Books of the Revolution.
61. Charles Knowles Bolton, *The Private Soldier under Washington* (New York: Charles Scribner's Sons, 1902), 75.
62. Sullivan had convinced Kirkland of the genuineness of his convictions. "I cannot but admire the ingenuity of the man," he wrote, for Sullivan had once been a "perfect Atheist" and then a "complete Deist—at length convinced by fair & impartial reasoning of the Existence of the Supreme Being, the perfection of his Character—the mediational undertaking—the inspiration of holy writ-except this doctrine Viz—the Depravity of human Nature—which he must deny or charge the

Deity with imperfection or what is worse—of being the author of sin." Samuel Kirkland to Jerusha Kirkland, 5 July 1779, in Papers of Samuel Kirkland, 78a.

63. Rev. William Rogers, 4 July 1779, in Cook, *Journals of the Military Expedition,* 250.

64. Dr. Ebenezer Elmer, 4 July 1779, in ibid., 82.

65. Israel Evans, "Discourse Delivered at Easton on the 17th of October 1779 to the Officers and Soldiers of the Western Army," Manuscripts Division, New York Historical Society, N.Y., 5–18.

66. Lt. William Barton, 25 September 1779, in Cook, *Journals of the Military Expedition,* 13.

67. Lt. Erkuries Beatty, 25 September 1779, in ibid., 34.

68. Davis, "Nathan Davis' History," 205.

69. Russell F. Weigley, "The Birth of an American Army: The Sullivan Expedition and the American Way of War," *Proceedings of the 201st Anniversary Wyoming Commemorative Association* (Wilkes-Barre, Pa.: Wyoming Valley Historical Society, 1979), 1.

70. Rev. William Rogers, 23 June 1779, in Cook, *Journals of the Military Expedition,* 248.

71. There is no doubt that Lt. Boyd and Pvt. Parker were tortured and killed while prisoners of Little Beard. The milder descriptions report that they had been decapitated and their eyes gouged out. For more detail, see James E. Seaver, *The Live of Mary Jemison: The White Woman of the Genesee* (Jersey Shore, Pa.: Zebrowski Historical Services and Publishing Company, 1991), 122; and Lt. Erkuries Beatty, 14 September 1779, in Cook, *Journals of the Military Expedition,* 32. The differences, however, were more imagined than real. Two of Sullivan's officers, Maj. Piatt and Lt. Barton, sent a patrol to look for Indian bodies left behind at Newtown. The patrol found two and brought them back to the officers. The bodies were then skinned from the waist down and the hides used to make leggings for the two officers. See Lt. William Barton, 30 August 1779, in ibid., 8.

72. Lt. Col. Henry Dearborn, 14 September 1779, in ibid., 75.

73. Martin and Lender, *Respectable Army,* 150–51.

74. Royster, *Revolutionary People at War,* 314–15.

75. See "Order Book of the German Regiment," *Pennsylvania Archives,* ser. 6, 14:24–65; and "Order Book of Hand's Brigade from Wyoming to Toga," ibid., 69–121.

76. Washington's courts adjudicated 424 separate charges, 77 of which dealt with desertion and related charges. See Paul G. Atkinson Jr., "The System of Military Discipline and Justice in the Continental Army: August 1777–June 1778," *Picket Post* (Winter 1972–73): 20–21.

77. Trussell, *Pennsylvania Line*, 222.

78. Hubley had written to Reed requesting money and authorization to reenlist them rather than let the unit disintegrate at such a critical time. See Hubley to Reed, 22 June 1779, in Records of Pennsylvania's Revolutionary Government, 1775–90 (Record Group 27), in the Pennsylvania State Archives (microfilm), Pennsylvania Historical and Museum Commission, Division of Archives and Manuscripts, 1978, roll 15, item 49.

79. John B. B. Trussell Jr., "The Forgotten Victory: The Sullivan Expedition of 1779," *Parameters* 5 (1976): 45.

80. This focus on the contractual relationship between the soldier and the state was not new to colonial society. New England soldiers had earned the disrespect of many British regulars by their insistence that the agreements made at the time of their enlistment be respected regardless of the operational situation at the time the enlistments expired. During the French and Indian War some colonial units went on strike when they believed the contract between themselves and the government had been violated. See F. W. Anderson, "Why Did Colonial New Englanders Make Bad Soldiers? Contractual Principles and Military Conduct during the Seven Years' War," *William and Mary Quarterly* 38 (July 1981): 406–7.

81. Lesser, *Sinews of Independence*, 76–77, 88–89, 124–25, 136–37.

82. Ibid.

83. See "Order Book of the German Regiment," in *Pennsylvania Archives*, ser. 6, 14:24–65; and "Order Book of Hand's Brigade from Wyoming to Toga," in ibid., 69–121.

84. Atkinson, "The System of Military Discipline," 20–21.

85. This fear of excessive swimming was an offshoot of "cold water disease." According to the medical thinking of the day, an overheated soldier who exposed himself to cold air and cold water could get fatally sick. Normally, the disease was associated with drinking cold water while overheated, but the ban against swimming in the heat of the day followed similar lines of thinking. The remedy for the ailment was to take a large spoonful of liquid laudanum, an opium derivative. The illness surgeons were treating with laudanum was heat exhaustion or heat stroke, depending on the circumstances. Swimming, of course, offered a better preventative and the cure no solution at all. Order Book of Lt. Col. Francis Barber, 24 June 1779, in Murray, *Notes from the Collections of Toga Point Museum*, 18; and DePauw, "Women in Combat," 215.

86. Order Book entry dated 8 July 1779, in American Revolution Orderly Book.

87. Order Book of Lt. Col. Francis Barber, 3 July 1779, in Murray, *Notes from the Collections of Toga Point Museum*, 27.

88. Lt. William Barton, 23 August 1779, in Cook, *Journals of the Military Expedition*, 7.
89. Journal of Edward Hand, 6–7 August 1779, in Joseph Brant Papers, Draper MSS 6F61.
90. Maj. Jeremiah Fogg, 22 August 1779, in ibid., 93.
91. Davis, "Nathan Davis' History," 201.
92. John Gano, "A Chaplain of the Revolution: Memoirs of John Gano," *Historical Magazine* 5 (November 1861): 330.
93. Ens. Daniel Gookin, 11 August 1779, in Cook, *Journals of the Military Expedition*, 104.
94. Carl von Clausewitz, *On War*, ed. Michael Howard and Peter Paret (Princeton, N.J.: Princeton University Press, 1976), 188.

CHAPTER 7: CIVIL-MILITARY RELATIONSHIPS

1. Washington to Pennsylvania's Executive Council, 5 July 1779, *Pennsylvania Archives*, ser. 1, 7:535.
2. Peter Paret, *Understanding War: Essays on Clausewitz and the History of Military Power* (Princeton, N.J.: Princeton University Press, 1992), 30.
3. Jack N. Rakove, *The Beginnings of National Politics: An Interpretive History of the Continental Congress* (New York: Alfred A. Knopf, 1979), 104.
4. Ibid., 199.
5. Kenneth Schaffel, "The American Board of War, 1776–1781," *Military Affairs* 50 (October 1986): 185.
6. Ibid.
7. Washington had absolutely no enthusiasm for this endeavor but acquiesced anyway rather than risk an open confrontation with the Congress and the Board. Lafayette found himself appointed to command the undertaking but soon regretted the honor. When it became clear that the Board had only a rudimentary idea of what it wanted Lafayette to accomplish and had not made adequate plans to support the effort, the French general wrote Washington in frustration, "Why am I so far from you and what business had the board of war to bring me through ice and snow without knowing what I should do, neither what they were doing themselves. . . . I have been shamefully deceived by the board of war." See Lafayette to Washington, 19 February 1778, in *Lafayette in the Age of the American Revolution: Selected Letters and Papers, 1776–1790*, ed. Stanley J. Idzerda (Ithaca, N.Y.: Cornell University Press, 1977), 299–300.
8. Douglas Southall Freeman, *Washington* (New York: Charles Scribner and Sons, 1968), 308–9.

9. William Nelson, *The American Tory* (Oxford: Oxford University Press, 1961), 87.

10. Ibid., 92.

11. Edward Countryman, "Out of the Bounds of the Law: Northern Land Rioters in the Eighteenth Century," in *The American Revolution: Explorations in the History of American Radicalism,* ed. Alfred F. Young (DeKalb: Northern Illinois University Press, 1976), 58.

12. Nelson, *American Tory,* 101.

13. Ibid.

14. William S. Hanna, *Benjamin Franklin and Pennsylvania Politics* (Palo Alto, Calif.: Stanford University Press, 1964), 196–97.

15. Richard Alan Ryerson, *The Revolution Is Now Begun: The Radical Committees of Philadelphia, 1765–1776* (Philadelphia: University of Pennsylvania Press, 1978), 213.

16. In fairness the radicals believed that they alone understood the potential offered by the revolt. They were idealists and linked the self-sacrificing republicanism talked of constantly among patriots to democracy, a concept generally scorned by the propertied classes of America. A democratic-republic, this was the new America the radicals hoped to see emerge from the war. Gordon S. Wood, *The Creation of the American Republic, 1776–1787* (New York: W. W. Norton, 1969), 230.

17. Margaret Burnham MacMillan, *The War Governors in the American Revolution* (New York: Columbia University Press, 1943) 70; and Robert L. Brunhouse, *The Counter-Revolution in Pennsylvania, 1776–1790* (Harrisburg: Pennsylvania Historical and Museum Commission, 1971), 14.

18. Ibid., 70.

19. Hooper to Samuel Johnson, 26 September 1776, in *Collected Records of North Carolina,* 10:819–20; quoted in Wood, *Creation of the American Republic,* 233.

20. Brunhouse, *Counter-Revolution,* 30.

21. Lawrence Delbert Cress, *Citizens in Arms: The Army and the Militia in American Society to 1812* (Chapel Hill: University of North Carolina Press, 1982), 5.

22. Brunhouse, *Counter-Revolution,* 23.

23. Ibid., 39.

24. Ibid.

25. Arthur F. Alexander, "Pennsylvania's Revolutionary Militia," *Pennsylvania Magazine of History and Biography* 69 (January 1945): 21.

26. Ibid.

27. Ibid.

28. Brunhouse, *Counter-Revolution,* 48.

29. Willard Sterne Randall, *Benedict Arnold: Patriot and Traitor* (New York: William Morrow, 1990), 439.
30. Ibid., 441.
31. Reed to Washington, 24 April 1779, in *Pennsylvania Archives*, ser. 1, 8:349–50.
32. Ibid., 67.
33. Edward Countryman, *A People in Revolution: The American Revolution and Political Society in New York, 1760–1790* (Baltimore: Johns Hopkins University Press, 1981), 159.
34. Ibid., 129.
35. Ibid., 161.
36. DeAlva Stanwood Alexander, *A Political History of the State of New York* (Port Washington, N.Y.: Ira J. Friedman, 1909), 9.
37. Peter Colt to George Clinton, 16 March 1779, in George Clinton, *Public Papers of George Clinton*, 4:638–39.
38. Nathanael Greene to Jacob Greene, 28 September 1776, in *The Papers of General Nathanael Greene*, ed. Richard K. Showman (Chapel Hill: University of North Carolina Press, 1986), 1:303.
39. Don Higginbotham, "The American Militia: A Traditional Institution with Revolutionary Responsibilities," in *Reconsiderations on the Revolutionary War*, ed. Don Higginbotham (Westport, Conn.: Greenwood Press, 1987), 93.
40. Potter to Armstrong, 17 May 1778, in Journals of Fort Augusta, vol. 24.
41. Ibid.
42. Hunter to Wharton, 14 May 1778, in ibid.
43. Ibid.
44. Clinton to Jay, 17 November 1778, in Clinton, *Public Papers of George Clinton*, 4:289.
45. Buchanan to Carothers, 11 May 1778, in Journals of Fort Augusta, vol. 24.
46. George Clinton to Washington, 15 October 1778, in Clinton, *Public Papers of George Clinton*, 4:164.
47. George Clinton to Washington, 17 October 1778, in ibid., 167–68.
48. George Clinton to New York's Congressional Delegates, 9 February 1779, in ibid., 555–56.
49. Ibid.
50. The beacons consisted of pre-positioned piles of dried timber ready for the torch. Washington to George Clinton, 15 March 1779, in ibid., 636–37.
51. Charles E. Miller Jr., Donald V. Lockey, and Joseph Visconti Jr., *Highland Fortress: The Fortification of West Point during the American Revolution, 1775–1783*

(West Point, N.Y.: United States Military Academy, 1988), 111.

52. Unlike traditional militia, the ranger companies consisted of volunteers contracted for a set period of service. The militia units sometimes functioned as the body from which the ranger units were recruited. Ranger companies were usually recruited from frontier settlements. Ideally, the soldiers who served in them were familiar with the nuances of frontier warfare and accustomed to the terrain in which they were to operate. Many of the ranger units were used for patrolling operations.

53. Washington to Reed, 19 April 1779, in Fitzpatrick, *Writings of Washington*, 14:406; and William B. Reed, ed., *Life and Correspondence of Joseph Reed* (Philadelphia: Lindsay and Blakiston, 1847), 2:85.

54. Hunter to Reed, 27 April 1779, in *Pennsylvania Archives*, ser. 1, 7:346–47.

55. Reed to Washington, 14 April 1779, in Reed, *Life and Correspondence of Joseph Reed*, 2:82.

56. Hunter's reply is unknown. Pennsylvania had employed a scalp bounty during the French and Indian War, with predictable results for both friendly and hostile Indians. The Executive Council did not authorize the bounty in 1779 but elected to do so in April 1780. See Reed to Hunter, 27 March 1779, in Unpublished Revolutionary War Papers of Major-General Edward Hand, ed. A. J. Bowden, New York Public Library, N.Y., 15; and Weslager, *Delaware Indians*, 302.

57. Bowden, Papers of Major-General Edward Hand, 15.

58. Reed to Hunter, 14 April 1779, in Journals of Fort Augusta.

59. Washington to Reed, 27 February 1779, in Fitzpatrick, *Writings of Washington*, 14:159.

60. Hand to Reed, 16 April 1779, in *Pennsylvania Archives*, ser. 1, 7:321.

61. Reed to Hand, 21 April 1779, in Reed, *Life and Correspondence of Joseph Reed*, 2:87.

62. Reed to Washington, 25 April 1779, in ibid., 91–92; and Reed to Washington, 24 April 1779, *Pennsylvania Archives*, ser. 1, 7:341–43.

63. Reed to Washington, 25 April 1779, in Reed, *Life and Correspondence of Joseph Reed*, 2:87.

64. Ibid.

65. Ibid.

66. Washington to Reed, 27 April 1779, in ibid., 2:95–96; and *Pennsylvania Archives*, ser. 1, 7:351–55.

67. Washington to Reed, 27 April 1779, in Reed, *Life and Correspondence of Joseph Reed*, 2:96; and Fitzpatrick, *Writings of Washington*, 14:452.

68. Reed to Washington, 1 May 1779, in Reed, *Life and Correspondence of Joseph Reed*, 97; and Reed to Washington, 8 May 1779, in ibid., 101.

69. Ibid.

70. Though unhappy about it, Reed intended to deliver at least some of the nonranger militia units that Washington had requested. Reed wanted Potter to command those Pennsylvania militia units assigned to Sullivan. Sullivan was happy with the idea and promised Potter a command "Equal to his Wishes" should he join the expedition. See Sullivan to Reed, 7 June 1779, in *Pennsylvania Archives,* ser. 1, 7:473.

71. Reed to the Board of War, 20 May 1779, in ibid., 424–25.
72. Sullivan to Reed, 31 May 1779, in ibid., 450–51.
73. Reed to the Board of War, 20 May 1779, in ibid., 424–25.
74. Hunter to Reed, 26 June 1779, in ibid., 510–12.
75. Sullivan to Reed, 7 June 1779, in ibid., 473.
76. Reed to Brown, 27 June 1779, in ibid., 515.

77. This was not an isolated incident. Only a month earlier another battalion commander had justified his refusal to move his battalion westward on the same grounds. Potter to Reed, 3 May 1779, in ibid., 10:159–60.

78. Petition from Penns Valley to the Executive Council, 21 August 1779, in ibid., ser. 2, 3:323.

79. Minutes of 15 September 1779, *Minutes of the Supreme Executive Council of Pennsylvania, from Its Organization to the Termination of the Revolution* (Harrisburg, Pa.: T. Fenn and Company, 1852–53), 12:104.

80. Two companies of local militia from the Wyoming Valley had joined the army by this time, but many of the men who made up these units had migrated from Connecticut when the Susquehanna Company opened the lands for settlement. Both Pennsylvania and Connecticut still claimed the Wyoming Valley, but the militiamen who accompanied Sullivan saw themselves as soldiers in the service of the latter.

81. Washington to Pennsylvania's Executive Council, 5 July 1779, in *Pennsylvania Archives,* ser. 1, 7:535.
82. Ibid.
83. Reed to Washington, 11 July 1779, in ibid., 555–56.
84. Ibid.
85. Minutes of 13 July 1779, *Minutes of the Supreme Executive Council,* 12:46.
86. Reed to Washington, 11 July 1779, *Pennsylvania Archives,* ser. 1, 7:555–56.
87. Sullivan to the Continental Congress, 21 July 1779, in ibid., 568; and Sullivan to Jay, 21 July 1779, in Hammond, *Sullivan Papers,* 3:83.
88. Ibid.
89. Wright, *Sullivan Expedition of 1779, Regimental Rosters of Men,* 5.
90. Brant to Bolton, 29 July 1779, in Sir Frederick Haldimand: Unpublished

Papers, reel 42; and William L. Stone, *The Life of Joseph Brant–Thayendanegea, Including the Indian Wars of the Revolution* (Cooperstown, N.Y.: H .and E. Phinney, 1846), 417–18.

91. Graymont, *Iroquois in the American Revolution*, 201.

92. Ibid., 202–3.

93. Frederick A. Godcharles, "The History of Fort Freeland," *Northumberland County Historical Society Proceedings* 2 (1930): 17.

94. McDonell to Butler, 5 August 1779, in Alexander C. Flick, "New Sources on the Sullivan-Clinton Campaign in 1779," *New York State Historical Association Quarterly Journal* 10 (July 1929): 276.

95. Ibid.

96. Ibid.

97. Ibid.; and McDonald's Report on Fort Freeland, 10 August 1779, in Joseph Brant Papers, Draper MSS 6F48.

98. MacDonald may have had an outside chance of taking Fort Augusta if he had been able to move on the post immediately after taking Fort Freeland. A high bluff across the river from the fort offered him an opportunity to gain accurate knowledge on the size of the garrison while remaining well beyond the range of the fort's guns. Immediately following the fall of Freeland, Augusta's garrison numbered only one hundred and fifty men. Given the sophistication of the post, this probably meant that MacDonald lacked the capacity to carry the fort. He certainly had it within his grasp to seize or destroy the powder stored at Maclay's house. It seems doubtful that this would have stopped Sullivan, however, as Fort Augusta's importance had diminished with the building of the depot at Wyoming.

99. Maclay to Reed, 26 July 1776, in *Pennsylvania Archives*, ser. 1, 7:586–87.

100. Sullivan to Hunter, 30 July 1779, in Hammond, *Sullivan Papers*, 3:89.

101. Sullivan to Cook, 30 July 1779, in ibid., 88–89.

102. Hubley to Reed, 30 July 1779, *Pennsylvania Archives*, ser. 1, 7:596–97.

103. Reed to the Board of War, in ibid., 640.

104. George Clinton to Udny Hay, 10 February 1779, in Clinton, *Public Papers of George Clinton*, 4:558.

105. Washington to George Clinton, 4 March 1779, in ibid., 617.

106. George Clinton to Washington, 7 June 1779, in ibid., 5:60.

107. Pawling to George Clinton, 22 July 1779, in ibid., 150.

108. George Clinton to Pawling, 22 July 1779, in ibid., 151.

109. George Clinton to Dr. Ker, 30 July 1779, in ibid., 161.

110. Washington to George Clinton, 3 August 1779, and Sullivan to George Clinton, 30 July 1779, in ibid., 177–78.

111. George Clinton to James Clinton, 5 August 1779, in ibid., 181.

112. George Clinton to Washington, 1 September 1779, in ibid., 252.

CHAPTER 8: CONCLUSIONS

1. Address of General William T. Sherman, in *Journals of the Military Expedition of Major General John Sullivan against the Six Nations of the Indians in 1779*, ed. Frederick Cook (Freeport, N.Y.: Books for Libraries Press, 1972), 439–40.

2. Kayangaraghta to Guy Johnson, 16 December 1779, Indian Records (Record Group 10), Federal Archives Division, National Archives of Canada, Ottawa, 1831, 92–97.

3. Ibid.

4. Cayuga Chief (speaker unknown), 3 November 1779, in ibid., 53–59.

5. Jack M. Sosin, *The Revolutionary Frontier, 1763–1783* (New York: Holt, Rinehart, and Winston, 1967), 134.

6. Maclay realized that Sullivan's failure to take Niagara lay at the heart of the problem. Maclay to the Executive Council, 9 April 1779, in *Pennsylvania Archives*, ser. 1, 7:172.

7. Reed to Potter, 16 September 1782, in *Minutes of the Supreme Executive Council of Pennsylvania, from Its Organization to the Termination of the Revolution* (Harrisburg, Pa.: T. Fenn and Company, 1852–53), 8:370.

8. *Pennsylvania Archives*, ser. 1, 9:641.

9. The second Treaty of Fort Stanwix, signed in 1784, showed the new direction the negotiations would take. Whereas the British had treated with them as equals, the Americans asserted that the United States held political sovereignty over the Iroquois. The treaty forced the Confederacy to relinquish all claims to the lands of the Ohio country and even required that they provide hostages until all prisoners taken during the war by Iroquois war parties were returned.

10. Daniel K. Richter, "War and Culture: The Iroquois Experience," *William and Mary Quarterly* 40 (October 1983): 103.

11. Ibid., 159.

SELECTED BIBLIOGRAPHY

I. MANUSCRIPT SOURCES

American Revolution Orderly Book. Military Records Collection, Wyoming Valley Historical Society, Wilkes-Barre, Pa.

Daniel Claus Papers. Manuscripts Division, National Archives of Canada, Ottawa.

Diplomatic Extracts of the Continental Congress. National Archives, Washington, D.C.

Emmett Collection. Manuscripts Division, New York Public Library, N.Y.

Evans, Israel. "Discourse Delivered at Easton on the 17th of October 1779 to the Officers and Soldiers of the Western Army." Manuscripts Division, New York Historical Society, N.Y.

Gansevort-Lansing Papers. New York Historical Society, N.Y.

Great Britain War Office Correspondence. Sir Henry Clinton's Correspondence with the War Office, General Washington, and Other Officers. Manuscripts Division, Library of Congress, Washington, D.C.

Indian Records (Records Group 10). Federal Archives Division, National Archives of Canada, Ottawa.

Iroquois Indians: A Documentary History of the Diplomacy of the Six Nations and Their League. Ed. Francis Jennings. Woodbridge, Ct., 1985.

Joseph Brant Papers. Draper Manuscript Collection (1727–1891), State Historical Society of Wisconsin.

Journals of Fort Augusta in the American Revolution. Vols. 15 and 24. Northumberland County Historical Society, Sunbury, Pa.

Orderly Books of the Revolution. Manuscript Division, New York Public Library, N.Y.

Papers of Zebulon Butler. Wyoming Valley Historical Society, Wilkes-Barre, Pa.

Papers of Henry Clinton. Clements Library, University of Michigan, Ann Arbor.

Papers of the Continental Congress. National Archives, Washington, D.C.

Selected Bibliography

Papers of Thomas Gage. Clements Library, University of Michigan, Ann Arbor.
Papers of Samuel Kirkland. Hamilton College, Hamilton, N.Y.
Papers of the Sullivan Indian Campaign. State Archives of New York, Albany.
Records of Pennsylvania's Revolutionary Government, 1775–90 (Record Group 27). Microfilm. Division of Archives and Manuscripts, Pennsylvania Historical and Museum Commission, Pennsylvania State Archives, 1978.
Revolutionary War Records (Records Group 93). National Archives, Washington, D.C.
Sackville Germain Papers. Clements Library, University of Michigan, Ann Arbor.
Sir Frederick Haldiman: Unpublished Papers and Correspondence, 1758–84. World Microfilms Publications Ltd. London, 1977.
Stephen Griffin Journal. Manuscripts Division, New York State Library, Albany.
Unpublished Revolutionary War Papers of Major-General Edward Hand. New York Public Library, N.Y.

II. Printed Primary Sources

Bleeker, Leonard. *The Order Book of Capt. Leonard Bleeker.* New York: Joseph Sabin, 1865.
Brophy, Marion, and Wendell Tripp, eds. "Supplies for General Sullivan: The Correspondence of Colonel Charles Stewart, May–September 1779." *New York History* 60 (July 1979): 274.
Carter, Clarence Edwin, ed. *The Correspondence of General Thomas Gage with the Secretaries of State, 1763–1775.* Vol. 1. New Haven, Conn.: Yale University Press, 1931.
Clausewitz, Carl von. *On War.* Ed. Michael Howard and Peter Paret. Princeton, N.J.: Princeton University Press, 1976.
Clinton, George. *Public Papers of George Clinton, First Governor of New York.* Vol. 4. Albany: State of New York, 1900.
Cook, Frederick, ed. *Journals of the Military Expedition of Major General John Sullivan against the Six Nations of the Indians in 1779.* 1887. Reprint. Freeport, N.Y.: Books for Libraries Press, 1972.
Davis, K. G., ed. *Documents of the American Revolution, 1779–1780.* Vols. 14 and 16. Dublin: Irish Academic Press, 1977.
Davis, Nathan. "Nathan Davis' History." *Historical Magazine* 3 (April 1868): 198–205.
Fitzpatrick, John C., ed. *The Writings of George Washington from the Original Manuscript Sources, 1745–1799.* Vols. 3–14. Washington, D.C.: U.S. Government Printing Office, 1936.

Flick, Alexander C. "New Sources on the Sullivan-Clinton Campaign in 1779." *New York State Historical Association Quarterly Journal* 10 (July 1929): 185–224.

———."New Sources on the Sullivan-Clinton Campaign in 1779." *New York State Historical Association Quarterly Journal* 10 (October 1929): 265–317.

Frederick the Great. "Instructions of Frederick the Great for His Generals, 1747." In *Roots of Strategy,* ed. Thomas R. Phillips, 343–44. Harrisburg, Pa.: Stackpole Books, 1985.

Gano, John. "A Chaplain of the Revolution: Memoirs of John Gano." *Historical Magazine* 5 (November 1861): 330–38.

Hammond, Otis G., ed. *The Letters and Papers of Major-General John Sullivan, Continental Army.* Vols. 2–3. Concord: New Hampshire Historical Society, 1931.

Hughes, Thomas. *A Journal by Thos. Hughes for His Amusement, & Designed Only for His Perusal by the Time He Attains the Age of 50 if He Lives So Long.* Cambridge: Cambridge University Press, 1947.

Idzerda, Stanley J., ed. *Lafayette in the Age of the American Revolution: Selected Letters and Papers, 1776–1790.* Ithaca, N.Y.: Cornell University Press, 1977.

Jordan, John W., ed. "Continental Hospital Returns, 1777–1780." *Pennsylvania Magazine* 23 (1898): 210–17.

Judd, Jacob, ed. *Correspondence of the Van Cortlandt Family of Cortlandt Manor, 1748–1800.* Vol. 2. Tarrytown, N.Y.: Sleepy Hollow Restorations, 1977.

Lauber, Almon W., ed. *Orderly Books of the Fourth New York Regiment, 1778–1780, the Second New York Regiment, 1780–1783 with Diaries of Samuel Tallmadge, 1780–1782 and John Barr, 1779–1782.* Albany, N.Y.: Division of Archives and History, 1932.

Lesser, Charles H., ed. *The Sinews of Independence: Monthly Strength Reports of the Continental Army.* Chicago: University of Chicago Press, 1976.

Lloyd, Henry. *History of the Late War in Germany between the King of Prussia and the Empress of Germany and Her Allies.* London: S. Hooper, 1781.

Luvaas, Jay, ed. *Frederick the Great on the Art of War.* New York: Free Press, 1966.

Minutes of the Supreme Executive Council of Pennsylvania, from Its Organization to the Termination of the Revolution. Harrisburg, Pa.: Printed by T. Fenn and Company, 1852–53.

Murray, Louise Welles, ed. *Notes from the Collections of Tioga Point Museum and Its Centennial Celebration of 1879.* Athens, Pa.: Tioga Point Historical Society, 1929.

Nicola, Lewis. *A Treatise of Military Exercise Calculated for the Use of the American.* Philadelphia: Styner and Cist Printers, 1776.

Pennsylvania Archives. Ser. 1, vols. 1–12; ser. 2, vols. 1–19; ser. 6, vols. 1–15. Philadelphia: J. Severns and Company, 1852–56; Harrisburg, Pa., 1874–1914.

Penrose, Maryly Barton, ed. *Indian Affairs Papers: American Revolution.* Franklin Park, N.J.: Liberty Bell Associates, 1981.

Phillips, Thomas R., ed. *Roots of Strategy.* Harrisburg, Pa.: Stackpole Books, 1985.

Pickering, Timothy, Jr. *An Easy Plan of Discipline for a Militia.* Salem, Mass.: Samuel and Ebenezer Hall, 1775.

Reed, William B., ed. *Life and Correspondence of Joseph Reed.* Vol. 2. Philadelphia: Lindsay and Blakiston, 1847.

Saxe, Maurice de. *The Reveries on the Art of War.* Harrisburg, Pa.: Military Service Publishing Company, 1944.

Seaver, James E. *The Life of Mary Jemison: The White Woman of the Genesee.* 5th ed. Jersey Shore, Pa.: Zebrowski Historical Services and Publishing Company, 1991.

Showman, Richard K., ed. *The Papers of General Nathanael Greene.* Vols. 3–5. Chapel Hill: University of North Carolina Press, 1986.

Shy, John, ed. *Winding Down: The Revolutionary War Letters of Lieutenant Benjamin Gilbert of Massachusetts, 1780–1783.* Ann Arbor: University of Michigan Press, 1989.

Sparks, Jared, ed. *Correspondence of the American Revolution Being Letters of Eminent Men to George Washington.* Vol. 2. Boston: Little, Brown, 1853.

———. *The Writings of George Washington.* Boston: Little, Brown, 1858.

Steuben, Frederick William Baron von. *Baron von Steuben's Revolutionary War Drill Manual: A Facsimile Reprint of the 1794 Edition.* New York: Dover Publications, 1985.

Stryker, William S. *General Maxwell's Brigade of the New Jersey Line in the Expedition against the Indians in the Year 1779.* Trenton, N.J.: W. S. Sharp, 1885.

Tustin, Joseph P., ed. *Diary of the American War: A Hessian Journal.* New Haven, Conn.: Yale University Press, 1979.

Vail, R. W. G., ed. *The Revolutionary War Diary of Lt. Obadiah Gore.* New York: New York Public Library Publications, 1929.

Vegetius. "Military Institutions of the Romans." In *Roots of Strategy,* ed. Thomas R. Phillips, 132–34. Harrisburg, Pa.: Stackpole Books, 1985.

Washington, George. "The Braddock Campaign." *American History Illustrated* 5 (November 1970): 16–17.

Willson, Beckles, ed. *The Life and Letters of James Wolfe.* London: W. Heinemann, 1909.

Wolfe, James. *Instructions to Young Officers.* London: Printed for J. Millan, 1768.

III. SECONDARY SOURCES

Abernethy, Thomas Perkins. *Western Lands and the American Revolution.* New York: Russell and Russell, 1959.

Alexander, Arthur F. "Pennsylvania's Revolutionary Militia." *Pennsylvania Magazine of History and Biography* 69 (January 1945): 15–25.

Alexander, DeAlva Stanwood. *A Political History of the State of New York.* Port Washington, N.Y.: Ira J. Friedman, 1909.

Alger, John I. *Definitions and Doctrine of the Military Art, Past and Present.* Wayne, N.J.: Avery Publishing Group, 1985.

Anderson, F. W. "Why Did Colonial New Englanders Make Bad Soldiers? Contractual Principles and Military Conduct during the Seven Years' War," *William and Mary Quarterly* 38 (July 1981): 395–414.

Armstrong, David A. "Order: Steuben's Contribution to the Patriot Cause." *Military Review* 56 (June 1976): 58–68.

Atkinson, Paul G., Jr. "The System of Military Discipline and Justice in the Continental Army: August 1777–June 1778." *Picket Post* (Winter 1972–73): 12–43.

Bancroft, George. *History of the United States from the Discovery of the North American Continent.* Boston: Little, Brown, 1875.

Billington, Ray A. "The Fort Stanwix Treaty of 1768." *New York Historical Association* 25 (April 1944): 184–85.

Bishop, Morris. "The End of the Iroquois." *American Heritage* 20 (October 1969): 28.

Bolton, Charles Knowles. *The Private Soldier under Washington.* New York: Charles Scribner's Sons, 1902.

Bowman, Allen. *The Morale of the American Revolutionary Army.* Washington, D.C.: American Council on Public Affairs, 1943.

Britt, Albert Sidney, and Jerome A. O'Connell. *The Dawn of Modern Warfare.* Wayne, N.J.: Avery Publishing Group, 1984.

Brunhouse, Robert L. *The Counter-Revolution in Pennsylvania, 1776–1790.* Harrisburg: Pennsylvania Historical and Museum Commission, 1971.

Carp, E. Wayne. *To Starve the Army at Pleasure: Continental Army Administration and American Political Culture 1775–1783.* Chapel Hill: University of North Carolina Press, 1984.

Countryman, Edward. "Out of the Bounds of the Law: Northern Land Rioters in the Eighteenth Century." In *The American Revolution: Explorations in the History of American Radicalism,* ed. Alfred F. Young, 37–69. DeKalb: Northern Illinois University Press, 1976.

———. *A People in Revolution: The American Revolution and Political Society in New York, 1760–1790.* Baltimore: Johns Hopkins University Press, 1981.

Craft, David. *The Centennial Celebration of General Sullivan's Campaign against the Iroquois in 1779.* Waterloo, N.Y.: Waterloo Public Library and Historical Society, 1879.

Cress, Lawrence Delbert. *Citizens in Arms: The Army and the Militia in American Society to 1812.* Chapel Hill: University of North Carolina Press, 1982.

Cruikshank, Ernest. *Butler's Rangers: The Revolutionary Period.* Niagara Falls, Ont.: Renown Printing Company, 1988.

Dederer, John Morgan. *War in America to 1775: Before Yankee Doodle.* New York: New York University Press, 1990.

DePauw, Linda Grant. "Women in Combat: The Revolutionary War Experience." *Armed Forces and Society* 7 (Winter 1980): 209–25.

Duffy, Christopher. *The Fortress in the Age of Vauban and Frederick the Great, 1660–1789.* London: Routledge and Kegan Paul, 1985.

Dunnigan, Brian Leigh. *Siege—1759: The Campaign against Niagara.* Youngstown, N.Y.: Old Fort Niagara Association, 1986.

Eid, Leroy V. "A Kind of Running Fight: Indian Battlefield Tactics in the Late Eighteenth Century." *Western Pennsylvania Historical Magazine* 71 (2 April 1988): 147–71.

Elting, John R. *Swords around a Throne: Napoleon's Grande Armeé.* New York: Free Press, 1988.

Everest, Allan S. *Moses Hazen and the Canadian Refugees in the American Revolution.* Syracuse, N.Y.: Syracuse University Press, 1976.

Ferling, John E. *A Wilderness of Miseries: War and Warriors in Early America.* Westport, Conn.: Greenwood Press, 1980.

Flexner, James Thomas. *Washington: The Indispensable Man.* New York: NAL/Penguin, 1984.

FM100–5 Operations. Washington, D.C.: Department of the Army, 1986.

Frazier, Patrick. *The Mohicans of Stockbridge.* Lincoln: University of Nebraska Press, 1992.

Freeman, Douglas Southall. *Washington.* New York: Charles Scribner's and Sons, 1968.

Frothingham, Thomas G. *Washington: Commander in Chief.* Boston: Houghton Mifflin, 1930.

Fuller, J. F. C. *British Light Infantry in the Eighteenth Century.* London: Hutchinson, 1925.

Gerlach, Donald R. *Proud Patriot: Philip Schuyler and the War of Independence, 1775–1783.* Syracuse, N.Y.: Syracuse University Press, 1987.

Gipson, Lawrence Henry. *The Great War for the Empire: The Victorious Years 1758–1760.* Vol. 7. New York: Alfred A. Knopf, 1949.

Godcharles, Frederick A. "The History of Fort Freeland." *Northumberland County Historical Society Proceedings* 2 (1930): 3–28.

Graymont, Barbara. *The Iroquois in the American Revolution.* Syracuse, N.Y.: Syracuse University Press, 1972.

Greene, George Washington. *The Life of Nathanael Greene.* Vol. 3. Boston: Houghton Mifflin, 1890.

Guerlac, Henry. "Vauban: The Impact of Science on War." In *Makers of Modern Strategy: From Machiavelli to the Nuclear Age,* ed. Peter Paret, 64–90. Princeton, N.J.: Princeton University Press, 1986.

Halsey, Francis Whiting. *The Old New York Frontier.* New York: Charles Scribner's Sons, 1901.

Hanna, William S. *Benjamin Franklin and Pennsylvania Politics.* Palo Alto, Calif.: Stanford University Press, 1964.

Harvey, Oscar J. *A History of Wilkes-Barre.* Wilkes-Barre, Pa.: Raeder Press, 1909.

Higginbotham, Don. "The American Militia: A Traditional Institution with Revolutionary Responsibilities." In *Reconsiderations on the Revolutionary War,* ed. Don Higginbotham, 83–103. Westport, Conn.: Greenwood Press, 1987.

———. *Daniel Morgan: Revolutionary Rifleman.* Chapel Hill: University of North Carolina Press, 1961.

———. *The War of American Independence: Military Attitudes, Policy, and Practice, 1763–1789.* Boston: Northeastern University Press, 1983.

Huston, James A. *The Sinews of War: Army Logistics, 1775–1953.* Washington, D.C.: Office of the Chief of Military History, 1966.

Hutson, James H. *Pennsylvania Politics 1746–1770.* Princeton, N.J.: Princeton University Press, 1972.

Jennings, Francis. *The Ambiguous Empire: The Covenant Chain Confederation of Indian Tribes with English Colonies from Its Beginning to the Lancaster Treaty of 1744.* New York: W. W. Norton, 1984.

Johnson, Allen, ed., *Dictionary of American Biography.* Vol. 4. New York: Charles Scribner's Sons, 1930.

Jones, Archer. *The Art of War in the Western World.* New York: Oxford University Press, 1987.

Kaplan, Roger. "The Hidden War: British Intelligence Operations during the American Revolution." *William and Mary Quarterly* 47 (January 1990): 115–38.

Kashatus, William C. "The Wyoming Massacre: The Surpassing Horror of the American Revolution, July 3, 1778." *Valley Forge Journal* 4 (December 1988): 107–22.

Kelsay, Isabel Thompson. *Joseph Brant, 1743–1807, Man of Two Worlds*. Syracuse, N.Y.: Syracuse University Press, 1984.

Lender, Mark Edward. "The Enlisted Line: The Continental Soldiers of New Jersey." Ph.D. diss., Rutgers University, 1975.

Lennox, John Herbert. "Samuel Kirkland's Mission to the Iroquois." Ph.D. diss., University of Chicago, 1932.

Lossing, Benson J. *Pictorial Field Book of the Revolution*. New York: Harper and Brothers, 1860.

Lykke, Arthur F., Jr. "Toward an Understanding of Military Strategy." In *The Strategic Environment: Selected Readings*. Fort Leavenworth, Kans.: U.S. Army Command and General Staff College, 1991.

Mackesy, Piers. "British Strategy in the War of American Independence." *Yale Review* 52 (June 1963): 539–57.

———. *The War for America, 1775–1783*. Cambridge, Mass.: Harvard University Press, 1964.

MacMillan, Margaret Burnham. *The War Governors in the American Revolution*. New York: Columbia University Press, 1943.

Mahon, John K. "Anglo-American Methods of Indian Warfare, 1676–1794." *Mississippi Valley Historical Review* 45 (September 1958): 258–75.

Mancall, Peter Cooper. "Environment and Economy: The Upper Susquehanna Valley in the Age of the American Revolution." Ph.D. diss., Harvard University, 1986.

Marcus, Robert D., and David Burner, eds. *America Firsthand: From Settlement to Reconstruction*. New York: St. Martin's Press, 1992.

Martin, James Kirby, and Mark Edward Lender. *A Respectable Army: The Military Origins of the Republic, 1763–1789*. Arlington Heights, Ill.: Harlan Davidson, 1982.

Martin, Tom. "Butler's Rangers." In *The American Revolution 1775–1783*, ed. Richard L. Blanco, 1:226–27. New York: Garland, 1993.

———. "Royal Greens." In *The American Revolution 1775–1783*, ed. Richard L. Blanco, 2:1440. New York: Garland, 1993.

Maurer, Maurer. "Military Justice under General Washington." *Military Affairs* 28 (Spring 1964): 8–16.

May, Elmer C., and Gerald P. Stadler. *Ancient and Medieval Warfare*. Wayne, N.J.: Avery Publishing Group, 1984.

McAdams, Donald R. "The Sullivan Expedition: Success or Failure." *New York Historical Society Quarterly* 54 (January 1970): 80.

Middlekauff, Robert. *The Glorious Cause: The American Revolution, 1763–1789.* New York: Oxford University Press, 1982.

Miller, Charles E., Jr., Donald V. Lockey, and Joseph Visconti Jr. *Highland Fortress: The Fortification of West Point during the American Revolution, 1775–1783.* West Point, N.Y.: United States Military Academy, 1988.

Miner, Charles. *History of Wyoming, in a Series of Letters from Charles Miner, to His Son William Penn Miner, Esq.* Philadelphia: J. Crissy, 1845.

Nelson, Paul David. *Anthony Wayne, Soldier of the Early Republic.* Bloomington: Indiana University Press, 1985.

Nelson, William. *The American Tory.* Oxford: Oxford University Press, 1961.

Norton, A. Tiffany. *History of Sullivan's Campaign against the Iroquois; Being a Full Account of That Epoch of the Revolution.* Lima, N.Y.: By the author, 1879.

Palmer, Dave Richard. *The Way of the Fox: American Strategy in the War for America, 1775–1783.* Westport, Conn.: Greenwood Press, 1975.

Paret, Peter. *Understanding War: Essays on Clausewitz and the History of Military Power.* Princeton, N.J.: Princeton University Press, 1992.

———. ed. *Makers of Modern Strategy: From Machiavelli to the Nuclear Age.* Princeton, N.J.: Princeton University Press, 1986.

Parker Geoffrey. Comments on "The Japanese Army as a Bureaucracy." Presented for the History of War as part of the General History Symposium, Institute for Advanced Studies, Princeton, N.J., 13 March 1993.

Patrick, Christine Sternberg. "The Life and Times of Samuel Kirkland, 1741–1808: Missionary to the Oneida Indians, American Patriot, and Founder of Hamilton College." Ph.D. diss., State University of New York at Buffalo, 1993.

Peckham, Howard H. *The Colonial Wars: 1679–1762.* Chicago: University of Chicago Press, 1964.

Perkins, Bradford. "The Peace of Paris: Patterns and Legacies." In *Peace and the Peacemakers: The Treaty of 1783,* ed. Ronald Hoffman, 190–229. Charlottesville: University Press of Virginia, 1986.

Preston, Richard A., Alex Roland, and Sydney F. Wise. *Men in Arms: A History of Warfare and Its Interrelationships with Western Society.* Fort Worth, Tex.: Holt, Rinehart, and Winston, 1991.

Rakove, Jack N. *The Beginnings of National Politics: An Interpretive History of the Continental Congress.* New York: Alfred A. Knopf, 1979.

Randall, Willard Sterne. *Benedict Arnold: Patriot and Traitor.* New York: William Morrow, 1990.

Richter, Daniel K. *The Ordeal of the Longhouse: The Peoples of the Iroquois League in the Era of European Colonization.* Chapel Hill: University of North Carolina Press, 1992.

———. "War and Culture: The Iroquois Experience." *William and Mary Quarterly* 40 (October 1983): 528–59.

Risch, Erna. *Supplying Washington's Army.* Washington, D.C.: Center of Military History, United States Army, 1981.

Robson, Eric. *The American Revolution in Its Political and Military Aspects, 1763–1783.* New York: W. W. Norton, 1966.

Royster, Charles. *A Revolutionary People at War: The Continental Army and American Character, 1775–1783.* New York: W. W. Norton, 1979.

Russell, Peter E. "Redcoats in the Wilderness: British Officers and Irregular Warfare in Europe and America, 1740 to 1760." *William and Mary Quarterly* 35 (October 1978): 629–52.

Ryerson, Richard Alan. *The Revolution Is Now Begun: The Radical Committees of Philadelphia, 1765–1776.* Philadelphia: University of Pennsylvania Press, 1978.

Schaffel, Kenneth. "The American Board of War, 1776–1781." *Military Affairs* 50 (October 1986): 185–89.

Sellers, Charles. *The Market Revolution: Jacksonian America, 1815–1846.* Oxford: Oxford University Press, 1991.

Shimmell, L. S. *Border Warfare in Pennsylvania during the Revolution.* Harrisburg, Pa.: R. L. Myers, 1901.

Shy, John. *A People Numerous and Armed: Reflections on the Military Struggle for American Independence.* Ann Arbor: University of Michigan Press, 1990.

———. *Toward Lexington: The Role of the British Army in the Coming of the American Revolution.* Princeton, N.J.: Princeton University Press, 1965.

Sosin, Jack M. *The Revolutionary Frontier 1763–1783.* New York: Holt, Rinehart, and Winston, 1967.

Steele, Ian K. *Warpaths: Invasions of North America.* New York: Oxford University Press, 1994.

Stone, William L. *The Life of Joseph Brandt-Thayendanegea, Including the Indian Wars of the Revolution.* Cooperstown, N.Y.: H. and E. Phinney, 1846.

Strachan, Hew. *European Armies and the Conduct of War.* London: Unwin Hyman, 1983.

Swiggett, Howard. *War out of Niagara: Walter Butler and the Tory Rangers.* Port Washington, N.Y.: Ira J. Friedman, 1933.

Symonds, Craig L. *A Battlefield Atlas of the American Revolution.* Annapolis, Md.: Nautical and Aviation Publishing Company of America, 1986.

Trussell, John B. B., Jr. "The Forgotten Victory: The Sullivan Expedition of 1779." *Parameters* 5 (1975): 40–53.

———. "He Never Missed His Aim." *Parameters* 6 (1976): 48–59.

---. *The Pennsylvania Line: Regimental Organization and Operations, 1776–1783.* Harrisburg: Pennsylvania Historical and Museum Commission, 1977.
Tully, Alan. *William Penn's Legacy: Politics and Social Structure in Provincial Pennsylvania, 1726–1755.* Baltimore: John Hopkins University Press, 1977.
Utley, Robert M. "Last Stand." *Quarterly Journal of Military History* 1 (Autumn 1988): 114–23.
Van Creveld, Martin L. *Command in War.* Cambridge, Mass.: Harvard University Press, 1985.
---. *Supplying War: Logistics from Wallenstein to Patton.* Cambridge: Cambridge University Press, 1986.
---. *The Transformation of War.* New York: Free Press, 1991.
Van Doren, Carl. *Mutiny in January: The Story of a Crisis in the Continental Army.* New York: Viking Press, 1943.
---. *The Secret History of the American Revolution.* Clifton, N.J.: Augustus M. Kelley, Publisher, 1973.
Veleker, Thomas Robert. "Pennsylvania's Performance under the Old Money Requisition System during the American Revolution." Master's thesis, Kansas State University, 1976.
Volwiler, Albert T. *George Croghan and the Westward Movement, 1741–1782.* Cleveland: Arthur H. Clark Company, 1926.
Wallace, Anthony F. C. *The Death and Rebirth of the Seneca.* New York: Alfred A. Knopf, 1970.
Wallace, Paul A. *Indians of Pennsylvania.* Harrisburg: Pennsylvania Historical and Museum Commission, 1981.
Ward, Christopher. *The War of the Revolution.* New York: Macmillan, 1952.
Weigley, Russell F. *The Age of Battles: The Quest for Decisive Warfare from Breitenfeld to Waterloo.* Bloomington: Indiana University Press, 1991.
---. "American Strategy: A Call for a Critical Strategic History." In *Reconsiderations on the Revolutionary War,* ed. Don Higginbotham, 32–53. Westport, Conn.: Greenwood Press, 1978.
---. "The Birth of an American Army: The Sullivan Expedition and the American Way of War." *Proceedings of the 201st Anniversary Wyoming Commemorative Association.* Wilkes-Barre, Pa.: Wyoming Valley Historical Society, 1979.
---. *A History of the United States Army.* New York: Macmillan, 1967.
Williams, Eugene Franklin. "Soldiers of God: The Chaplains of the Revolutionary War." Ph.D. diss., Texas Christian University, 1972.
Wood, Gordon S. *The Creation of the American Republic, 1776–1787.* New York: W. W. Norton, 1969.

———. *The Radicalism of the American Revolution.* New York: Alfred A. Knopf, 1992.
Wright, Albert Hazen. *New York Historical Source Studies: The Sullivan Expedition of 1779, The Losses.* Series no. 34. Albany: New York State Historical Society, 1965.
———. *New York Historical Source Studies: The Sullivan Expedition of 1779, Regimental Rosters of Men.* Series no. 34. Albany: New York State Historical Society, 1965.
Wright, John W. "Some Notes on the Continental Army." *William and Mary Quarterly* 11 (April 1931): 81–105.
———. "Some Notes on the Continental Army." *William and Mary Quarterly* 12 (July 1931): 185–209.
Wright, Robert. "Green's Southern Campaign." Paper presented for Special Warfare Command at Fort Bragg, N.C., 13 December 1994.
York, Neil R. "Pennsylvania Rifle: Revolutionary Weapon in a Conventional War." *Pennsylvania Magazine of History and Biography* 103 (July 1979): 302–24.

Index

Abraham, 17
Adams, John, 159
Adolphus, Gustavus, 64
Albany, N.Y., 24, 25, 43, 44, 48, 54, 107, 116
Allegheny, 15, 40, 42, 44–47, 49–51, 57, 59, 107, 108, 115, 121, 127, 173
Allegheny River, 40, 44, 115
Ambuscade, 59, 72, 82, 86, 87, 89–93, 95, 96, 234n. 59
Amherst, Gen. Jeffery, 61
Amish, 161
Andrustown, N.Y., 29
Angels, Capt. W. "Gans," 146
Annihilation, Battle of, 197
Antes, Frederick, 181
Aristocracy, 136, 158
Arnold, Gen. Benedict, 53, 54, 167, 211, 212n. 73, 225n. 21
Arquebus, 64
Articles of War, 144, 167
Artillery, 4, 40, 46, 56, 57, 62, 69, 75, 77, 81, 83, 84, 90, 95, 100, 101, 173, 189, 213n. 4, 218n. 43, 218n. 45, 220n. 70, 223n. 125, 230n. 10
  batteries, 63
  heavy siege, 39
  light, 73, 218n. 45
Assembly, 158, 162–165, 168, 169, 231n. 18

Associators, 165
Athens, Pa., 5
Austrians, 66, 67
Avenues of Approach, 15, 43

Baldwin's Creek, 87
Bancroft, George, 4
Barber, Col. Francis, 137
Barrels, 114, 117, 118, 228n. 62, 229n. 82
Barton, Lt. William, 143, 235n. 71
Base of supply, 112, 125
Base of operations, 43, 45, 104
Bateaux, 44, 46, 54, 74, 77, 100, 106, 113, 115, 116, 122, 123, 233n. 37
Bayonet, 65, 66, 68, 69, 92, 95, 124
Beatty, Lt. Erkuries, 156
Beaujeau, Daniel, 134
Bible, Holy, 147
Bishop, Morris, 6, 199,
Bland, Humphrey, 70
Blockhouse, 27, 77, 175, 176, 183, 184
Board of Trade, 10
Board of War, 109, 120, 121, 159, 166, 178, 185, 186, 225n. 21, 227n. 50, 228n. 62, 237n. 7
Bolton, Lt. Col. Mason, 28, 40, 53, 58, 84, 86, 101, 219n. 57
Bonaparte, Napoleon, 65
Boone, Capt. Hawkins, 183
Boston, 1, 7, 18, 24, 35, 39, 61, 114, 129, 195, 198, 199

INDEX

Board of Commissioners, Boston, 24
Bouquet, Henri, 67, 70
Boyd, Lt. Thomas, 6, 96, 97, 99, 144, 149, 223n. 125, 235n. 71
Braddock, Gen. Edward, 19, 71, 72, 104, 134, 162, 221n. 91
Brandywine, Battle of, 2, 20
Brant, Joseph [Thayendanegea], 21, 23, 25, 29, 31, 79, 83, 84, 86, 87, 90, 95, 96, 134, 182–84, 188, 192, 193, 206n. 67
Brant, Molly (sister of Joseph) 21
British army, 4, 7, 19, 20, 32, 35, 53, 155, 161, 168, 197
British Articles of War, 144
Brodhead, Col. Daniel, 37, 40, 47, 49–51, 59, 103, 114, 115, 121, 127, 173, 176, 182, 186
Brooklyn Heights, Battle of, 2
Brown Bess, 68
Brown, Lt. Col. Alexander, 179, 198
Bunker Hill, Battle of, 129
Burrowes, Maj John, 123
Butler, Maj. John, 21–25, 27, 53, 56–59, 83, 84–89, 96, 101, 134, 143, 182, 183, 188, 192, 204n. 41, 205n. 52, 222n. 109, 223n. 125, 233n. 45
Butler, Capt. Walter, 29–30
Butler, Lt. Col. William, 30, 174
Butler, Col. Zebulon, 45, 205n. 52, 210n. 36
Butler's Rangers, 27, 30, 43, 53, 56, 82, 84, 85, 86, 87, 92, 101, 162, 182, 183, 187, 204n. 41, 205n. 52, 222n. 109, 233n. 45

Camp followers, 62
Canada, 2, 4, 7, 19, 20, 23, 29, 32, 38, 40, 52, 54–57, 62, 107, 117, 132, 159, 170, 186, 193
Canajoharie, N.Y., 29, 41, 49, 52
Cannawago, N.Y., 51
Cannon, 39, 54, 77, 148, 187, 213n. 57
Carleton, Gen. Guy, 19
Carlisle, Earl of, 27

Carlisle, Pa., 53, 109, 114
Carlisle Commission, 27
Carolinas, 1, 15
Carrying Place, the, 77
Cartographers, 11
Cattle, 84, 85, 114, 118, 119, 122, 123, 128, 182, 228n. 69, 229n. 82
Cavalry, 62, 64, 69, 100, 105, 111, 151
Cayuga, 15, 23, 25, 43, 192, 194, 201n. 14, 209n. 30, 34, 214n. 5
Cedars, Battle of, 23
Ceremony, use of, 147, 149
Certificates of service, 114, 115
Challenge and password, 79, 195
Chaplains, 63, 111–12, 146, 147
Charleville musket, 68
Chemung, 75, 77, 79, 80, 81, 83, 86, 89, 90, 95, 99, 100, 195, 210n. 36
Chemung Raid, 137
Chemung River, 4, 31, 44, 45, 47, 77, 80, 81, 95, 125
Chemung (village), 29, 44, 47, 125, 154
Chenussio, 96, 97, 123
Cherokee, 14, 15
Cherry Valley 13, 30, 171, 193
Chivalry, 140
Chonowataline, N.Y., 120
Ciley, Col. Joseph, 139
Civil-military relations 5, 157, 196
Clark, George Rogers, 7
Claus, Daniel, 21
Clausewitz, Carl von, 156
Clinton, Gen. Henry, 1, 20, 32, 43, 46, 52, 53, 54, 55, 62, 79, 85, 162, 212n. 73, 226n. 30
Clinton, Gen. James, 37, 41, 59, 62, 75, 83, 103, 115, 119, 120, 134, 147, 150, 153, 155, 182, 186, 187, 214n. 4, 219n. 53, 234n. 58
Clinton, Gov. George, 29, 49, 55, 115, 116, 160, 161, 169–73, 177, 187, 188, 189, 193
Cobleskill, 29

257

Coehorn mortar, 39, 62, 81, 100
Colonial charters, 7
Combined operations, 35
Committee of Correspondence, 23
Common law, 144
Conesus Lake, 96, 97
Connecticut, 13, 21, 33, 35, 52, 54, 56, 57, 59, 131, 173, 195
Connecticut River, 33, 54, 57
Connecticut Valley, 52
Conoy, 15, 23
Constitution, 164, 165, 168–70
Continental Army, 4, 7–9, 20, 29, 31, 33, 36, 42, 45, 47, 52–55, 62–64, 68, 71, 77, 99, 100, 103, 108, 114, 115, 117, 122, 123, 126, 127, 130–32, 135, 140, 144, 146, 150, 152, 153, 156–58, 160, 165, 166, 170, 172, 174–78, 182, 186–91, 195–98, 214n. 6, 218n. 44, 225n. 17, 226n. 30
Continental Association of Congress, 170
Continental Congress, 7, 8, 14, 23, 24, 28, 31, 33, 35, 36, 42, 66, 106, 110, 133, 140, 150, 157, 158, 160, 162, 163, 167, 171, 172, 184 196, 199n. 25, 203n. 28, 205n. 51, 220n. 70, 237n. 7
Continentals, 54, 99, 133, 172, 187
Converging columns, 59
Conway cable, 159
Cook, John, 185
Coopers, 117
Coos, N.H., 52
Cornplanter, 7, 183, 192
Council of War, 91, 94
Courts-martial, 129, 140, 143–45, 151, 154, 167
Covenhoven, Robert, 28
Craft, Rev. David, 5, 6
Craik, James, 214n. 6
Creveld, Martin van, 127
Crissé, Turpin de, 70
Culminating Point, 105, 224n. 5
Cumberland County, 179, 185

Cummings, Capt. John, 80–81

Dartmouth, Earl of, 19
Davis, Deputy Quartermaster John, 114
Davis, Nathan, 93, 139, 141, 142, 148
Dearborn, Lt. Col. Henry, 81, 92, 149
Deception, 37, 47, 77
Declaration of Independence, 140, 158
Defiles, 73, 81, 134, 218n. 44
Deism, 146
Deist, 146, 234n. 62
Delaware, 9, 11, 15, 23, 30, 47, 57, 82, 87, 92, 106, 107, 189, 207, 209n. 30
 as allies, 84, 86
 chiefs, 86
Delaware River, 29, 108, 161, 224n. 9
Delaware (village), 4, 57, 86
Demonstration, 31, 52, 59
Depot, 104, 107, 108, 112–14, 121, 123, 128, 207n. 4
Depot system, 105, 127
Derrstown (Lewisburg), Pa., 28
Desertion, 29, 63, 145, 150–152, 235n. 76
Detroit, 17, 37, 38, 54, 56, 107, 199n. 25, 212n. 74
Discipline, 63, 65–8, 70–72, 85, 99, 124, 130, 132, 140, 144–46, 151, 153, 154–56, 196
Diversion, 20, 26, 31, 32, 43, 44, 50, 52, 56, 175–77, 182, 184, 195
Doctrine, 8, 59, 71, 75, 99, 213n. 4
Douw, Volckert, P., 17
Drout, Pvt. Richard, 139
Drum ruffles, 79
Dumas, Jean, 134
Durham boats, 106, 224n. 9

Easton, 52, 73, 107–12, 116, 117, 125, 128, 134, 137, 145, 147, 149, 151, 155, 166, 173, 178, 212n. 81, 217n. 28
Eighth Regiment of Foot, 40
Eleventh Pennsylvania, 28, 69, 96, 114, 149, 234n. 58

Index

Elmer, Dr. Ebenezer, 142
Elmira, N.Y., 4, 125, 191
Engineers, 39, 53, 208n. 13
England, 1, 10, 11, 15–17, 19, 23, 32, 55, 61, 85, 129, 130–32, 161, 163, 168, 196
Esprit de corps, 147
Essay on the Art of War (Crisse), 70
Estaing, Comte Charles Hector, 27
Estherton, Pa., 103, 113, 118
Ethnocentrism, 5
European armies, 8, 63–67, 69, 70, 79, 105, 127, 135
Evans, Israel, 147
Ewald, Capt. Johann, 70
Executive Council, Pennsylvania, 46, 108–10, 115, 126, 137, 157, 164, 166, 167, 174, 180, 181, 185, 225n. 21, 240n. 56
Eyre, Benjamin, 113, 115

Fabian strategy, 34, 207n. 1
Feint, 50, 54, 56, 57
Feu de Joie, 148
Fifth New Jersey, 123
Finger Lakes, 5, 36, 83, 95, 209n. 34
Firepower, 39, 68, 69, 73, 99
First Continental Congress, 17
First New Jersey, 91, 138, 153
Fithian, Philip Vickers, 13, 14
Flexner, James Thomas, 34, 36
Flick, Alexander, 6, 7
Flintlock musket, 65, 68
Flints, 154, 171
Florida, 32
Flying Crow, 22
Fodder, 9, 20, 31, 104, 105, 123
Fogg, Maj. Jeremiah, 83, 84, 124
Folard, Jean Charles de, 65
Food, 9, 20, 31, 35, 50, 57, 59, 84, 85, 103, 104, 113–17, 119, 122, 123, 124, 125, 128, 133, 140, 141, 143, 153, 155, 169, 171, 182, 190, 214n. 6, 227n. 50
Foraging, 84, 119, 123, 125, 127, 128, 196
Forbes, John, 70

Fort Augusta, 14, 28, 85, 114, 118, 119, 124, 174, 176, 183–85, 242n. 98
Fort Clinton, 160
Fort Duquesne, 71, 134
Fort Freeland, 142, 182, 183, 185, 242n. 98
Fort Jenkins, 27, 176, 179
Fort Montgomery, 160
Fort Niagara, 2, 23, 25, 26, 28, 37, 38, 40, 80, 115, 183, 194, 195, 208n. 13, 213n. 4, 214n. 4
Fort Oswego, 25
Fort Pitt, 38, 40, 44, 50, 57, 103, 107, 114, 115, 176, 182, 186
Fort Reed, 125, 147, 148, 155, 208n. 11, 229n. 87
Fort Stanwix (Schuyler), 6, 11, 13, 23, 25, 26, 43, 44, 48, 49, 193, 208n. 11
Fort Sullivan, 2, 77, 219
Fort Wintermoot, 27
Forty-fort, 27
Fourth Pennsylvania, 30, 90, 189
France, 1, 16, 19, 27, 35, 61, 65, 66, 103, 194, 197
Francis, Turbutt, 17
Franklin, Benjamin, 80, 162
Frederick the Great, 15, 53, 65, 66, 69, 70, 135, 208n. 9
French and Indian War, 65, 69, 70, 135, 162, 213n. 4, 236n. 80
French army, 65, 194
French navy, 20, 27
Fruit, Robert, 2, 23, 108, 153, 168
Funerals, 149
Furloughs, 53, 152

Gage, Gen. Thomas, 18, 19, 203n. 31
Gansevoort, Col. Peter, 79
Gates, Gen. Horatio, 1, 2, 159
Genesee, 84, 94, 125, 127, 193
Genesee River, 96, 100, 123, 137
Genesee Valley, 59
George III, 25, 32, 52, 58
Georgia, 1, 15

259

Index

Germain, Lord George, 18, 20, 30–32, 39, 55
German battalion, 150, 151, 177
German Flats, N.Y., 13, 29, 193
Germans, 14, 150, 163
Germantown, Pa., 20
Glacial esker, 87
Glorious Cause, The (Middlekauff), 7
Glover, Gen. John, 2
God, 146, 147
Gookin, Ensign Daniel, 118, 156,
Goodrich, William, 214n. 5
Goshen, 183
Grant, Thomas, 27, 41, 109, 137
Graymont, Barbara, 6, 7
Great Britain, 15, 35, 158, 174
Great Lakes, 6, 7, 20, 21, 38
Great Warrior's path, 206n. 58, 211n. 55
Greene, Quartermaster General Nathanael, 102, 103, 105–9, 112–16, 118, 120, 121, 126, 136, 166, 170, 178, 187, 207n. 4, 226n. 39, 227n. 46, 229n. 73
Guerrilla war, 26, 103, 190
Gunpowder, 64, 128, 160

Haldimand, Sir Frederick, 40, 52–58, 79, 85, 193, 212n. 74, 210n. 36, 219n. 57, 232n. 29
Half-rations, l, 124, 139, 155
Hand, Gen. Edward, 31, 33, 45, 53, 56, 62, 69, 73, 75, 79, 81–83, 89–93, 95, 97, 100, 112, 114, 116–18, 123, 131, 135, 137, 142, 149, 150, 154, 168, 175–77, 179, 194
Hard currency, 14, 106
Harris Ferry, Pa., 14, 113
Hart, Maj. William, 110
Hartley, Lt. Col. Thomas, 28–31, 172, 174, 222n. 101
Harvard College, 24
Hathorn, Col. John, 183
Hazen, Col. Moses, 52, 182, 195, 211n. 55

Herkimer, Gen. Nickolas, 25, 26
Hessians, 62, 70, 135
Higginbotham, Don, 7, 36, 170
Historians, 4–6, 34, 131, 132, 192
History of the American Army, A (Weigley), 64
History of the Late War in Germany, (Lloyd), 70
History of the United States (Bancroft), 5
Hooper, Col. Robert L. 108, 110–12, 164, 166, 167, 225n. 21
Howitzers, 39, 62, 74, 100, 220n. 70
Hubley, Lt. Col. Adam, 82, 114, 116, 118, 119, 143, 176, 179, 185, 186, 217n. 28, 236n. 78
Hudson Highland, N.Y., 20, 173
Hudson River, 19, 33, 55, 107, 125, 162, 169
Hudson Valley, 19, 37, 47, 173
Hughes, Thomas, 52, 53
Hunter, Samuel, , 171, 174, 175, 178, 179, 181, 184, 185, 240n. 56
Hunter, Rev. Andrew, 147

Impressment, 108–10, 126, 187
Indians, 4, 6, 9, 11, 17–19, 23–27, 29–32, 38, 41, 42, 44, 49, 51, 52, 54, 59, 67, 71, 81, 83, 85–87, 89, 90, 92, 93, 96, 97, 100, 101, 143, 144, 149, 170, 182, 183, 191, 194, 200n. 2, 200n. 6, 205n. 46, 205n. 52, 219n. 64, 221n. 91
Infantry, 4, 40, 41, 62–69, 71, 79, 81, 83, 84, 95, 111, 152, 177, 189, 216n. 17
  heavy, 64, 67
  light, 62, 64, 65, 67–9, 73, 74, 81, 83, 89, 92, 95, 100, 134, 154, 189, 216n. 21
Instructions for His Generals (Frederick the Great), 70
Intelligence, 4, 8, 36, 37, 42, 46, 52, 54, 55, 57, 59, 60, 120, 180, 226n. 30
Invalid Corps, 177

Index

Irondequoit, N.Y., 25
Iroquois, 1–6, 9–11, 13, 15–7, 20–27, 30, 31, 36, 38, 39, 40–47, 49, 50, 52–55, 57–60, 62, 77, 79, 84–87, 92–96, 99, 102–107, 110, 116, 119, 122, 123, 128, 134, 141, 147, 148, 149, 158, 169, 172, 179, 182, 184, 187, 188, 192, 193, 194–97, 202n. 19, 221n. 86, 243n. 9
Iroquois in the American Revolution, The (Graymont), 6

Jay, John, 7, 171
Jenkins, Lt. John, 47, 80
Johnson, Guy, 21, 192
Johnson, John (son of William), 10, 17, 21, 39, 57, 162, 192, 204n. 41, 219n. 57
Johnson, Sir William, 10, 21, 39, 204n. 41
Jones, John Paul, 85
Jury, 144

Kayashuta, 22
Kegs, 117, 118
Kentucky, 11, 37
Kimball, Capt. Benjamin, 154
Kinship, 132
Kirkland, Jerusha (wife of Samuel), 146
Kirkland, Samuel, 23, 24, 41, 142, 146, 193, 205n. 46, 234n. 62,
Knox, Gen. Henry, 39, 69

Lafayette, Gen. Marquis de Marie Joseph, 33, 237n. 7
Lake Erie, 40, 48, 49, 106
Lake Oneida, 43, 48, 49, 106
Lake Ontario, 38, 40, 44, 48, 54, 58
Lake Otsego, 13, 25, 29, 41, 44, 49, 52, 73, 105, 115, 116, 119, 122, 127, 134, 145, 147, 153, 186, 187, 189
Lancaster Treaty of 1744, 13
Leadership, 5, 8, 9, 44, 66, 67, 84, 86, 95, 129–31, 133–36, 140, 150, 154–56, 158, 159, 189, 197, 230n. 6

Lee, Gen. Charles, 160
Lewis, Col. Morgan, 10, 107
Lexington, Mass., 129, 131, 132
Line of advance, 47, 59, 71, 104, 107
Line of communications, 37, 39, 40, 48
Linear combat, 62
Little, John, 183
Lloyd, Henry, 70
Logan, James, 202n. 19
Logistics, 31, 33, 42, 43, 49, 50, 102–5, 114, 116, 121, 122, 125, 152, 181, 186, 197
London, 6, 162
Long Island, 35, 62
Lossing, Benson, 5
Louisbourg, 37
Loyalist, 17, 20, 21, 24, 162, 170

Maclay, William 85, 184, 193
Magazines, 39, 104, 107, 184
Malcolm, Col. William, 111
Manifest Destiny, 147
Maryland, 150
Matchlock, 64
Maxwell, Gen. William, 76, 83, 91, 138
McAdams, Donald R., 6, 7
McDonald, Capt. John, 57, 85, 87, 101, 222n. 109, 242n. 98
McIntosh, Gen. Lachlan, 40
McNeill, Samuel, 90, 93
Mennonites, 161
Mercenaries, 40
Middlebrook, N.J., 2, 106, 108
Middlekauff, Robert, 7
Middletown, Pa., 113
Mifflin, Thomas, 166
Military Institutions of the Romans (Vegetius), 70
Militia, 7, 18, 20, 25, 27–29, 38, 47, 52, 54, 61, 101, 114, 115, 129, 158, 160, 162, 165, 166, 170–82, 185, 187, 189, 190, 193

261

INDEX

Militiamen, 170, 173, 176, 179, 182, 190, 205n. 52, 240n. 52, 241n. 70, 241n. 80
Mingo, 9, 209n. 30, 203n. 28, 209n. 30
Minisink, N.Y., 29, 142, 182–84, 188
Mississauga, 23
Mississippi, 10, 193
Mohawk, 14, 15, 17, 21–23, 25, 26, 30, 50, 54, 106, 107, 115, 162, 182
Mohawk River, 13, 41, 43–44, 48, 49, 52, 105
Mohawk Valley, 162
Mohicans, 18, 19, 203n. 28, 214n. 5,
Money, 24, 52, 106, 107, 156, 181
Monmouth, Battle of, 27, 62
Montour, Esther, 28, 233n. 45
Montour, Capt. Roland, 82, 83
Montreal, 20, 33, 56
Moravian ministers, 15
Moravian mission, 13
Morgan, Daniel, 30, 62, 68, 69, 73, 95, 107
Morristown, N.Y., 119, 133
Mourning War, 94
Muncy, Pa., 28, 85, 175, 176, 179, 206n. 58
Muskets, 24, 65, 66, 68, 71, 73, 83, 100, 148, 153, 154, 176, 195
Musketeers, 65, 93, 100
Mutiny, 131, 133, 138, 230n. 9, 231n. 18

Nanticoke, 15, 23, 209n. 30
Napoleonic army, 127
Nassau, Maurice de, 64, 215n. 11
Native Americans, 67, 94, 100
New England, 19, 32, 129, 130
New Hampshire, 2, 52, 92, 118, 153, 178
New Jersey, 2, 11, 13, 27, 35, 43, 47, 55, 56, 58, 75, 76, 80, 81, 91, 119, 123, 131, 138, 152, 153, 167, 177
New Jersey Line, 137, 142
New York, 1, 3, 5, 6, 9, 11, 13, 15, 16, 20, 21, 23, 25, 29, 31, 32, 34, 35, 36, 38, 40, 43, 44, 47, 48, 55, 56, 58, 76, 81, 96, 103, 104, 107, 114–17, 126, 132, 133, 157, 160–62, 168, 169, 170–73, 175, 177, 186, 187, 189, 192, 212n. 81
Newburgh, N.Y., 133
Newport, R.I., 1, 27, 31, 33, 104
Newtown, N.Y., 6, 4, 57, 59, 80, 86, 93–95, 100, 101, 137, 140, 144, 145, 195, 221n. 86
North Carolina, 15
Northumberland County, Pa., 23, 171, 174, 175–79, 185
Northumberland (village), 14
Norton, A. Tiffany, 5, 6, 192
Nurses, 63, 140, 214n. 6

Officer Corps, 111, 129, 130, 132, 133, 135, 136, 149, 150, 154, 155, 160, 195
Ogden, Col. Matthias, 91, 145, 234n. 59
Ohio country, 38
Ohio River, 11, 16, 19,
Ohio Valley, 7, 9, 10, 13, 15
Oneida, 15, 23, 24, 26, 40, 43, 48, 49, 62, 96, 106, 143, 144, 193, 194, 205n. 46, 209n. 30,
Oneida contingent, 40
Onondaga, 15, 23, 24, 194, 209n. 30
Onondaga River, 48
Onondaga (village), 21
Operations, 5, 14, 19, 20, 31, 32, 34–38, 43, 45, 55, 56, 58, 59, 62, 70, 72, 84, 99, 104, 105, 107, 115, 122, 127, 159, 161, 168, 172, 173, 195, 197, 213n. 4
Order of battle, 53, 223n. 125
Oriskany, Battle of, 25, 26
Ottawa, 6, 209n. 30

Pack saddles, 53, 110, 226n. 30
Pack trains, 73
Palmer, Dave R., 34
Parker, Michael, 97, 129, 149, 235n. 71
Parr, Maj. James, 73, 83, 90, 92, 96
Partisan combat, 70
Partisan warfare, 72
Penn, Gov. John, 202n. 19
Penn, Gov. Thomas, 162

INDEX

Pennsylvania, 2, 5, 6, 9, 11, 13, 14, 16, 18, 20, 21, 21, 25, 27, 28, 30, 31, 35, 36, 38, 42, 45, 46, 49, 50, 56, 58, 69, 70, 90, 96, 103, 106–11, 113–15, 117, 126, 131, 133, 137, 140, 149, 150, 157, 160–62, 164–72, 176–82, 186–90, 192, 193, 196, 202n. 19, 240n. 56, 241n. 80
Pennsylvania Line, 133, 150, 231n. 18
Pension, 150
People Numerous and Armed (Shy), 131
Philadelphia, 14, 46, 53, 109, 110, 150, 151, 161–64, 167, 171, 174, 226n. 30 231n. 18
Pickets, 77, 155
Pictorial Field Book of the Revolution (Lossing) 5
Pike, 64
Pine Creek, 13
Pioneer crews, 95
Pioneer teams, 83
Pocono Mountains, 111, 151
Poor, Gen. Enoch, 73, 76, 81, 83, 91–93, 124, 219n. 53, 234n. 59
Post, Frederick, 15
Potter, Gen. James, 170, 193, 241n. 70
Prideaux, Gen. John, 39
Proclamation of 1763, 10
Proctor, Col. Thomas, 62, 53, 69, 74, 77, 90, 91, 93–95, 100
Providence, R.I., 2

Quakers, 161, 163
Quartermasters, 44, 50, 104, 108, 109, 114–16, 120, 123, 125–27, 137, 178, 216n. 25, 228n. 62, 229n. 73
    agents, 109, 126, 166
    general, 65, 102, 103, 108, 121, 166
    officers, 45, 109, 113, 123, 136
Quebec, 20, 56, 62, 85

Radicalism of the American Revolution, The (Wood), 132
Radicals, 163–69, 180, 238n. 16
Rage Militaire, 132

Ramparts, 39
Rangers, Pennsylvania militia, 174, 175, 178
Rations, 124, 125, 227n. 50, 228n. 69, 229n. 82
Reading, Pa., 14, 95, 146
Reconnaissance, 62, 73, 75, 76, 80, 91
    patrols, 73, 91
    plan, 73
Reed, Gov. Joseph, 45–7, 109, 110, 125, 147, 148, 155, 160, 161, 167, 173–82, 184, 185, 186–88, 193
Reveries upon the Art of War (Saxe), 70
Rhode Island, 1, 2, 19, 27, 31, 55, 104, 121, 131, 169
Richelieu, Cardinal, 102
Rifles, 30, 62, 68, 69, 73, 90, 96, 100, 154, 215n. 13n, 217n. 26, 222n. 101
Rifleman, 69
Rogers, Rev. William, 112, 149
Rome, 64
Romney, George, 31
Roslin Castle, 149
Running the gauntlet, 144
Rutledge, Edward, 159

Sachems, 10, 17, 21, 23
Saratoga, Battle of, 1, 19, 26, 35, 68, 223n. 118, 223n. 123
Saxe, Maurice de, 65, 70, 135,
Scalp bounty, 240n. 56
Schenectady, N.Y., 43, 54, 116
Schoharie, N.Y., 30, 193
Schuyler, 23, 24, 26, 41–44, 47–50, 56, 57, 105, 125, 193
Second Continental Congress, 35, 163
Second New Hampshire, 92, 118
Second New Jersey, 76, 80
Second New York, 76
Security, 14, 15, 41, 45, 49, 52, 60, 70–75, 77, 79, 89, 96, 99, 103, 105, 107, 110, 113, 134, 150, 169, 172, 175, 176, 179, 186, 190, 195, 210n. 49, 212n. 73, 218n. 44, 221n. 91

INDEX

Seneca, 7, 15, 22, 23, 25, 26, 30, 42, 43, 45, 48–50, 57, 59, 93–96, 105, 123, 125, 142, 183, 194, 209n. 30, 209n. 34
Sermon, 146, 147
Shamokin, 15
Shawnee, 9, 11, 13, 15, 94, 202n. 19
Shelburne, Lord, 7
Sherman, William, 159, 191, 192
Sheshequin, 28
Sheshequin trail, 206n. 58
Shikellamy, 15
Shippen, Peggy, 167
Shipwrights, 107, 113, 115
Shock action, 64, 65, 68
Shreve, Col. Israel, 76, 77, 123–25, 128
Shy, John, 131
Six Nations, 7, 10, 17, 24, 41, 194, 203n. 28, 221n. 86, See Iroquois
Skirmishers, 64, 67
Social Darwinism, 6
Society of Friends, 161
South Carolina, 3, 4, 15
Speculators, land, 7, 11
Spencer, Col. Oliver, 111
Springfield, N.Y., 29
St. Lawrence River, 20, 33
St. Lawrence Valley, 38
St. Lucia, 32
Standard combat procedures, 72
Stansbury, Joseph, 46
Steele, Alexander, 117
Steuben, Gen. Frederick William Baron von, 65, 66, 68, 135, 153, 216n. 25
Stoicism, 140, 233n. 39
Stony Point, N.Y., 55
Strategy, 1, 19, 20, 26, 32–35, 157, 182, 207n. 1
Street, Col. John, 145
Stuart, John, 17
Sullivan, Gen. John, 1–9, 36, 37, 40, 41, 43, 44, 48, 49, 50–54, 56–60, 62, 63, 68–73, 75–77, 79, 84, 86, 87, 89, 90, 91–97, 99–106, 108, 128, 130, 133, 134, 136, 137, 139, 140, 141–58, 160, 162, 164–66, 168, 170, 173, 175, 176, 178, 179–97, 198n. 9, 208n. 11, 213n. 4, 214n. 5, 217n. 28, 218n. 53, 219n. 57, 222n. 111, 223n. 125, 225n. 24, 227n. 50, 228n. 62, 228n. 69, 229n. 73 230n. 88, 232n. 29, 234n. 58, 234n. 59, 234n. 62, 241n. 70
Sunbury, Pa., 14, 15, 23, 28, 85, 103, 112, 113, 139, 140, 174, 175, 178, 179, 184, 201n. 14, 206n. 58, 233n. 37
Supplies, 4, 6, 9, 20, 24, 35, 38, 41, 43, 44, 47, 50, 53, 57, 84, 85, 102, 103–9, 112–26, 128, 137, 138, 143, 157–60, 165, 166, 172, 175, 178, 186, 187, 193, 195, 199n. 25, 207n. 4
Supply trains, 75
Supply War (Creveld), 127
Supporting attack, 44–46, 59
Surgeons, 139, 140, 153, 236n. 85
Surveyors, 63
Susquehanna Company, 241n. 80
Susquehanna depot, 112
Susquehanna River, 13–15, 26–29, 31, 41, 42, 44–50, 53, 54, 56, 59, 73, 75, 77, 79, 83, 86, 102, 105–8, 110–115, 116, 118, 119, 121, 122, 126, 154, 155, 179, 172, 178, 183–85, 187, 188, 195, 206n. 58, 227n. 50, 233n. 37
Susquehanna Valley, 5, 10, 11, 14, 15, 28, 45, 57, 103, 112, 113, 127, 175, 193, 201n. 13, 202n. 19, 206n. 58
Swiggett, Howard, 6

Tactics, 8, 18, 42, 61, 64–68, 72, 81, 94, 99, 100, 134, 135, 170, 215n. 13, 215n. 14, 221n. 91
Teamsters, 63, 117
Thaosagwat, 96, 97, 144
Third New York, 96
Thirty-Fourth Regiment of Foot, 40
Thomas, John, 141
Tiadaghton (Pine) Creek, 11
Tioga, Pa., 2, 5, 13, 28, 30, 41, 45–47, 51,

INDEX

Tioga *(continued)*
 58, 59, 62, 69, 73, 75, 77, 79, 80–83, 100, 101, 119, 123–25, 127, 128, 139, 140, 143, 147, 148, 149, 155, 172, 187–89, 206n. 58
Tory, 2, 4–6, 8, 21, 25–27, 29, 31, 35, 37, 38, 40, 43, 48, 53, 56, 57, 77, 80, 86, 87, 93, 95, 99, 101, 110, 123, 142, 144, 161, 167, 170, 171, 176, 177, 182, 184, 193
Towanda, Pa., 206n. 58
Town Destroyer, 7
Treatise of Military Discipline, 70
Treaty of Fort Stanwix, 6, 11, 13, 23, 25, 193, 201n. 10,
Treaty of Fort Stanwix (second), 243n. 9
Treaty of Paris, 22
Trenton, N.Y., 2, 138, 160
Tuscarora, 15, 23, 24, 26, 62, 143, 144, 193, 202n. 18, 205n. 46, 209n. 30, 214n. 5, 227n. 24

Unandilla River, 11
Unandilla (village), raid on, 29–30
United States Military Academy, 134
U.S. Army, 59, 99, 100, 125

Valley Forge, Pa., 65, 102, 133, 150, 153
Van Cortland, Col. Phillip, 76
Vattel, Emmeric, 141
Vegetius, 70, 72
Vermont, 32, 169, 187
Virginia, 11, 15, 16, 18, 103, 177
Volley Fire, 66, 67, 72

Wadesworth, Commissary General Jeremiah, 114
Wait, Capt. Jason Wait, 32, 55, 89, 122, 134, 188
Wallis, Samuel, 46–47
War of American Independence, The (Higginbotham), 7
War Out of Niagara (Swiggett), 6
Way of the Fox, The (Palmer), 34
Ward, Christopher, 6

Warrants, 108–10
Warrior, 44, 89, 95, 99, 127
Washington, Gen. George, 1, 2, 4–9, 20, 23, 26, 27, 30–50, 52–56, 58–63, 65, 67–72, 82, 102–8, 110–12, 114–23, 125, 126, 128, 129–42, 150, 152–55, 157, 159–62, 164, 165, 167, 168–70, 172–82, 185–90, 193–97, 207n. 4, 210n. 36, 211n. 55, 212n. 73, 212n. 82, 214n. 5, 214n. 6, 215n. 13, 216n. 21, 226n. 39, 227n. 46, 227n. 50, 229n. 80, 233n. 39, 235n. 76, 237n. 7, 241n. 70
Washington, Lund (brother of George), 130
Waverly, N.Y., 81
Weare, President Meshech, 52
Weigley, Russell, 34, 64
West Indies, 19, 20, 32, 103
West Point, N.Y., 20, 36, 55, 134, 173, 212n. 73, 214n. 5
Westmoreland County, 175, 179
Wharton, Thomas, 170, 171
Whitehall, 1, 17, 19, 26, 27, 31, 54, 55, 84, 200n. 2, 204n. 41, 212n. 81, 231n. 10,
Wilson, James, 159
Wolfe, Gen. James, 61, 230n. 6
Women of the Army, 63
Wood, Gordon, 132
Wood Creek, 11, 43, 48, 105, 106
Wright, Albert Hazen, 182
Wright's Ferry, Pa., 103, 106, 107, 113, 117, 118, 207n. 4,
Wyalusing, Pa., 13, 154
Wyoming, 13, 27, 30, 43, 45, 47, 52, 53, 56, 60, 69, 73, 77, 79, 100, 102, 103, 106, 109, 111, 113, 114, 116–19, 121–15, 127, 137, 139–45, 147, 149, 151, 169, 171, 175, 177, 179, 185, 186, 187–89, 210n. 36, 214n. 5, 218n. 43, 226n. 39, 241n. 80
Wyoming depot, 116

Young, Arthur, 38

Zeisberger, David, 15

265

www.ingramcontent.com/pod-product-compliance
Lightning Source LLC
Chambersburg PA
CBHW021145160426
43194CB00007B/695